CW00839979

GALLOWAY: LAND AND LORDSHIP

Edited by
Richard D. Oram
and
Geoffrey P. Stell

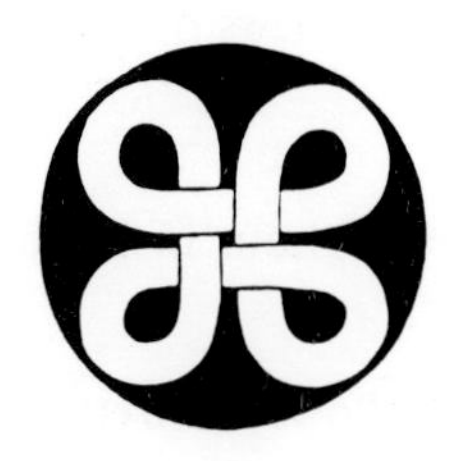

Published in Scotland by:
The Scottish Society for Northern Studies
c/o School of Scottish Studies
University of Edinburgh
27 George Square
Edinburgh
EH8 9LD

ISBN 0 9505994 6 8

Copyright © 1991. Scottish Society for Northern Studies and individual contributors.

All rights reserved. No part of this publication may be reproduced, stored in a retrieval system or transmitted in any form, in any quantity, or by any means electronic, mechanical, photocopying, recording, or otherwise without the prior written permission of the Society and appropriate contributors. Multiple copying of any of the contents of the publication is always illegal.

The Scottish Society for Northern Studies gratefully acknowledges financial assistance in the publication of this volume from:

THE MOUSWALD TRUST

STEWARTRY DISTRICT COUNCIL

Cover: Loch Ken and Kenmure Castle; painting by John Fleming engraved by Joseph Swan (from Swan's Views of the Lakes of Scotland (1837), ii, facing p.191).

Text set throughout in English Times.

Printed by The Galloway Gazette, Newton Stewart.

CONTENTS

CONTRIBUTORS

IAN A. MORRISON lectures in the Department of Geography, University of Edinburgh.

JOHN MACQUEEN is Emeritus Professor of Scottish Studies, School of Scottish Studies, University of Edinburgh.

PETER H. HILL is Excavation Director of the Whithorn Excavations.

DEREK J. CRAIG was formerly a research student in the Department of Archaeology, University of Durham.

EDWARD J. COWAN is Professor of History, University of Guelph, Ontario.

GILLIAN FELLOWS-JENSEN is based in the Place-Name Institute of the University of Copenhagen.

DAPHNE BROOKE, Auchencairn, is a local historian who has undertaken extensive research on the place-names and society of early Galloway

RICHARD D. ORAM was formerly a research student in Medieval History in the St John's House Centre for Advanced Historical Studies, University of St Andrews.

HECTOR L. MACQUEEN lectures in the Department of Scots Law, University of Edinburgh.

GEOFFREY P. STELL is an investigator with the Royal Commission on the Ancient and Historical Monuments of Scotland, Edinburgh.

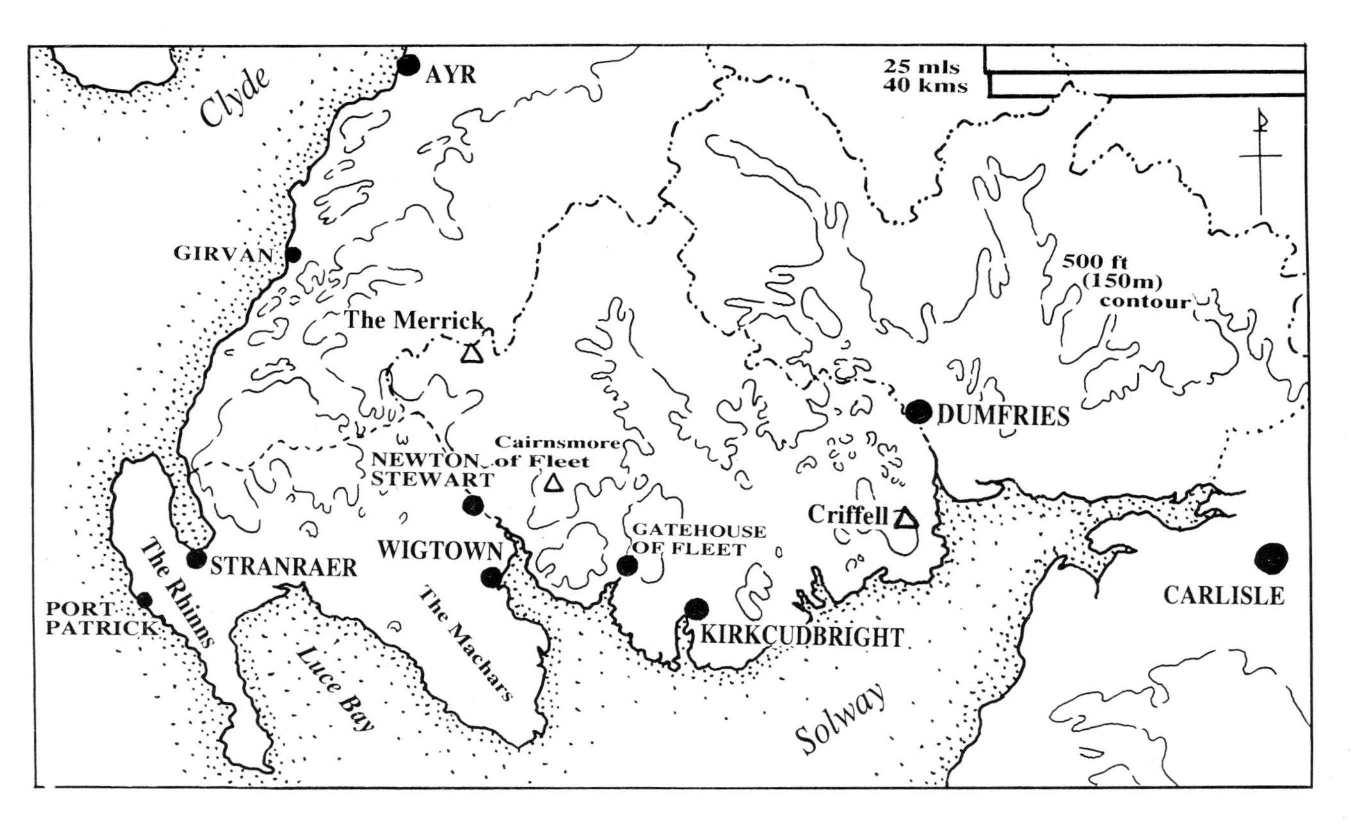

Dumfries and Galloway showing 150m contour and principal places mentioned in the text.

St Ninian's Cave: general view from south.

INTRODUCTION

Galloway 1986

The Annual Conference of the Scottish Society for Northern Studies has become something of an institution. The Society exists to foster links, historical and contemporary, between Scotland and the Scandinavian world. The Conference has taken on a life of its own and functions both as an annual social event and as a local history travelling roadshow. At its best it provides a forum where amateur and professional can meet, relax and speculate across a wide range of disciplines — history, geography, archaeology, place-name studies and others. When the Conference takes place in the Gaidhealtachd, as in Benbecula in 1985, it functions as a *ceilidh* in the best and widest sense, and draws inspiration from the Gaelic tradition. But the Scandinavian credentials of the Society are never forgotten. In the Northern Isles and in Caithness they are very much to the fore. In other parts of Scotland Scandinavian connections can be uncovered where least expected. However, the reverse is also true: the rumour of Scandinavian influence can prove to be much exaggerated. Such was the case with Galloway.

The belief that the Vikings once played a key role in Galloway is widespread, fostered by such local historians as M'Kerlie, Wentworth Huyshe, W. G. Collingwood and John E. Robertson. At the Conference, however, speaker after speaker searched for Scandinavian influence, but could find little or none. The Society's past president, Ted Cowan, now professor of History at Guelph, Ontario, launched a particularly telling attack on the Scandinavian hypothesis, the swash-buckling delivery of which did not entirely mask its scholarly credentials. His strictures were not confined to historians, but extended also to allied disciplines. 'It is truly alarming,' he writes in his published paper in this volume, 'to note the extent to which archaeologists are imprisoned in historical structures totally fabricated by local historians'. 'The overwhelming conclusion,' he believes, 'must be that the Viking presence in Galloway was not significant'.

Despite this, the tone of the Conference was far from negative. On the contrary, it was remarkable how well conclusions pieced together from stray clues in one discipline tallied with those from another and helped to form a composite picture. If the Vikings were hard to find, one surprise was the strength of the evidence for Cumbric survival throughout the Dark Ages. Several papers — John MacQueen, Craig, Brooke and Fellows-Jensen — point towards this conclusion. One difficulty which faces the historian of early Galloway, apart from the lack of record evidence, is the sheer complexity of the settlement pattern within a relatively short compass: Britons, Angles, Gaels and Vikings (both Danish and Norse), Normans and Gall-Gaidhil all stalk through these pages. So too do Fergus, lord of Galloway, and his unruly sons and grandsons.

In this volume, based mainly on papers read at the Conference, Ian Morrison sets the scene with a finely judged piece on landscape and locality. His description of Galloway, viewed by the modern airborne traveller, is a memorable one: the uplands 'a rumpled tweed coast in rich moorit browns' and the coastal lowlands 'a neatly worked scarf patterned in many greens, tossed down between the tweedy roughness of the interior and the sleek grey skein of the Solway'. Professor John MacQueen returns to the study of St Ninian after many years; not indeed to Ninian himself, but to the early medieval *Lives* of the saint, which he considers throw an 'interesting light on the literary culture of Whithorn in the eighth century'. Whithorn is to the fore again in Derek Craig's study of the pre-Norman sculpture in Galloway. Given the lack of record evidence, sculpture is a valuable historical source. He argues for 'an organised professional school of carving' operating in Galloway, and he believes that its strength points to the 'continued survival of Whithorn as a regional centre in the undocumented period between 802 and 1128'.

One achaeologist to whom Professor Cowan's strictures do not apply is Peter Hill, director of the dig at Whithorn. At the Conference he gave a report on work in progress, but his paper in this volume rests mainly on excavations carried out since that date. In it he considers the archaeological record in the light of recent research and postulates 'a settlement of Hiberno-Norse artisans and traders at Whithorn' in the dark years between 802 and 1128. This is an exciting suggestion which brings the Vikings right back into contention.

In another paper Daphne Brooke is sceptical about received views on the Gall-Gaidhil, and tentatively proposes a new etymology for the place-name 'Galloway'. Her appendices listing the main reference to the Gall-Gaidhil in Irish sources and the forms of the name for both province and people of Galloway in early record sources should prove an invaluable quarry for future scholars. The paper also touches on the lordship of Galloway in the twelfth century. Gillian Fellows-Jensen reviews the place-name evidence for Scandinavians in Dumfriesshire and Galloway. She finds considerable evidence for Scandinavian settlement in Dumfriesshire, probably mainly Danish laid on an Anglian foundation; the name 'Tinwald', however, with its strong Norse associations, remains something of a puzzle. In Galloway, there is far less evidence for settlement, although there are pointers to Norse influence in centres of power. She argues that the much-discussed inversion compound names beginning 'Kirk-' reflect Scandinavian influence overlaid on Gaelic, although some may be ascribed to twelfth-century parochial reorganisation.

Three papers direct our attention to the Galloway of Fergus and his sons. Richard Oram reflects on the likely antecedents of Fergus and the composition of his principality. He conjectures Fergus to have been of mixed Norse-Celtic origin, and portrays him as an independent lord of Galloway proper, west of the river Urr. Kirkcudbright and Cruggleton may have been his centres of power. Geoffrey Stell comments on the 'size and sophistication' of the three Cistercian monasteries founded by the lords of Galloway — Dundrennan, Glenluce and Sweetheart; and argues for conservatism and continuity in the structures associated with secular lordship. He notes the great antiquity of many castle sites, including Morton, Buittle and Cruggleton, and comments on the number of island fortifications. In a paper commissioned for this volume, Hector MacQueen gathers what is known of the 'laws of Galloway', the separate existence of which was acknowledged and confirmed by the Scottish Parliament in 1384. He is able to draw many parallels between these laws and the laws of the Gaelic-speaking Scots elsewhere, providing valuable clues to the social and administrative structure of Galloway under its native lords. Like other contributors, he also raises the possibility of Cumbric survival.

The Murray Arms Hotel at Gatehouse-of-Fleet provided a most congenial base for the Conference. One of its many claims to fame is that it was here that Robert Burns wrote 'Scots wha hae . . .'. It is therefore most appropriate that in his second paper in this volume Ian Morrison, discarding the mantle of geographer for that of musicologist, should investigate the tune to which Burns composed the words. In Burns's own day the tune was known as 'Hey, tuttie taitie', and was popularly believed to have been the air to which the Scots army marched to Bannockburn. In a fascinating piece of detective work Ian traces the tune back through Alexander Montgomerie and Gavin Douglas in the sixteenth century to William Dunbar in the fifteenth, thus establishing that the traditional account may not be so far-fetched as might appear at first sight.

At the Conference, Alfred Truckell gave a spirited and erudite account, liberally spiced with extracts from chronicle sources, of the tough nature and fearsome reputation of Galwegians in the Middle Ages. Unfortunately, it has not been possible to reproduce that account here, but the editors and organisers of the Conference wish to record their deep gratitude to Mr Truckell for his willingness to share with them — in the lecture-hall and on site visits — his encyclopaedic knowledge of his native province.

Finally I should like to thank the editors of this volume, Richard Oram and Geoffrey Stell, for their patience and persistence in gathering the papers and seeing them through the press. This is, remarkably, the first of the Society's monograph series in which John Baldwin has not played a leading part, but I hope that readers familiar with the earlier volumes on Shetland, Caithness, Cumbria and the 'firthlands' of Ross and Sutherland will agree that the high standard set there has been admirably maintained.

DAVID SELLAR, President 1986

Lincluden College: aerial view from south-east.

GALLOWAY: LOCALITY AND LANDSCAPE EVOLUTION

Ian A. Morrison

Writing of Scotland as a whole, Stuart Piggott has suggested on more than one occasion[1] that

> To understand a people, one must first understand their country. Without a knowledge of the routes of access and of egress by land and sea, of the regions of mountain and moorland over against those of forest and flood plain, of the conditions of climate and natural environment — in a word, without a geographical setting — any study of human communities in past or present times must be a meaningless abstraction.

This certainly rings true of Galloway, which traditionally embraces what was in pre-Regionalisation days Wigtownshire and the Stewartry of Kirkcudbright, from the Mull of Galloway in the west to the River Nith at Dumfries in the east. Though this south-western corner of Scotland has an undeniable character of its own, its identity does not reflect an internal homogeneity. Instead, it arises from characteristic juxtapositions of contrasting elements. As Geoffrey Stell remarked recently,[2] the heart of the region is a subtly different blend of all the scenic qualities which visitors expect to find in Scotland at large. There is a rugged mountainous core, with crags, corries and dark forests reminiscent of the Highlands; rolling sheep-speckled moorlands look typical of the Border country; and in its lowlands are farmlands with as fertile soils as any in the Merse.

Gordon Donaldson[3] tells us that an uncharitable seventeenth-century visitor remarked that the map of Scotland looked like a pillory-coat, bespattered by dirt and rotten eggs. The present-day traveller, flying over Galloway, may perceive more attractive garb: the uplands as a rumpled tweed coat in rich moorit browns, with the coastal lowlands as a neatly worked scarf patterned in many greens, tossed down between the tweedy roughness of the interior and the sleek grey silk skein of the Solway.

SCALE AND MARITIME LOCATION

A flight over the area can also give a feeling for the compact size of Galloway, and of its relationship to the lands and seas around. Even from the low altitude of the little commuter flight from Dublin to Edinburgh, one finds that one can take in the whole panorama from Dumfries to Stranraer in one sweep of the eye. Indeed, those who toil wingless up the Merrick (at 2764ft, 843m, the highest peak in southern Scotland) reckon that on a good day they can see not only Goat Fell in Arran, but Ben Lomond, the English Lakeland peaks, and the Mournes in Ireland. Even from sea-level on the Solway, one can look across not only to Cumbria but to the Isle of Man; and Ulster is just twenty miles across the water.

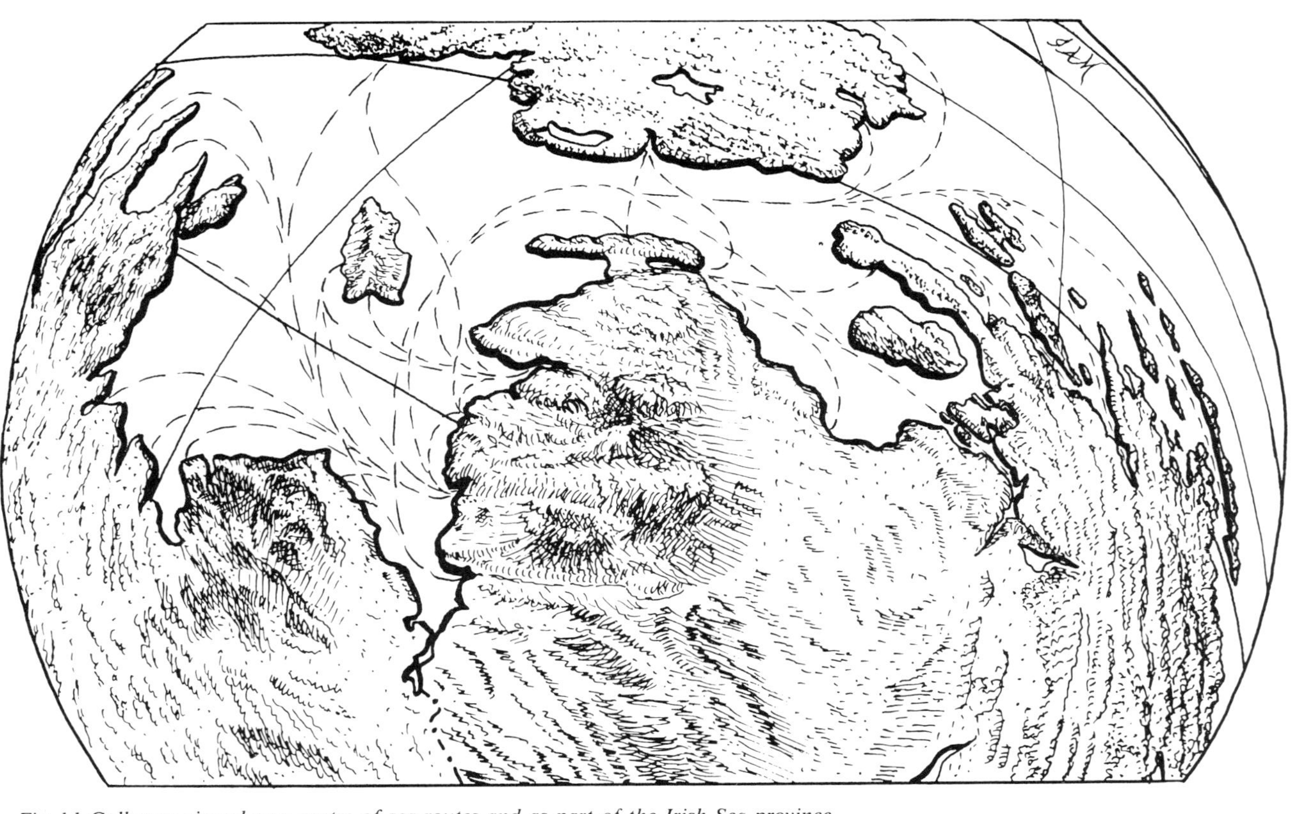

Fig. 1.1 Galloway viewed as a centre of sea-routes and as part of the Irish Sea province.

By simply using their eyes directly, our medieval and indeed prehistoric forbears may well have had a better perception of Galloway's location than our map-ridden generation. As Innes Macleod puts it:[4]

> To look at a map of Scotland on its own is a sure and certain way of starting with a false sense of the geography and history of this south-west corner . . . it does seem to be tucked away on its own, rather a long way from 'important' Scottish towns and cities, and involving a long journey through the moors and hills of Ayrshire and Dumfriesshire to get there.

Historically, at many periods it seems more profitable to regard Galloway as less of an out-of-the-way corner of Scotland than as an intrinsic part of the Irish Sea province, in terms of economic, political and demographic links. As Stuart Piggott pointed out,[5] we have to take access and egress by water as well as by land.

For Galloway, sea links and river access were of considerable importance from prehistory right through until the coming of the railways. This Victorian invention heralded the shift for traders and travellers alike to land-based thinking, which has been consolidated so completely in the present century by modern road transport. By and large, however, in Galloway the rail and road links which have developed over the last century and a half have grown to serve the pre-existing communities, which had evolved during the long previous eras when water transport was of much greater local significance. Thus, though today movement by water figures little in the lives of the people of the region, appreciation of its importance in the past gives a necessary insight into the settlement pattern we now see.

In the days of small coasting traders, under sail and latterly under steam, the string of sheltered inlets and river mouths along the Solway gave havens for craft plying in and out of the Clyde, across to Kintyre, and to the Hebrides beyond. Cumberland, Lancashire and Cheshire were familiar neighbours, and in the 18th and 19th centuries, merchants from Wigtown and Kirkcudbright formed partnerships in commerce and insurance with their opposite numbers in Whitehaven and Liverpool. There were more possibilities then than now if one wished to travel directly from Kirkcudbright or Stranraer to Peel in the Isle of Man, or on to Denbigh, Caernarvon and Anglesey in Wales. Galloway seamen were trading regularly in and out of Dublin, Down, Antrim, Derry and Donegal. By no means all of the trafficking figured in official records. Galloway's long and complex coastline bordering the North Channel, Irish Sea and Solway Firth gave great scope for those plying illegal trades, and from what one gathers of the scale of the smuggling tradition, it is hardly surprising that Robert Burns's service there should have inspired 'The Diel's awa' wi the Excise Man'. With the Isle of Man on the horizon, temptation must have remained great for a century after Burns, for it was not until 1876 that Man was brought within the orbit of British Customs regulations.

Although for small vessels the coves and little estuaries were ideal for running contraband or more mundane cargos for the local communities, their havens and channels are hardly scaled to the demands of modern container ships. Neither are the rivers, though these used to be busy with craft wending their way through the fields as far as Palnackie, and indeed Dalbeattie up the Urr, or Dumfries up the Nith. Even the smaller of the steam coasters of half a century ago were reaching the limit of practical access, and woe betide those which did not pay close attention to the tides and sandbanks. Dr C. V. Wayne has recently published a delightful volume of first-hand reminiscences of the coasting trade, in which Captain Owen Spargo illustrates this vividly.

In 1930 he was 2nd mate on SS *Kyle Firth,* heading for Palnackie, which still then had a thriving trade in grain and animal feed, with coal and general cargo coming in from the Mersey and fertilisers from Continental Europe. This was despite the winding channel (with a rock called the Porter Stone on a horseshoe bend). It was so shallow that for steamers it was regarded as a 'Spring Tide Port', i.e. only workable when tides are at their greatest amplitude. Since the Spring Tides were almost over, the captain of the *Kyle Firth* took the risk of sailing by night from Kirkcudbright, though this was customarily regarded as a daylight port.

> The crew arrived on board well 'lubricated' . . ., and the Captain and Pilot supporting each other . . . After we had been steaming for about an hour . . . I was ordered to let go the anchor. The mate then told me 'you don't need watches here . . . she won't drag; how true that was. I got up at six o'clock the next morning, and I could not see the sea! We were high and dry on a sand bank . . .

The next tide took them off, but they lost a propellor blade on the Porter Stone:

> We eventually arrived at Palnackie but . . . she took the ground in the middle of the river and remained fast. With the tide falling and the following day's tide smaller still, she was 'neaped' and would have to remain where she was for about a fortnight . . . the swans swimming peacefully around her.[6]

Though as Geoffrey Stell[7] rightly points out, places like Kirkcudbright and Garlieston still maintain a traditional seafaring atmosphere, they and the many other agreeable harbours which are Galloway's legacy from earlier centuries are now mostly limited by their miniscule scale to local fishing craft and yachts. Loch Ryan, however, offers a haven of a quite different order of size. Portpatrick, outside, had been the usual option for a direct Galloway-Ulster crossing in the days of sail, but as the wreckage of the outer harbour there shows, it is vulnerable to westerly gales. Stranraer, sheltered within Loch Ryan, took over with the coming of the Irish steam packet and ferry service. It soon developed some of the characteristics of a major port, including the dubious distinction[8] of being one of the few country towns in Scotland with a prostitution problem. The women congregated there to cull cash from homeward-bound Irish navvies. During World War II the size of the secure roadstead offered by the loch led to Cairnryan being refurbished to become a terminus for trans-Atlantic convoys. Though the naval connections of the area have faded, Stranraer has retained its importance to the present day as the commercial port offering the shortest sea-crossing between Britain and Ireland.

THE EVOLUTION OF GALLOWAY'S SCENERY

Having given some thought to routes of access and egress, let us now take the next steps advocated by Piggott, and consider the combinations of terrain and climate which have provided the Galwegians with their characteristic environment.

Space here does not allow a detailed descriptive 'setting of the stage' area-by-area within Galloway for the human action to be played out in the later chapters. An attempt will therefore be made to identify processes in the physical development of the terrain which have produced characteristic landscape elements. The aim in this is to provide keys the reader may use in their own interpretation of the scenery of areas of Galloway of particular interest to them.

We suggested above that the relationship of land and sea has been perceived in different ways at different phases in the history of Galloway. As in so much of Scotland, however, although the way that the terrain has been recorded and utilised has changed radically in the brief span of recorded human activity, the basic layout of the region (and indeed much of its topographic detail) reflects events long antecedent to its human past. Beneath our cultural imprint of field-patterns and settlements, the ancient structure of the bedrock provides the bones of the landscape; during the past few million years, these have been both sculpted and fleshed out in the processes of the Ice Age, and by sea-level changes.

An appreciation of even the sheer age of the rocks can give insights into the aspects of the cultural landscape, such as the characteristic nature of the preferred building stones. In Galloway, some of the bedrock is more than five hundred million years old, and little is less than half that age. This makes the Alps (which have only appeared during the last sixty-five million years) seem young, and puts us back into periods when the whole layout of the land masses on planet Earth were very different from what we are familiar with now. Thus, the agreeable pinkish stones of Caerlaverock Castle or Sweetheart Abbey reflect tropical sunlight beating down on red desert sands, long before the dinosaurs lived, when our part of the Earth's crust lay down by the equator. Nearby, Locharbriggs Quarry, close to Dumfries, once provided around half the freestone used by Scottish masons, and its desert colour dominates street after street of the more stylish tenements in Glasgow. Dumfries itself stands over a basin of Permian sandstone, dating from around two hundred and fifty million years ago.

This not only gave good quality artesian water for 19th-century industries there, but more red sandstone for the architects of its Victorian and Edwardian prosperity.

Structural basins like this in the bedrock have often been eroded out to give hollows in the terrain, and an appreciation of their layout can give an insight into the pattern of the Galloway landscape. Thus, the southern part of the Dumfries basin is now drowned by the Solway, creating the bay between Caerlaverock Castle (with its once-tidal moat) and Sweetheart Abbey. Then from there to Abbey Head (south of Kirkcudbright, named after Dundrennan Abbey) the sweep of the coast follows the northern margin of a flooded basin of Carboniferous and New Red Sandstones, with the more resistant rocks of Bengairn and Criffel rising immediately inland. Wigtown Bay may have a similar underlying structure. In the west, much of Luce Bay and Loch Ryan appear to have been eroded into a basin of Permian sandstones. The repeating pattern does not cease there; Belfast

Fig.1.2 Caerlaverock Castle; sketch from an aerial viewpoint.

Lough and Strangford Lough match the New Red Sandstone basin around Stranraer, just as the tougher materials of the Ards Peninsula in County Down provide a structural counterpart for the upstanding Rhinns of Galloway.

These ancient sandstones of Galloway are soft enough to encourage elaborate carving, so they were used extensively in the medieval ecclesiastical architecture of the area. Sometimes, however, it was felt necessary to employ some of the stronger rocks of the region, though they were more difficult to work. Thus, for example, Sweetheart Abbey also made use of granite, from close-by Criffel.

We tend to assume from their use in architecture that all granites are outstandingly durable, but this is not so. It is certainly true that the main highland areas of Galloway are associated with granites, emplaced during the Caledonian mountain building period (around four hundred million years ago, in Old Red Sandstone times). But as the plutons of granitic material were intruded at depth into the country rock, they baked and metamorphosed the pre-existing sedimentary strata. The intrusions are thus surrounded by 'metamorphic aureoles'. It is another key to understanding the scenery of Galloway to realise that these zones of heat- and pressure-tempered metamorphic rocks have sometimes proved even more resistant to erosion than the granites which they surround.

Thus, the heart of the Criffel granite massif has been hollowed out by glaciation. Similarly, the outcrop of granite by the Cairnsmore of Fleet (711m), has been ground out by the ice to form the scenery at the western extremity of the area. Just north of the Mull of Galloway itself, where an intrusion gives the spectacular cliffs of Crammag Head and Laggantallach Head, it is sedimentaries toughened by metamorphosis which form hills that ring the worn-down granite.

The most striking example of this pattern forms the highest part of Galloway. A figure-of-eight-shaped intrusion of granite runs for almost 20km from Loch Doon to Loch Dee. There, only the ridge of Mullwharchar (692m) is of granite; the higher surrounding peaks are not. These include the Merrick (as we noted, at 843m the highest peak in southern Scotland), the Rhinns of Kells (813m), Shalloch on Minnoch (768m) and Lamachan Hill (716m). They all lie on or around the metamorphic aureole. Their material was once vulnerable sedimentary rocks such as shales and flagstones, but it was transformed by the heat and chemical action associated with the intrusion of the granites into resistant schists. They form a rugged ring around the central Mullwharchar ridge. The white granite of that is relatively tough, but between it and the metamorphics there now lies a trench 500m below the peaks, with a moat of lochans. This has been excavated from tonalite, a less resistant variety within the granite.

The repeated glaciations of the last two or three million years have certainly had a major role in sculpting the present landscape, by picking out differences in the hardness of the bedrock. Dr Grahame Jardine believes, however, that the present drainage system of Galloway shows hints of origin as far back in pre-glacial times as the mid-Tertiary, say thirty million years ago. As time passed, the initial pattern was modified not only by the interplay between glaciation and geological structure, but by river captures.

For example, the waters of the Ken and Dee converge, and combine on a south-easterly heading. Though the resulting river now turns away to the south-west, a through valley continues on a south-easterly course past Castle Douglas to the coast of the Solway at Orchardton Bay. It would seem that the original outlet that way was superseded by the present south-westerly one into Kirkcudbright Bay. Threave Castle is set at the elbow of capture, where it dominates the bifurcation of the valley system. It thus seems that pre-glacial events have set patterns of natural routeways which have helped to set the stage for strategic decisions in medieval times.

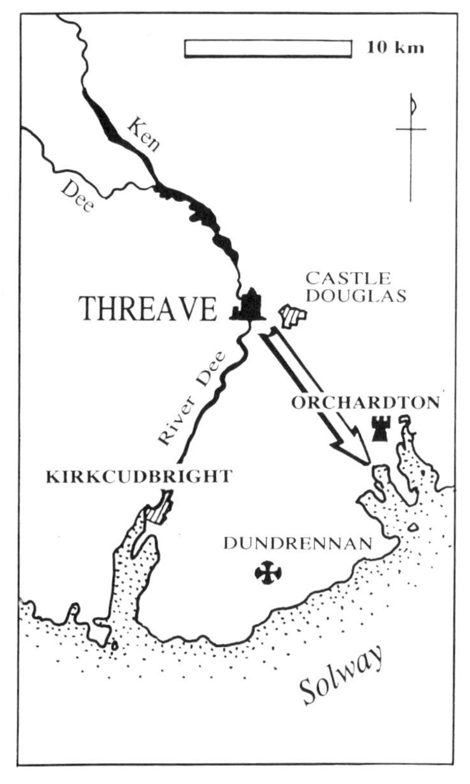

Fig.1.3 Threave Castle; sketch-map showing site in relation to routes created by river capture.

In reconstructing past landscapes and interpreting historical events in Galloway, it has to be kept in mind that the drainage pattern has been changed in very recent times by reservoir and hydro-electric schemes. The major Clatteringshaws Loch is artificial; many other mountain lochs have been extended by dams; and instead of draining to the Ayrshire coast, Loch Doon now discharges into the Solway, *via* a mile-long tunnel to the Dee and the artificially-deepened Loch Ken.

Compared to the works of man or of rivers, in Galloway, as in so much of Scotland, it is clear that the dominant land-sculpting agent has been the ice of the Quaternary Ice Age. We do not know how many glaciations there have been, but Galloway was certainly wholly buried in the ice sheets many times. Erratic boulders of Loch Doon granite were carried up onto the tops of the Merrick and the Cairnsmore of Fleet; Cairnsmore and Criffel boulders are to be found in Cumberland (and indeed pieces of Ailsa Craig have been carried past Galloway as far as Snowdonia!).

The uplands of Galloway contain classic examples of landscapes of glacial erosion: lochs like Doon and Trool occupy troughs gouged from the bedrock by the ice (Loch Trool's valley is of the characteristic Alpine U-shaped cross-section); the cold north-eastern faces of the Rhinns of Kells and the Merrick are bitten into by corries, where snow patches developed into small glaciers.

With the scenery having been reworked again and again by numerous glaciations over at least two million years, we cannot now tell how far the features of glacial erosion we see in Galloway are the product of the last major period of glaciation, or of former phases. Certainly, the whole of the Scottish mainland was completely buried by an ice sheet around 20,000-18,000 years ago. This retreated in stages, and Galloway may have become ice-free by (or soon after) 14,000 years ago (dates are in uncalibrated radiocarbon terms). But between 11,000 and 10,000 years ago (i.e. just 9-8,000 bc) there was a sharp cold spell. Many valley glaciers developed in the Scottish Highlands, and one which pushed into the lowlands from the trough where Loch Lomond now lies has been used to name this stage.

In Galloway, Dr Roger Cornish[9] has mapped eleven little glaciers dating from this Loch Lomond Advance, around the Merrick, Corserine and Loch Doon. Most occupied north- and east-facing corries, and apart from two which covered two and three square kilometres, the rest were less than one sq. km. in area. Their effect on the broad view of the present landscape was therefore limited; but they are a salutary reminder that even in Galloway (which we tend to think of as the bland South-West of Scotland), Ice Age conditions prevailed as recently as 8,000 bc, when elsewhere in the world various peoples were well on the road to the domestication of plants and animals, and what we consider as the roots of civilisation.

So far, we have been considering glacial erosion. Though there is certainly plenty of evidence of this, the distance of the area from the main centres of ice accumulation means that we see neither the fjord-coastline of Highland Scotland, nor the intractable ice-scoured bedrock landscapes of the crofting counties. Instead, it is the deposits left by the ice which often dominate the scenery and land-use potential of the Galloway lowlands. There, the bedrock is often thickly plastered with glacial drift. There are many lochans and boggy hollows even now in the depressions in the boulder clay, despite the canny drainage work of generations of farmers, and in the past there were certainly many more.

Particularly in the western lowlands, the feeling of being in the Irish Sea province (an impression encouraged by both the structural and the cultural links) is enhanced even further by tracts of landscape dominated by drumlins. These are rolling hillocks of glacial till, streamlined by the ice sheet. They occur elsewhere in Scotland (parts of Glasgow are built on them), but on this side of the North Channel they seldom dominate the eye as much as they do in the country around Wigtown. Folk who have retired to Galloway to escape the troubles in Ulster have remarked that they often feel that they are back in the landscape of County Down.

The end, around 8,000 bc, of the latest phase of glaciation in Scotland

Fig.1.4 Lochar Moss; stratigraphic change as reported in the old rhyme: 'First a wood, then a sea / Noo a Moss, and ever will be.'

did not mark the cessation of major structural changes in the landscape of Galloway. It is not just modern scientists who have appreciated this. The antiquary Daniel Wilson noted a century and a half ago that the locals had a rhyme about Lochar Moss:

> First a Wood and then a Sea,
> Noo a Moss, and ever wull be . . .

Perfectly accurately, they had observed stratigraphy which expressed the interaction there between land- and sea-levels: a forest had been drowned, and buried in marine clay with sea-shells; then when the mud-flats eventually emerged above sea-level, they were colonised by a peat bog.

When the last ice left Galloway, world sea-level was low, because of the amount of water still locked up in the glaciers elsewhere. But the land-level in Galloway was also lower than at present, because of the isostatic depression caused by the weight of the superincumbent ice during the previous glacial episodes. For several millennia, a race ensued between the rising ocean and the rising land. Sometimes the ocean won, and there were extensive inundations of Galloway's coastal margins; sometimes the land drew clear, exhibiting raised beaches above the contemporary tideline. Although ocean level tended to be uniform from place to place (water finding its own level), differences in isostatic loading and response meant that the land-level movements vary, and former shorelines are thus often tilted. The local histories of relative level change therefore also vary, not only between Galloway and other parts of Scotland (depressed differentially by the ice) but even along the length of the Solway.

In Galloway, between the headlands of ancient rocks we are repeatedly confronted by long stretches of mud-flats, marshes, raised beaches and carse lands (raised estuarine deposits like those of the Forth and Tay). For many years, Dr Grahame Jardine has played a leading part[10] in working out the interplay between land- and sea-levels which has given us the present coastal landscape. In the following summary, based on his investigations, dating is by radiocarbon (uncalibrated), and heights are given in terms of Ordnance Datum (OD), which is modern mean tide-level.

Between 9,000 and 8,000 years ago, mean relative sea-level was two to four metres below OD at the eastern end of the Solway, but about one metre above OD in Wigtown Bay (this tilting of the shoreline is due to differential land movement continuing after that date). For the next millennium or so, the rise of the world ocean level appears to have outstripped the upward movements in Galloway. By about 7,200 years ago (i.e. 5,200 bc) the sea had attained its maximum lateral extent in south west Scotland during our post-glacial period. It had not, however, reached its maximum height. It was still rising, but the Lochar Gulf ceased to be affected by salt water about 6,600 years ago (*c.* 4,600 bc), possibly because of the growth of sand and gravel bars about its mouth. Elsewhere in the

Solway, the main post-glacial transgression did not finish until around 5,600 years ago in the east, or 5,000 (i.e. 3,000 bc) in the west.

It was not just around Lochar Moss by Dumfries that these level changes had major topographic implications. Wigtown Bay formerly extended almost to Newton Stewart, but was then filled in with carse clays, which were capped by the Moss of Cree when they eventually emerged above sea-level. Raised beach deposits can be traced across the isthmus between Luce Bay and Loch Ryan, suggesting that the Rhinns of Galloway were cut off from the mainland in late glacial and early post-glacial times. Indeed,

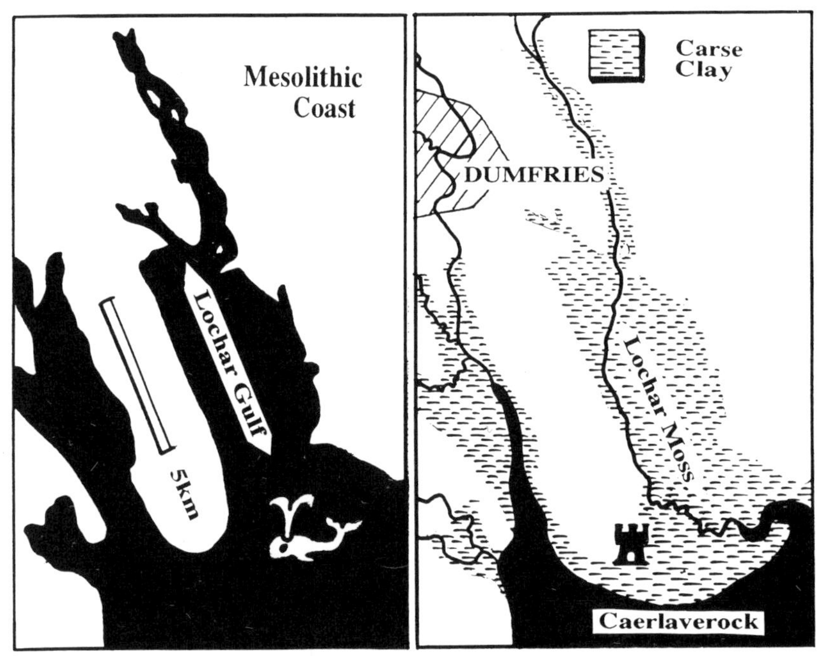

Fig.1.5 Dumfries, the Nith Estuary and Lochar Moss; sketch-map showing shoreline change from mesolithic to modern times.

former shoreline remnants on the Rhinns themselves suggest they sometimes only showed as a string of islets. In phases when the area emerged, and stretches of sandy seabed were exposed, coastal dunes built up. Those around Luce Bay surpass 15m (50ft) in height, and sand-blows can reveal Mesolithic sites.

As we have seen, in parts of Galloway the main post-glacial transgression did not culminate until around 3,000 bc, i.e. a millennium or so after the local arrival of Neolithic peoples, and only perhaps five hundred years before bronze working is evident. The complex interaction of land- and sea-level changes went on long after the local maxima of the transgression.

Thus it is by no means only during the Mesolithic that we have to take into account the possibility of the changes in coastline when considering the environments of settlement sites.

Even in the later era of the fully historical period, when the amplitude of contemporary natural change is much diminished, we cannot afford to disregard these earlier events. Their legacy of deposits and landforms has implications for the patterns of historical and indeed present-day coastal land use and settlement. Sometimes their influence has been negative, and sometimes positive. Where they can be stripped of peat and drained economically, the old estuarine muds of the carse lands can provide fertile soils. Sometimes, however, the task has proved daunting, as in the case of the Lochar Moss, the largest of these areas. Though the peat there was once used for industrial as well as household fuel (and, more recently, bagged for horticulture), reclamation has only proceeded around the edges. In contrast, elsewhere the admixture of raised beach materials or blown sand has helped to lighten the texture of what would otherwise have been heavy soils of glacial boulder clay, so that they drain better and warm sooner in the spring.

CLIMATE AND LAND

Ameliorating factors such as these have especial importance, because of the particular nature of Galloway's climate. To those who dwell elsewhere in Scotland, conscious of their snell winters, the climate of the south-west has a reputation for blandness. Summer holiday visits reinforce this impression, with images of lush lowland greenery. But compared to what we are used to on the east coast of Scotland, upland bleakness starts low in Galloway. Improved land reaches only up to about 500ft (just 150m) above sea-level; and often three-quarters of that 'improved' land is under permanent grass even down by the coast, because of the combination of the rainfall with the heavy clay soils. These lowlands of Galloway have been nicknamed the dairy-farm of Scotland, but above, we move rapidly into sheep country: S. R. Crockett's Galloway of misty hills 'of brown bent and red heather . . . and grey gnarled thorn'.

Dr Joy Tivy[11] has made a comparative study of the upland vegetation of Galloway and the Border Country lying to the east. The higher rainfall and the humidity of the west, and its greater cloudiness and exposure, favour peat growth more than in the relative rain shadow to the east. Thus, in the Galloway mountains the quality of the grazing is poorer, with more bog myrtle, purple moor grass and deer sedge than in the dryer grasslands of the high Border Country. The higher level of precipitation on the Atlantic side held true during the Ice Age too, and the resulting rather more severe glacial activity there has left more patches with sparse soil cover. Compared to the better Border sheep-runs, in upland Galloway only half the density of stocking is possible, five or more acres being needed to support one ewe. It is perhaps not surprising that much more of the hill land has been turned over to forestry than in the more productive east. Glen Trool Forest Park alone runs to over 100,000 acres.

On the eastern side of Scotland, even as far to the north as Aberdeenshire, cereal crops can be grown successfully at considerably higher altitudes than in Galloway. This is despite notably colder winters. The seeming paradox is due to the oceanic influence on Galloway's climate, compared to the relative continentality of the east coast climate. It is not just the way that the weather coming in off the Atlantic gives high rainfall, and persistent cloud cover which inhibits evaporation. Having a major ocean up-wind tends to lower the amplitude of the march of temperature through the year.

Thus, in the winter, the more 'continental' east coast tends to cool down to a greater extent, while the great mass of ocean water responds slowly and holds up the temperature in the west. This gives Galloway its blander winter. Unfortunately, this is of scant advantage for arable farming, since little crop growth occurs then.

In summer, while the temperature curve can rise quite steeply in areas protected from the influence of a major ocean, the heat-sink effect of the Atlantic now works the other way, and inhibits the rise of summer temperatures in areas such as Galloway. This flattening of the curve means that relatively few day-degrees of energy are available above the threshold temperatures for plant growth and ripening. Everything is more marginal; not only is there less scope for evaporating excess soil moisture, but the cooling effect of increasing height above sea-level becomes critical at a much lower altitude than in regimes where summer temperatures show a higher peak. Crops ripen in the Alps and other inland continental locations at far greater heights than the Merrick, let alone the practical limits of arable cultivation in Galloway. In a European perspective, it is notable that despite the marked contrast in their winters, Galloway has been mapped by Dr Martin Parry[12] as having a much more marginal climate for cereal cropping than Finland, let alone Buchan.

LANDSCAPE IMAGERY: IN WORDS AND PAINT

The landscapes of Galloway should not, however, be regarded merely in such mundane matters as 'land use potential'. At the start of this essay, it was suggested that the region was not characterised by homogeneity. This is to its advantage, in terms of delights for the eye. Galloway gains a particular attractiveness from its juxtapositions of the rich variety of the vistas evolved through the local interactions of climate with terrain, and of people with place. This has made it a ready source of imagery for painters and writers alike. It was to Galloway that the Glesga' Boys (the 'Scottish Impressionists') sallied out from their sooty city at the turn of the century. And many artists, professional and amateur, have followed them since.

Along the Solway, the sea can retreat towards the horizon, leaving the cloudscape reflected in a vast beige mirror of wet sand; but the tide can come racing in, to send gurly seas surging around rugged headlands, licking towards caves reputed to be the lairs of smugglers, or worse. The villainous Dirk Hatteraick (adopted by Sir Walter Scott in *Guy Mannering*) seems positively benign compared to the Bean clan of Galloway cannibals. According to John Wilson, a rhymer from Gatehouse, in their cave:

The limbs o' men, women an' weans on the wa's,
Like beef that is dried were hung up in grim raws,
An' some laid in pickle fu' sune tae be ta'en
By that horde in the Hades o' aul' Sawney Bean.

Along the coast, *The Raiders* of Samuel R. Crockett's fiction lurked on a thinly disguised version of Hestan Island, off the mouth of the Urr.

One feels in safer territory when one leaves the wilder stretches of shore for the neat little towns, sheltered by the inlets which were the main focus of their prosperity when the sea was the main highway for legal trade too. Well built from local stone, they combine the couthiness of their miniscule scale with confident and distinct identities. Local pride is evident in the pleasant pretentiousness of many of their 18th- and 19th-century buildings, and harmonious colour washes lend them vividness, even under lowering skies, as many painters have appreciated. Here, too, however, there is a smell of adventure, and violence. This comes out in regional writings, long and short. Consider the laconic epitaph of the luckless James Montgomery of Portpatrick, who perished in 1652:

Sir James by pirates shot, and therefore dead
By them i' the sea was solemly buried

The quill of the more verbose Walter Scott turned Gatehouse of Fleet into the Kippletringan of *Guy Mannering;* Robert Louis Stevenson took up Borgue for *The Master of Ballantrae;* and more recently Dorothy L. Sayers brought genteel skullduggery to the area with *Five Red Herrings.*

Both the authors and the artists have found the lowland scenery between the little towns more than agreeable; Thomas Carlyle, that Ecclefechan arbiter of refined taste, fairly frothed about the prospects from the shoreside road betwixt Creetown and Gatehouse. Farther west, painters have caught the whalebacks of the drumlins, netted in a mesh of hedgerows.

If, however, one turns inland, that low limit for the 'improved land' means that one often moves with quite startling rapidity up out of the lowlands, manicured by centuries of canny husbandry, into scenery that has lost little of the wildness which was the legacy of the Ice Age to Highland Galloway. There has been a tradition of wildness amongst the denizens of those uplands, too. Tales of their nefarious doings were combined with graphic descriptions of the moor and mountain landscapes by Crockett in books such as *The Men of the Moss Hags, Bog Myrtle and Peat,* or *Raiderland.* John Buchan, too, found the rugged country around the Cairnsmore of Fleet an appropriate setting for the hunting of Hannay in the *Thirty-Nine Steps.*

At the end of his introduction to the *Exploring Scotland's Heritage* volume on Dumfries and Galloway, Geoffrey Stell commented that the region.

> may not have everything, but many of its antiquities stand high in their respective national league tables.

Many of those who explored the area with the Scottish Society for Northern Studies would be willing to extend that judgement from antiquities to landscapes, and most would certainly agree with him that

> every resident knows, and every visitor will find out, what — in the best possible sense — a fascinating region this is![13]

Bibliography

Useful general surveys, setting the geological and geomorphological evolution of Galloway in its Scottish perspective include:

Craig, G. (ed.), *Geology of Scotland* (Edinburgh, 2nd edition 1983);

Whittow, J., *Geology and Scenery in Scotland* (London, 1977); and

Price, R., *Scotland's Environment During the Last 30,000 Years* (Edinburgh, 1983).

Notes

1. Piggott, S., *Scotland Before History* (London, 1958), 1; Piggott, S., and Ritchie, G., *Scotland Before History: with Gazetteer of Ancient Monuments* (Edinburgh, 1982).
2. Stell, G., *Exploring Scotland's Heritage: Dumfries and Galloway* (Edinburgh, 1986), 9.
3. Donaldson, G., *Scotland: The Shaping of a Nation* (Newton Abbot, 1974).
4. Macleod, I., *Discovering Galloway* (Edinburgh, 1986), 5.
5. Piggott, *Scotland Before History,* 1.
6. Spargo, O., and Thomason, T., *Old Time Steam Coasting* (Wolverhampton, 1982), 42.3.
7. Stell, *Dumfries and Galloway.*
8. Smout, T. C., *A Century of the Scottish People: 1830-1950* (London, 1986).
9. Cornish, R., 'Glaciers of the Loch Lomond Stadial in the western Southern Uplands of Scotland', *Proceedings of the Geographical Association,* xcii (1981), 105-14.
10. e.g. Jardine, G., 'Holocene raised coastal sediments and former shorelines of Dumfriesshire and eastern Galloway', *TDGAS,* 55 (1980), 1-59.
11. e.g. Tivy, J. (ed.), *The Organic Resources of Scotland* (Edinburgh, 1973).
12. Parry, M., *Climatic Change, Agriculture and Settlement* (Folkestone, 1978), 85.
13. Stell, *Dumfries and Galloway,* 13.

THE LITERARY SOURCES FOR THE LIFE OF ST NINIAN

John MacQueen

There are three major documentary sources for St Ninian. One, which will be referred to as HE, is the first paragraph of Bede, *Historia Ecclesiastica* III.iv., written, as seems likely, in 731.[1] Second (MNE) is the *Miracula Nynie Episcopi*,[2] a poem composed by a monk at Whithorn towards the end of the eighth century, and some fifty years later than Bede. Third (VN) is the *Vita Niniani*[3] by Ailred of Rievaulx, probably composed between 1154 and 1160 (Ailred died in 1166).

As has long been realised, there is a particularly close relationship between MNE and VN. MNE is the religious epyllion composed in Latin heroic (hexameter) verse, as were many other important saints' *Lives* during the eighth and ninth centuries. Examples that come readily to mind include Bede's metrical *Life* of St Cuthbert, written before 705, Alcuin's metrical *Life* of St Willibrord (*c.* 785-797), Milo of St Amand's *Life* of Amandus, completed between 845 and 855, and Heiric of Auxerre's *Life* of St Germanus of Auxerre, completed in 877.[4] Each of these poems has as its source an earlier prose narrative — for Bede, the anonymous *Life* of St Cuthbert, for Alcuin, his own prose *Life* of Willibrord, for Milo, his own prose narrative, for Heiric, the much earlier (*c.* 480) *Life* of Germanus by Constantius.[5] It is probable that MNE is also based on a prose source, no longer extant, which may be called *PV. At several points MNE can be understood only if one makes a comparison with VN, a fact which presumably indicates that both are ultimately based on *PV, which Ailred's prose version reproduces with more precision of detail than does the compressed and often allusive verse of MNE.

The existence in both of a series of posthumous miracles associated with the distinctively Anglo-Saxon personal names shows that at least some of the material had its origins in the period of the Anglian bishopric at Whithorn, which had just been established when Bede completed his *Historia Ecclesiastica*, but as there is nothing similar in the actual life-story as related in either work, there is a suggestion that this part at least antedates the Anglian supremacy.

It should be added that there is evidence[6] to suggest that VN was based, not directly on *PV, but on an intermediate lost Anglo-Saxon translation (*ASV), one phrase (*Farres Last*) of which Ailred preserves in his chapter VIII.

How is HE related to this? Bede's knowledge of Ninian is likely to be derived from his friend Pecthelm, first Anglian bishop of Candida Casa, who died in 735.[7] Pecthelm is acknowledged by Bede as the source of two anecdotes in *Historia Ecclesiastica*: one (V.xiii.) is the story of the Mercian who on his deathbed was shown by an angel the slender volume which recorded his good acts, and by a demon the massive record of his evil acts; the other (V.xviii.) is the story of the miraculous cures affected at the tomb of Haedde, the saintly bishop of the West Saxons who died in 705. Pecthelm's recent election to the see of Candida Casa is recorded in *Historia Ecclesiastica* V.xxiii., but he is there described as *first* bishop of the see, a remark earlier contradicted by HE. Bede, I suggest, knew nothing of the history of Candida Casa when he recorded the election; shortly afterwards Pecthelm or an intermediary gave him more information, which he then incorporated in his text at III.iv., without however making any correction at v.xxiii.. This may result from nothing more than a lapse of memory. HE certainly gives the appearance of having been inserted into a chapter dealing primarily with Columba, which itself, as Plummer noted,[8] is not included in the *capitula*, or in the late Anglo-Saxon translation, and thus may well be a later interpolation. The decision to include some account of Columba was itself possibly a late one — Columba, after all, had nothing directly to do with the history of the English church and people — and the decision to include Ninian later still. Pecthelm is the most likely source of information. He must have gained this in turn from traditions, or more probably a ducument, preserved at Whithorn, a document which basically, I suggest, was *PV, the existence of which has already been postulated. As against this, it has commonly been said that there is nothing factual, or apparently factual, in MNE and VN which is not also in HE, with the implication that HE is therefore the source of both. Certainly HE compresses a surprisingly high factual content into very few words. There are ten main items:-

(i) Ninian's *floruit* was long before Columba's arrival in Iona.
(ii) He converted the Southern Picts.
(iii) He was a reverent bishop and a holy man (i.e. monk) of the nation of the Britons.
(iv) He was regularly instructed at Rome.
(v) His monastic episcopal seat included a church named for Martin of Tours (ob. 397).
(vi) This contained the relics of St Ninian and of many other saints.
(vii) An Anglican bishop had recently been appointed to the see.
(viii) The church was now in the province of the Bernicians.
(ix) It was called in the vernacular The White House.
(x) The explanation of the name is that it was built of stone in a manner to which the Britons were not accustomed.

MNE and VN, however, contain additional, apparently factual statements:

(i) Ninian visited St Martin on his way home from Rome (VN).
(ii) Martin provided masons for the building of Candida Casa (VN).
(iii) The Picts converted by Ninian were called Niduari (MNE).
(iv) Ninian had dealings with a king called Tuduael, Thuuahel, Tuduvallus.

(v) A place called Farres Last was somewhere in the vicinity of Whithorn. (VN).
(vi) Ninian was accustomed to make use of a cave (MNE).
(vii) A name Plebia occurs in connection with Ninian (VN).
(viii) Stories of posthumous miracles include four Anglo-Saxon personal names — Pethgils, Plecgils (MNE), Adefridus, Desuit (VN).

The possible significance of this additional material has been discussed elsewhere.[9] In addition, MNE suggests that the Pope of Ninian's visit to Rome was called Clement,[10] or had a particularly close relationship to Pope Clement. The latter was commonly but erroneously regarded as St Peter's immediate successor, and if the reference is to him, it shows merely that the author of MNE had no idea of Ninian's historical period. On the other hand, Siricius, who was Pope from 384 to 399, built San Clemente, an important church in Rome, on a site which was believed to have connections with his predecessor.[11] It is just possible that a reference to Siricius is intended.

Despite this, most writers (including myself) have tended to concentrate on HE, not least because MNE and VN contain much fabulous material in the shape of miracle stories, none of which is to be found in HE. MNE includes four attributed to the lifetime of the saint; VN adds two others. MNE and VN each has in addition four posthumous miracles, three of which correspond in both works, but the fourth differs. It is generally assumed, at least implicitly, that these miracle stories are subsequent additions to the straightforward factual account of HE. For several reasons, this is unlikely.

(1) A general characteristic of the early hagiographical tradition in the Western as in the Eastern church is the emphasis placed by it on the miraculous.

The *Life of Martin* by Sulpicius Severus (*c.* 363-*c.* 420/5), written during the lifetime of the saint by one of his immediate followers, and Constantius' *Life of Germanus*, already mentioned,[12] are striking and influential examples. Both appear to have been well-known in Britain. The performance of miracles formed a necessary part of a saint's *dossier.* It is extremely unlikely that any account of a much earlier monastic luminary would have come down to Bede unaccompanied by miracle stories.

(2) In historical work, Bede's general habit is to include miracle stories only when they are sanctioned by a tradition still powerful in his own time, or by the eye-witnesses with whom he has some kind of personal acquaintance. The frequency with which miracle stories are included in *Historia Ecclesiastica* actually increases as Bede moves towards his own present. It is not likely that he would have included specimens dating from a remote period, and originating in a community with which he was personally unfamiliar.

(3) Bede sometimes suppresses miracle stories for which he cannot obtain first-hand evidence. Thus his own *Historia Abbatum*[13] omits the story of the miracles which followed the death of Abbot Ceolfrid (642-716) and which are related in the final paragraph of the anonymous *Historia Abbatum*, his main source. Ceolfrid was Bede's own abbot, but presumably he was unable to find eye-witnesses of the occurrences.

All in all, it seems improbable that Bede should have received the story in the form in which he has preserved it, and probable that a closer approximation to the older form is provided by MNE and VN. The probable line of descent may be represented by a stemma:

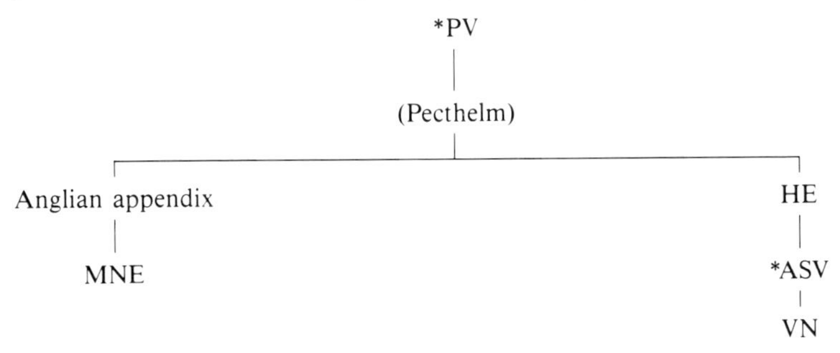

MNE and VN nevertheless are themselves characterised by internal differences of three main kinds. First is the order of events. In MNE the conversion of the Picts follows immediately upon Ninian's return from Rome, and precedes the foundation of Candida Casa, whereas in VN the foundation of Candida Casa, together with the miracles involving Tudwal and the priest accused of fornication, have first place. The result is that in MNE the four miracle stories form a group, and are separated only by the single chapter from the four posthumous miracles; the author may well have changed the order of his source simply to obtain such a grouping.

Second is the fact that MNE and VN each contain one posthumous miracle not present in the other. In MNE the story of the priest Plecgil's physical experience of the presence of the Christ child in the elements of the Mass forms the climax of the series; VN substitutes a rather colourless story of the healing of two lepers. The Plecgils story was known on the continent during the 9th century; it is utilised for serious theological purposes by St Paschasius Radbertus (*c.* 785-*c.* 860) in his treatise *De Corpore et Sanguine Domini*, written in 831 and revised in 844.[14] The doctrine put forward by Paschasius, an extremely material form of Transubstantiation, was sharply attacked by two notable contemporaries, Ratramnus of Corbie (ob. 868), and Rabanus Maurus (776 or 784-856), abbot of Fulda and archbishop of Mainz, one of the greatest theologians of the age.[15] It is conceivable that the known hostility of such opponents to the doctrines implicit in the story led Ailred to exclude it from VN —

this despite the fact that he was a Cistercian, and that a very similar miracle, derived possibly from Paschasius or even MNE, twice appears (chapters 14 and 15), and is given great emphasis, in the Cistercian *Queste del Saint Graal*,[16] a prose romance or spiritual fable written about 1225.

Third is the fact that VN contains two lifetime miracles not present in MNE. One is the story of the *illicita cogitatio*, the sinful thought which momentarily destroyed the spiritual umbrella protecting Ninian and his psalter from the rain. The emphasis on the book as part of the story suggests that the narrative was originally linked to a supposed relic of the saint — a psalter which showed traces of exposure to the elements. If this is so, the story is likely to be early. The second is the record of the miracles of the staff of St Ninian in the sea and on land, the details of which more resemble sensational romantic fiction than anything in the other miracle stories.

Both stories may simply be later additions to the original *Life*. More probably, as I see it, they fall outside the scheme set for himself by the author of the MNE. As has been mentioned, his primary concern was with the miracles performed by the saint. The *illicita cogitatio*, however, illustrates not so much the exercise of spiritual power as a failure on the part of St Ninian. At least to the superficial reader, the second story illustrates the power resident in the saint's crozier rather than in his person. The crozier makes an early appearance in VN's version of the story of the bull and the thieves, the version of which in the MNE to a degree lacks point simply because the miracle-working staff makes no appearance. There are hints that it has been suppressed by the author.

An alternative possibility should also be noted. MNE is written in the complex literary tradition of the Latin saint's *Life* in metrical form, seen at its most advanced in Heiric's *Life of Germanus*, which has already been mentioned in the course of this essay. Numerological structure is one feature of the tradition. Elsewhere,[17] I have attempted an analysis of Heiric's use of the Hexad, the number 6. Similar features are also to be found in the prose tradition as may be illustrated by the tenth century *Navigatio Sancti Brendani*, but it also appears in works written at a much earlier date. In Bede's prose *Life of St Cuthbert*[18] (c.720), for instance, the life, death and entombment of the saint is narrated in forty chapters. Death and entombment mark his entrance into the life, the promised land, towards which his mortal life had been, as it were, a prologue, a pilgrimage. Correspondingly, the Israelites spent forty years in their journey through the wilderness to the Promised Land. The symbolism is clear: it is used in the *Navigatio*, and also in the dedicatory acrostics which Milo used to introduce his metrical *Life of Amandus*.[19] Milo's poem, moreover, is divided into four books which correspond to the four Gospels, and also to the idea of Concord, illustrated in the four figures of the saint and King Dagobert, reconciled in Book III by means of the two close friends, the laymen, Dado (Ouen, Audoin) and Eligius, who afterwards themselves became saints and bishops, in Rouen and Noyon respectively. The situation is summarised in the line *Salve, fida fides; felix concordia haveto,*[20] which occurs (III.291) when the pair are introduced. Concord is also implicit in the names of the saint and his parents, Amandus, Serenus and Amantia:

Rem stupidus miror divino munere gestam,
Quod sibi conveniunt genitor, genetrix genitusque,
Nominibus dignis donorum munera fantes.[21]

(I.134-6)

The word *conveniunt*, 'come together, agree, harmonise,' is particularly significant in this passage.

MNE is on a smaller scale than the other *Lives* mentioned. It contains fourteen short chapters, of which the first nine are devoted primarily to the miracles performed by the saint during his earthly lifetime, the succeeding five to his posthumous miracles. Nine is also prominent in that *all* the miracles are narrated in the course of nine chapters, V-XIII. The number nine appertains primarily to the angels, corresponding as it does to their nine orders, and to the nine celestial spheres, for the movements of which the angels have responsibility. Nine is also the square of three, which is the number of the Trinity, whose place is above even the angels.[22].

MNE begins with the descent to incarnation of Christ from his place with the Father beyond the celestial spheres, and continues with the labours undertaken by the community of saints generally, the bright stars, who carried on his earthly work after the Ascension, the return to the Father. Ninian was one who joined in the task of bringing humanity from death to the golden-glowing stars in the starry sky (*Sic hominum cuneos graui de morte uocatos/Duxit ad astriferi rutilantia sidera celi.*[23] Candida Casa sparkles like a star. Ninian restores light and life by curing blindness and raising the dead, and eventually is carried by the shining host, the angels, beyond the starry sky to the glory of the Trinity:

Ergo ubi utilitas morientes liquerat artus,
Spiritus extimplo precinctus agmine claro,
Tegmine iam niueo fulgens ceu fosforus axe,
Angelicis uectus ulnis super astra polorum,
Inter sanctorum globos cuneosque perennes
Transit et, altithroni penetralia uisere regis
Lectus, in aula poli turmis celestibus ille
Iunctus conspicue cernit trinitatis honorem.[24]

(269-276)

His work, which during his life has been an extension of Christ's, continues after his death. The climax is proclaimed by an angel, and forms a kind of Second Coming; the venerable Plecgils, like Simeon in the Temple, is permitted to hold the Christ-child in his arms as he celebrates Mass in the church of St Ninian.

The movement of the poem, that is to say, is one of emanation from beyond the celestial spheres, emanation, however, which throughout earthly existence retains stellar quality, and which is climaxed by subsequent triumphant return through the spheres, with angelic accompaniment. The entire series of Ninianic miracles is completed by the union of mortal and transcendent, Plecgils and Christ, in the sacrament of the altar. The number nine bears an obvious relationship to this movement, and the author of MNE may well have felt that its inclusion was essential to his purposes, even if it led to the exclusion of certain miracle stories.

Evidence confirming an interest at Anglian Whithorn in numerology and related literary techniques is provided by the *Hymnus Sancti Nynie Episcopi*, which accompanies MNE in the Bamberg manuscript.[25] This poem is constructed on the model of Bede's hymn to the virgin saint Aedilthryd (*Historia Ecclesiastica* IV.18.), and on the analogy of the Hebrew alphabetic (acrostic) psalms. The hymn contains twenty-seven couplets. In the first twenty-three, the sequence of the initial letters follows the order of the alphabet from A to Z, omitting J, U and W. The initials of the final four couplets constitute the word AMEN. The alphabetic reference is probably to the phrase which in the first and last of the twenty-two chapters of *Revelation* John places in the mouth of Christ, 'I am Alpha and Omega, the beginning and the end.' (The Hebrew alphabet has twenty-two characters.) The final four couplets accept and confirm the message of the first twenty-three in terms, particularly, of the saint celebrated in the hymn. The number twenty-seven, finally, is not only the cube of three, but is also associated with the Third Person of the Christian Trinity, the Holy Spirit. The numerology of the hymn thus has strong trinitarian overtones, with the emphasis falling on God the Son and God the Holy Spirit.

Whatever its relationship to the historical fact of the life of St Ninian, MNE certainly throws some interesting light on the literary culture of Whithorn in the eighth century.

Notes

1. I have used the edition by C. Plummer (2 vols., Oxford, 1896). There is a later edition with translation by R. A. B. Mynors and B. Colgrave (Oxford, 1969). The Penguin translation, with the slightly misleading title *A History of the English Church and People* (Harmondsworth, 1955), is by Leo Sherley-Price. Later editions of this last have been revised by R. E. Latham.
2. Strecker, K. (ed.), *Monumenta Germaniae Historica: Poetae Latini Aevi Carolini* IV.iii. (Berlin, 1923), 943-962. Also included is the *Hymnus Sancti Nynie Episcopi*, discussed at the end of this paper: with translation, MacQueen, W. M., *TDGAS*, (1959-60), 21-57. All quotations are from the latter.
3. Ed. with translation, Forbes, A. P., *Lives of S. Ninian and S. Kentigern, The Historians of Scotland* 5, Edinburgh, 1874), 6-26 (translation), 137-157 (text).
4. Bede's metrical *Life* is edited by Jaager, W., *Bedas metrische Vita sancti Cuthberti, Palaestra* 198 (Leipzig, 1935); Alcuin's *Vitae* of Willbrord will be found in Migne, *Patrologia: Series Latina* CI (Paris, 1863), with the prose version

occupying columns 694-714, the verse 714-722. The poems by Milo and Heiric are edited by Traube, L, in *MGH: Poetae Latini Aevi Carolini* III (Berlin, 1896), 561-609 and 432-517 respectively.

5. Levison, W. (ed.), *MGH, Scriptores Rerum Merovingicarum* VIII (Berlin, 1920), 247-283; translation by Hoare, F. R., *The Western Fathers* (London, 1954; Harper Torchbrook (ed.), (New York, 1965), 284-320.
6. MacQueen, J., *St. Nynia* (Edinburgh, 1961), 4-5.
7. The suggestion sometimes made, that Bede received his information from Pictavia, perhaps on the occasion of the embassy sent in 710 by the Pictish king, Nechtan mac Derili, to Ceofrith, abbot of Wearmouth, is contradicted by the general Whithorn emphasis of Bede's narrative, and also by the fact that Bede's account of Ninian appears to be a late addition to the *Historia Ecclesiastica*.
8. *Bede,* II.127.
9. See, for instance, on the interpretation of the literary evidence, Levison, 'An Eighth Century Poem on St. Ninian,' *Antiquity* 14 (1940), 280-291; Anderson, A. O., 'Ninian and the Southern Picts,' *SHR*, 27 (1948), 25-47; Chadwick, N. K., 'St. Ninian: A Preliminary Study of the Sources,' *TDGAS*, 27 (1950), 9-53; Grosjean, P., 'Les Pictes apostats dans l'epitre de S. Patrice,' *Analecta Bollandiana*, 75 (1958), 354-78; MacQueen, J., *St. Nynia*, 7-12, 'History and Miracle Stories in the Biography of Nynia,' *Innes Review*, 13.2 (1962), 115-29; Fahy, D., 'The Historical Reality of St Ninian,' *Innes Review*, 15 (1964), 35-46, Wilson, P. A., 'St Ninian and Candida Casa: The Literary Evidence From Ireland,' *TDGAS*, 41 (1964), 156-85, 'St Ninian: Irish Evidence Further Examined,' *TDGAS*, 41 (1969), 140-159; Kirby, D. P., 'Bede's Native Sources for the *Historia Ecclesiastica*,' *BJRL*, 48 (1966), 341-371, 'Bede and the Pictish Church,' *Innes Review*, 24 (1973), 6-25; Boyle, A., 'Saint Ninian: Some Outstanding Problems,' *Innes Review* 19 (1968), 57-74.
10. The phrase used (v.42) is *cuius in aduentu gaudet clementia Rome*; I give the translation in its immediate context: 'Then he proceeded on sacred foot, seeking to be confirmed by the holy offices of the Pope who happened at that time to be holding this high office, deemed worthy to guard the memorials of his predecessors of old and the hill of apostolic triumphs: at his coming the clemency of Rome rejoiced.'
    The reference to 'predecessors' suggests that the poet was well aware that Ninian was not a contemporary of the very early Pope Clement; the use of the word 'memorials' may, as suggested in the text, be a reference to Pope Siricius.
11. The evidence is partly archaeological, partly based on Jerome, *De viris illustribus* 15, written in 392. The church was built on the site of a private house used for Christian worship, the *titulus Clementis.* See Guglielmo Matthiae, *Le chiese di Roma dal IV al X secolo,* vol. III of *Roma cristiana,* Paluzzi, C. G. (ed.), (Rome, 1962), 59, 70-71. For help in preparing this note, I am much indebted to my colleague, Mr J. C. Higgitt, Dept of Fine Art, University of Edinburgh.
12. Above, n.5.
13. Plummer, Bede, I.364-387; this is immediately followed by the anonymous *Historia Abbatum* (I.388-404).
14. Migne, *Patrologia Latina*, CXX. Paschasius' *De Corpore et Sanguine Domini* occupies columns 1267-1350, his later defence of his position, the *Epistola ad Frudegardum*, columns 1351-1366.

15. *Oxford Dictionary of the Christian Church s.v.* 'Rabanus Maurus.' His refutation of Paschasius occupies chapter XXXIII, 'De eucharistia', of his *Poenitentiale ad Heribaldum* (Migne, *Patrologia Latina,* CX, 492-494). Ratramnus' *De Corpore et Sanguine Domini* will be found in Migne, *Patrologia Latina*, CXXI, 123-170.
16. Pauphilet, A. (ed.), (Paris, 1923): translated Matarasso, P. M., *The Quest of the Holy Grail* (Harmondsworth, 1969).
17. MacQueen, J., *Numerology* (Edinburgh, 1985), 58-63.
18. Ed. and translated, Colgrave, B., *Two Lives of St. Cuthbert* (Cambridge, 1940).
19. Above, n.4.
20. Hail, faithful faith! Happy concord, hail!'
21. 'I am lost in astonishment at the outcome of divine grace, that begetter, bearer and borne should harmonise in proclaiming graces with names that are appropriate to the gifts.'
22. *Numerology,* 81-94.
23. 'Thus he brought hosts of men summoned from grevious death to the golden-glowing stars in the starry sky,' (25-26).
24. 'Thus when the breath of life had left his dying limbs, immediately surrounded by the shining host and now blazing bright in snow-white vestment, like Phosphorus in the sky, he was carried in angel arms beyond the stars of the sky, and passing through the companies of the saints and the everlasting hosts, joyful at visiting the innermost shrine of the King throned on high, he clearly perceived, united as he was with the heavenly hosts in the halls of heaven, the glory of the Trinity.'
25. Codex Bambergensis BII.10. of the eleventh century.

Dunskey Castle: general view from south.

WHITHORN: THE MISSING YEARS

Peter H. Hill

Whithorn is perilously central to any study of Galloway in the Christian era. Apart from the various Lives of St Ninian and the Northumbrian records of the eighth-century bishops of Whithorn,[1] there are no reliable historical records of Galloway in the first millennium other than Ptolomey's topography,[2] the Ravenna Cosmography[3] and the brief inscriptions on memorial stones. Without the Whithorn sources regional historians would have to rely solely on place-names, excavation evidence and the extrapolation of patterns and processes from neighbouring areas with fuller documentation. The centrality of Whithorn is perilous because it tends to conceal our fundamental ignorance of the history of the rest of Galloway.

Daphne Brooke has evolved a useful model for the chronology of Whithorn from *c.*400 AD until the Reformation.[4] She identifies three bishoprics:

The First Bishopric pertains to the ministry of Ninian. It has no contemporary historians and information about it has been transmitted through the writings of the eighth and later centuries. The writers came from an alien cultural milieu, followed contemporary conventions and had their own ends firmly to the fore. They and their informants were responsible for the confection of an earlier, mythic 'history' of Whithorn and for its transmission to distant places and later centuries. The history and historic implications of this first bishopric is a favoured resort of scholars who have endowed it richly with circumstance despite the mythic quality of the evidence.[5]

The Second Bishopric comprises the Northumbrian succession of the eighth and early ninth centuries. This phase has an impeccable historical provenance founded on Bede and the Northumbrian annalists. It has left a unique testament in the Miracula Nyniae Episcopi[6] which reveals the benign exploitation of a founder legend to instruct contemporary audiences and to attract status — and pilgrims — to a shrine remote from other Anglo-Saxon centres. The success of this Northumbrian propaganda is evident in the subsequent adoption of Whithorn and Ninian by retrospective Irish hagiographies.[7] The last records of the Second Bishopric name one Heathured as bishop in *c.*833-6.[8]

The Third Bishopric begins some three centuries later in the third decade of the twelfth century with the consecration of Gilla-Aldan at York. Historical sources became more plentiful from then on, and, while there is still much to debate, the essential chronological framework is secure.

There were three main phases in the ecclesiastical history of Whithorn

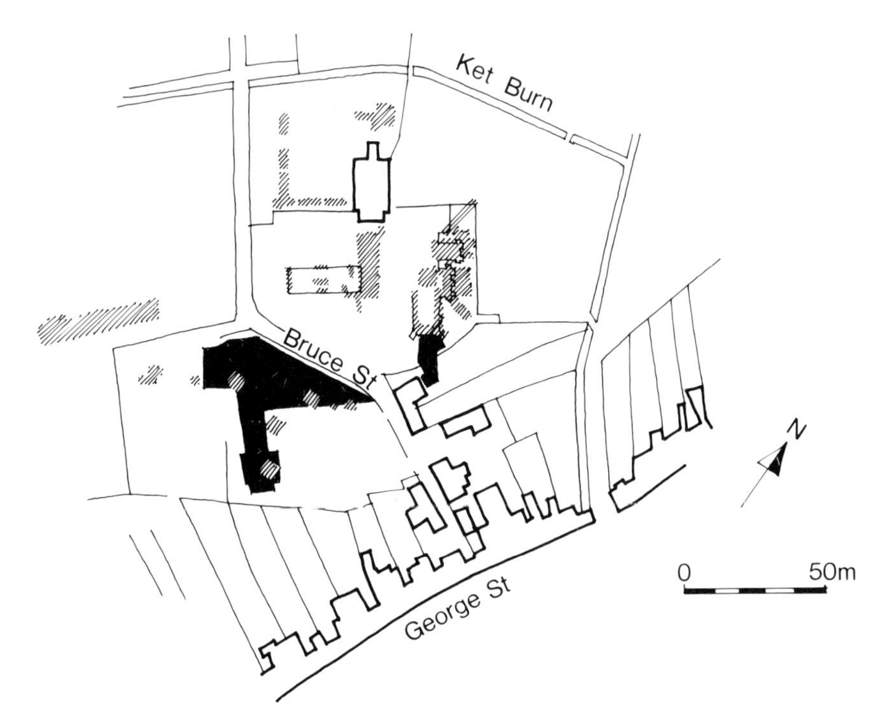

Fig.3.1 Excavations at Whithorn Priory; Whithorn Trust excavations in black, earlier work shaded.

before the Third Bishopric. The first phase, which encompasses the First Bishopric and whatever preceded and followed it, is beyond the scope of this paper. The second phase encompassing the Second Bishopric spans a hundred years or so from 731 to 833-6. The episcopal succession is certain, the existence of a monastery probable[9] and organisational parallels can be sought elsewhere in the Northumbrian and English Churches. The third phase, which is the principal subject of this paper, is, perhaps, the most obscure. It encompasses the years from *c.*833 until the establishment of the Third Bishopric in *c.*1128. It has no contemporary historians and was of such little interest to later writers that it passed virtually unrecorded.[10] In terms of historical records it represents the missing years in the development of Whithorn.

The Galloway Conference of the Scottish Society for Northern Studies effected an invaluable spring-cleaning of some of the dustier corners of Galwegian history. The mythic casualties included the no-longer-eponymous Gall-Gaidhil[11] while an incisive assault was launched against the fabulous eleventh-century Viking earldom of Galloway, and the

Fig.3.2 Aerial view of Whithorn Priory in 1989 showing location of main excavation trench.

attempts of archaeologists to create a history of this period from their scraps of evidence.[12]

The writer reported, *inter alia,* tantalising archaeological evidence of an Hiberno-Norse settlement close to the ruins of the medieval priory at Whithorn.[13] These discoveries ran counter to the prevailing thrust of the conference, which in reviewing the extant evidence of Scandinavian contact with Galloway had found little of substance. The writer was rewarded to

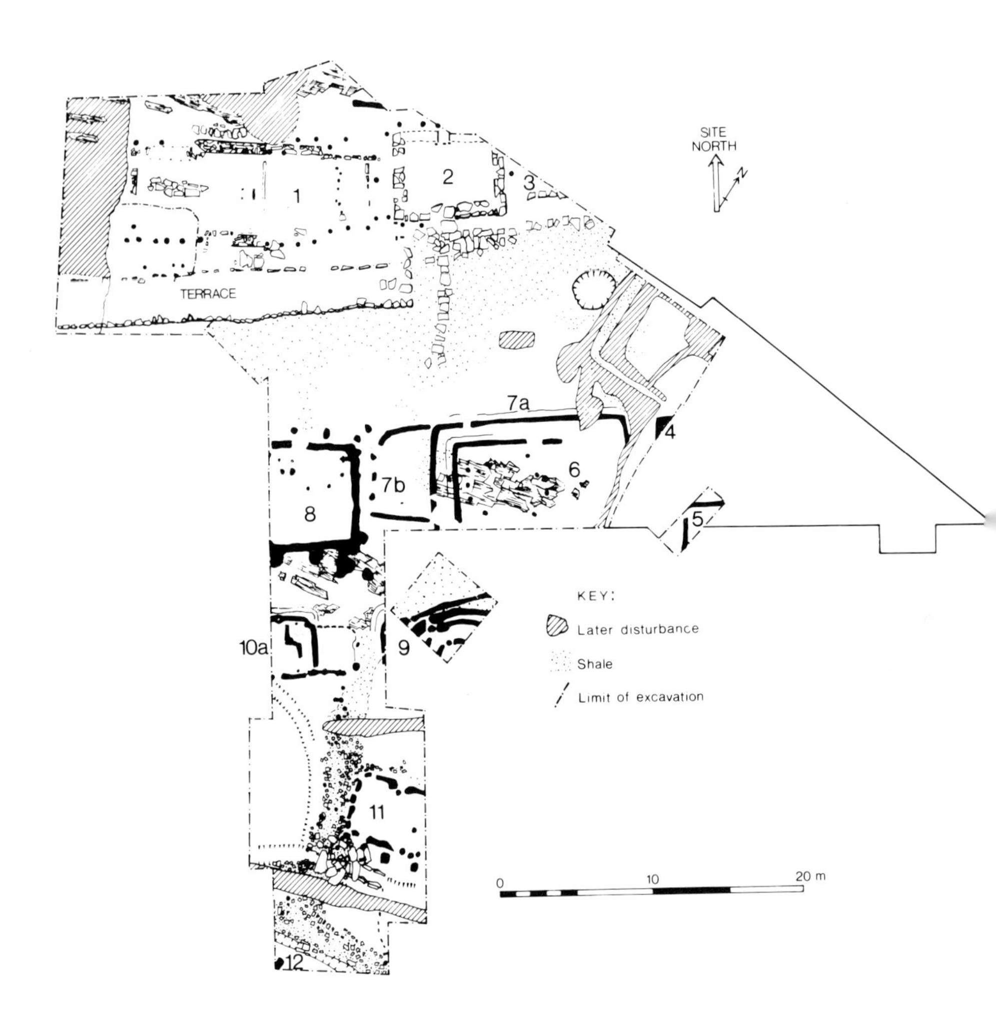

Fig.3.3 Northumbrian features of the eighth/ninth centuries.

see a significant contribution to the debate from the results of a small-scale excavation.

There have been major developments since the conference. Shortly afterwards the Whithorn Trust was established to continue the exploration of the site and five seasons of excavation are now complete (Figures 3.1 and 3.2). Much has been learnt of the 'Hiberno-Norse' settlement and still

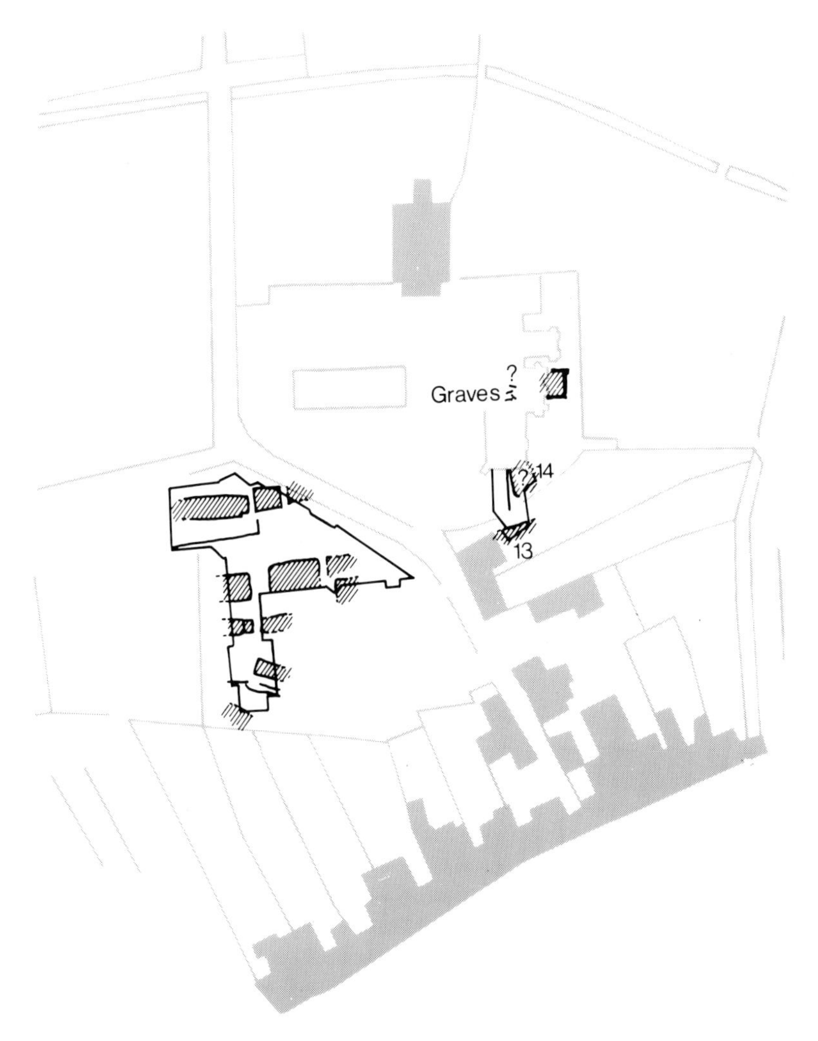

Fig.3.4 General plan of Northumbrian features at Whithorn.

more will be revealed when the structures and finds have been analysed in full.

The 'Hiberno-Norse' settlement occupied the south slope of the low hill now crowned by the priory ruins. This ground had been intensively settled by the Northumbrians by the early eighth century.[14] Their regularly planned settlement (Figure 3:3) comprised a range of ecclesiastical buildings on the high ground (a church, burial chapel and children's graveyard); a terrace of large timber buildings on level ground half-way down; and smaller

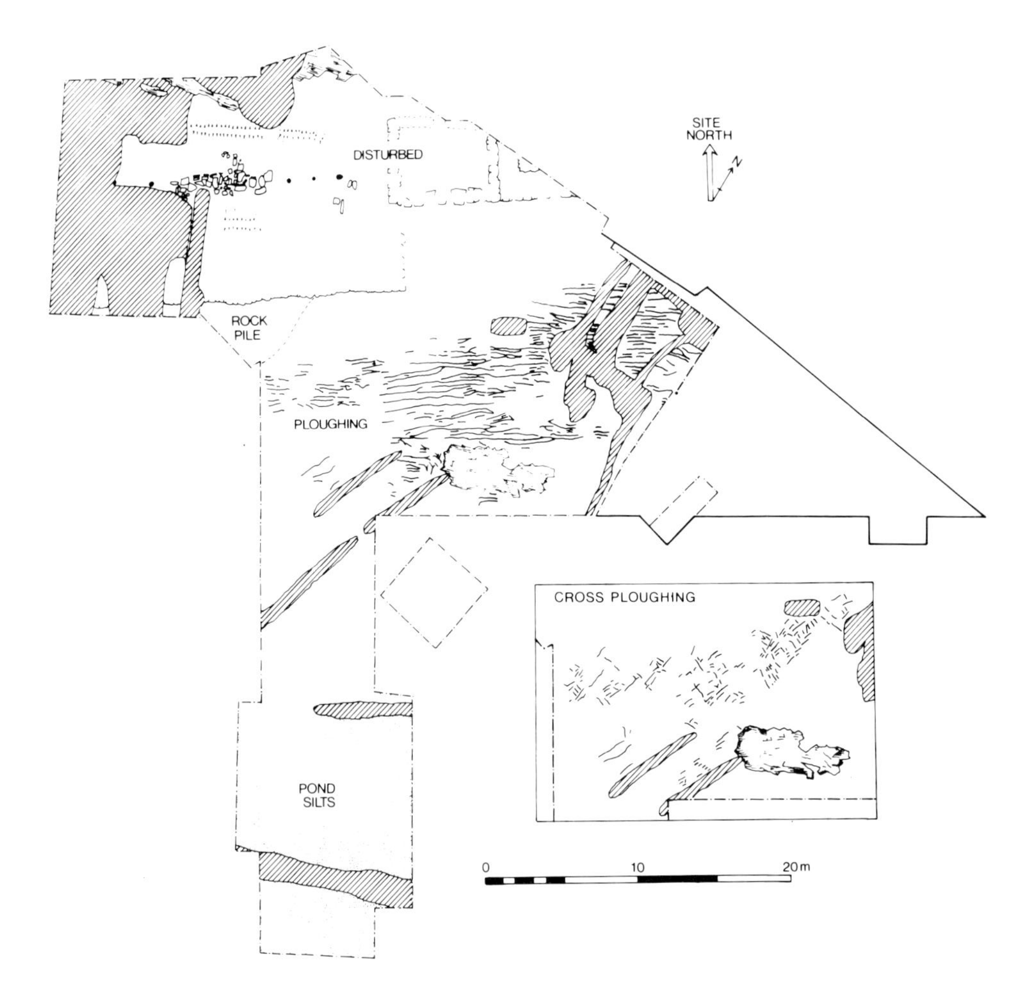

Fig.3.5 Whithorn in c.850 AD.

timber buildings on poorly-drained ground at the foot of the slope. Reassessment of earlier excavation evidence[15] suggests that a further range of buildings underlies the twelfth-century cathedral and possibly included the principal church[16] (Figure 3.4). The Northumbrian settlement had been abandoned by the mid ninth century. The ecclesiastical buildings were apparently ruinous, a shallow pond covered the remains at the foot of the slope while the intervening level ground had been ploughed (Figure 3.5).

The deposits above and below the plough soil have produced a rich assemblage of Northumbrian coins which date the ploughing with unusual precision (Table 1 below). Assuming that these finds give reliable evidence, the ploughing can be dated to the ultimate years of Eanred's reign or the first reign of his successor Aethelred II. The chronology of the Northumbrian kings at this time is debateable[17] but the first reign of Aethelred II probably belongs within the period 840 to 860.

Table 1: Ninth-century events and coin finds.

Occupation — paving, fires, etc.
One coin of Osberht and a related irregular issue:
*c.*849-855[18]

|

Fallow, demolition of church and related deposits
Six coins of Aethelred II and one of Archbishop Wigimund:
*c.*843-9[19] and *c.*840-5[20]

|

Midden
Twenty-three coins of Aethelred I and Eanred: *c.*790-6, 810-41

It is tempting to compress the evidence of decay and change into a picture of catastrophe and to correlate this with the known pattern of Viking raids on the British Isles in the late 830s and 840s[21]. This is inadmissable as the Northumbrian timber buildings were probably abandoned many years previously, while the church seems to have been dismantled with care rather than wantonly destroyed. The ploughing of a formerly settled area does, however, hint at troubled times — perhaps the same troubles that according to some sources brought Alpin, king of Scots, to a violent death in Galloway in 841.[22]

A new phase of settlement, which began shortly after the ground was ploughed, survived for almost four hundred years until the ecclesiastical precinct was reorganised in about 1240.[23] Initial activity was marked by coins of the second reign of Aethelred II and subsequent occupation by two later Northumbrian issues (Table 1). Deposits on the middle and upper ground have produced small assemblages of ninth/tenth-century artefacts, while the structures on the lower ground date at the earliest to the eleventh century. The end of the settlement is marked definitively by the redevelopment of the occupied area as a cemetery in the mid-thirteenth century. The archaeological evidence of the evolving settlement was complex and many of the deposits had been destroyed or damaged by later graves. Three principal phases of activity can be distinguished.

Phase 1 lasted from about 850 until about 1000.[24] There was occupation to either side of a road crossing the site comprising formless areas of paving without walls, doors or hearths. These structural remains probably represented a settlement, although the plans of individual buildings were elusive. A sparse collection of finds included late Northumbrian coins (Table 1), a penny of Eadgar (*c.*959-75), a Scandinavian harness fitting , antler combs and ring-headed pins. Manufacturing debris, which characterised Phases 2 and 3, was rare. There was clearly Scandinavian contact, but neither Scandinavian settlement or dominion can be demonstrated.

Phase 2 (Figure 3.6) lasted from about 1000 until perhaps the mid-twelfth century. The earlier settlement was expanded by draining the shallow pond at the foot of the slope, probably by cutting ditches where the Ket Burn heads eastwards from modern Whithorn. Drains were then cut through the moist silts of the former lake bed and new houses were built. A radiocarbon date of 1015 to 1220 AD[25] was obtained from a stake used in one of these houses. There were numerous phases of rebuilding after the original houses decayed, suggesting a thriving community replacing and renovating its homes.

The economic basis of the settlement was indicated by the manufacturing debris and imported artefacts. The ditch at the foot of the slope produced abundant evidence of leather-working, while antler-working debris (often reflecting the manufacture of single-sided combs) was spread over most parts of the site. Iron-working was demonstrated by ore, bloomery slag, smithying waste and finishing tools; lead-working by spilt metal, scarfs and hack-metal awaiting recasting. Finer crafts were poorly represented. Glass tesserae suggested an episode of jewellery-work,[26] and occasional crucible sherds indicated work in copper alloy, silver or gold. Certain crafts were strikingly absent. There was little evidence of wood-turning and, indeed, mature timber was rare. No fabrics were found in the waterlogged deposits and evidence of thread and fabric production was sparse. Relatively late deposits produced Hiberno-Norse stick-pins, beads and distinctive jars with a red, gritty fabric.

The Hiberno-Norse label attached to this settlement depends upon the artefacts associated with it and must be treated circumspectly. Almost all the articles — stick-pins, beads, knives, soapstone and the like — were readily portable, and the whole collection would scarcely fill a pedlar's pack. The most telling artefacts were the houses which were, by definition, non-portable. The best-preserved house (Figure 3.7) is strikingly similar to Viking buildings at Dublin[27] (Figure 3.8) and Waterford,[28] themselves believed to be a unique adaptation of an Irish vernacular tradition to the

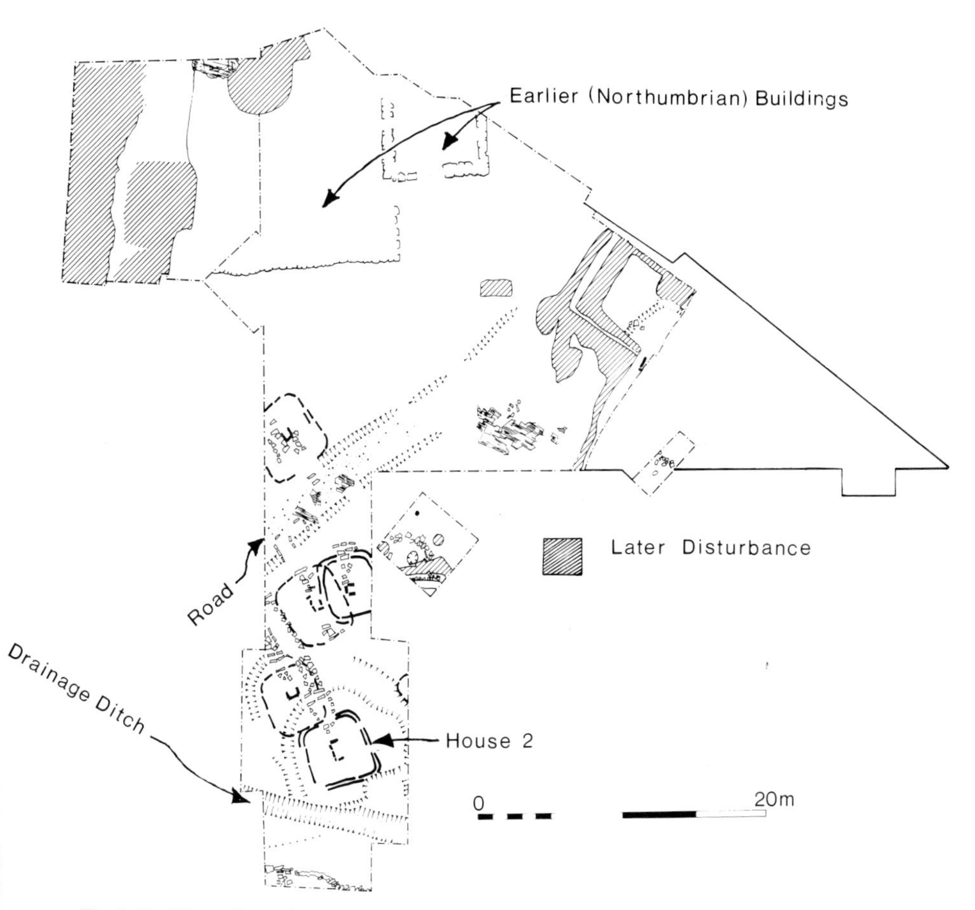

Fig.3.6 Phase 2 settlement.

specialised needs of Hiberno-Norse towns. There is as yet no corpus of tenth/eleventh-century buildings in southern Scotland to compare and contrast with the Whithorn examples. The significance of their Irish affinities is difficult to assess. They might have been a local adaptation of the Irish style, or could equally indicate the presence of settlers from the Irish towns.

Phase 3 lasted from the mid-twelfth century until the mid-thirteenth century. The former settlement layout survived, while a new building type appeared. Manufacture remained important, and one building was abutted by a dump of smelting and smithying debris associated with broken or discarded finishing tools. By this time trading patterns had changed. New

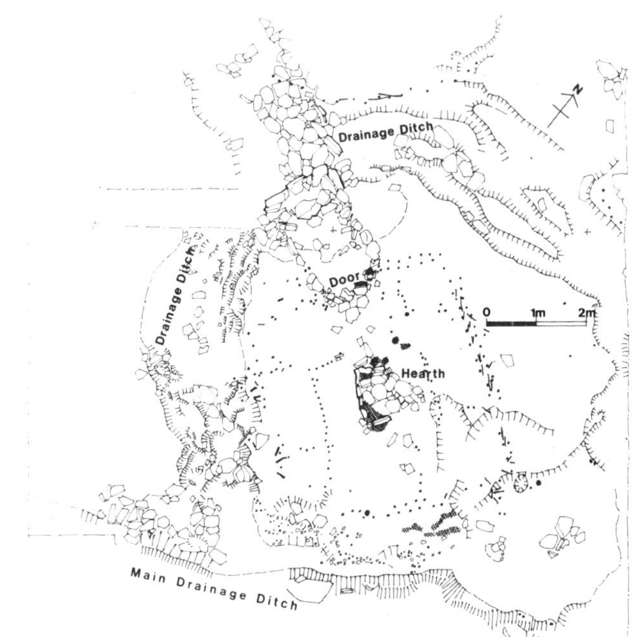

Fig.3.7 Whithorn: House 1.

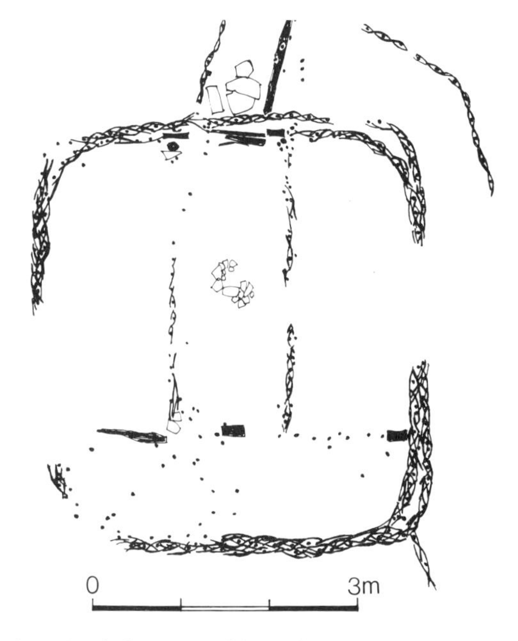

Fig.3.8 House 9/1, High Street, Dublin (after Murray, 1983).

wheel-turned pottery types and been introduced from the east and the supply of distinctive Hiberno-Norse artefacts had dried up.

This phase probably followed the reformation of the church and was contemporary with the building of the new cathedral and priory, representing the continuing development of the earlier settlement in a changing economic climate. The demise of the settlement in the mid-thirteenth century may have reflected the final subjugation of Galloway to the Scottish Crown in 1235 or, perhaps, the transfer of Whithorn's status

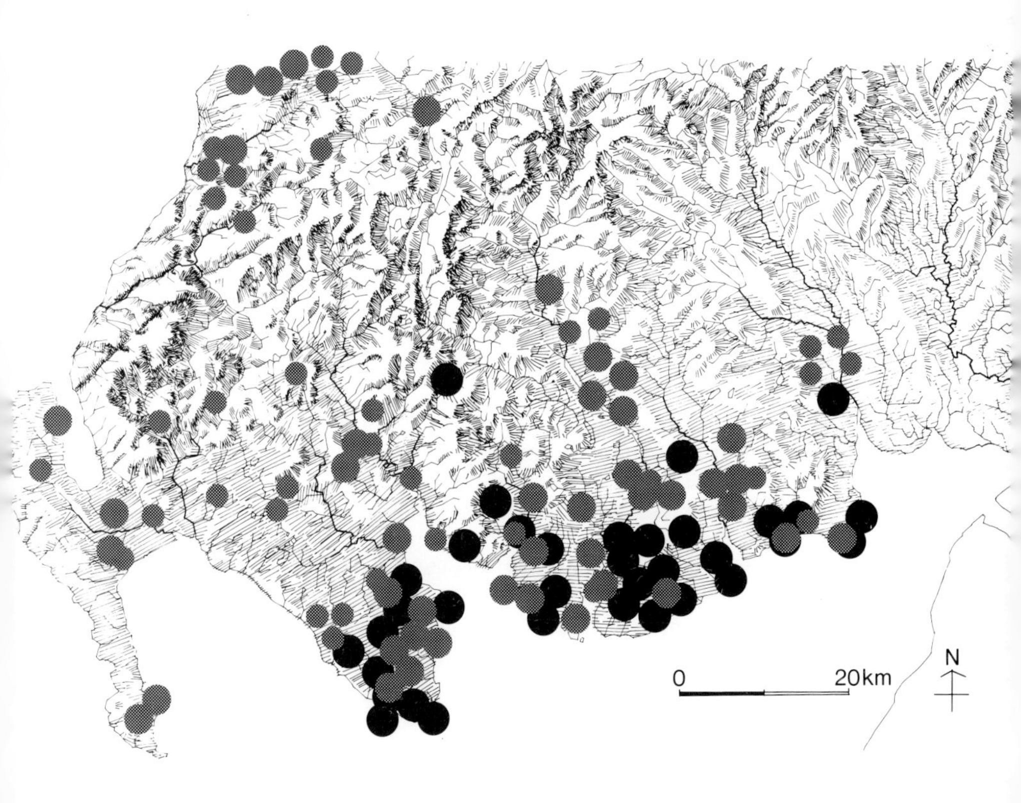

Fig. 3.9 Scandinavian place names (black) superimposed on British and Anglian place names (grey).

as a centre of trade to Wigtown, which became the seat of the new royal sheriff and the shire administration by the middle of the thirteenth century.

The foregoing paragraphs attempt an objective summary of the excavation evidence. Dating is imprecise, the evolving status of the settlement unknown and the origin of its inhabitants uncertain. Isolated from the wider context of contemporary society, it is of limited value. A fuller picture requires further evidence.

The most important contribution comes from the place-names. Gillian Fellows-Jensen's valuable contribution in this volume is supplemented by published and unpublished papers by Daphne Brooke[29] on place-name patterns throughout Galloway. These studies reveal a striking correspondence in the distribution of Northumbrian and Scandinavian place-names in Galloway (Figure 3.9), indicating a coherent link between these apparently distinct phases of settlement. The Northumbrian names occur in extensive geographical blocks separated by blank areas where British names survive. Several possible centres can be identified, such as the ecclesiastical site at Whithorn, Kirkcudbright and Edingham[30] and the secular strongholds at Arsbotl in the Glenkens and Cruggleton[31] on the east coast of the Machars. These 'blocks' were probably estates, or more properly multiple estates settled by Anglian speakers and under Northumbrian control.[32] The intervening areas were presumably still occupied by the original British inhabitants and controlled by British potentates. This territorial landscape was probably organised, or perhaps merely redistributed, as the Northumbrians took control of Galloway in the late seventh or early eighth centuries.

There is nothing remarkable in this picture. It reflects a pattern recorded reliably in the eastern parts of Northumbria[33] and reconstructable elsewhere in southern Scotland.[34] It seems to have been an enduring pattern of both organisation and settlement.[35] Many of the British and Northumbrian place-name elements emerge uncorrupted in the charters of the twelfth and thirteenth centures, indicating that the fabric and peoples of the territorial landscape survived the collapse of Northumbrian control in the ninth century.

The Scandinavian names are less widespread than their Anglian precursors and generally occupy smaller, more compact areas within the large blocks of Northumbrian settlement. These areas seem too small to have been won by conquest and then held against hostile neighbours. They were probably acquired as the result of negotiations[36] equally appropriate to all the *coastal* territories of the former Northumbrian hegemony. The striking absence of Scandinavian names from the 'British' territories suggests that either they were excluded from the deal if it was favourable, or else were strong enough to resist if it were unfavourable.

The regional pattern of Scandinavian settlement within the former Northumbrian coastal territories suggests the context for the tenth- to twelfth- century settlement at Whithorn. Throughout this period, activity was focused on a road leading south from the crown of the hill towards the Isle of Whithorn[37] (Figures 3.10 and 3.11). By the eleventh century this road was lined with the dwellings of artisans processing raw materials probably produced in the hinterland of the Machars (antler and hides) and more distant parts of Galloway (iron and lead). The settlement was probably a trading post processing a limited range of locally produced raw materials, trading on the products and importing luxuries and commodities from a trade network linking the lands around the Irish Sea with the main

Fig.3.10 General plan of Whithorn in c.1050 AD showing possible site of church.

Scandinavian seaways. The natural harbour at the Isle of Whithorn would have been an ideal port for carrying these products outwards.

Why was Whithorn chosen as a production centre? Physical geography does not seem to commend it and, indeed, the settlement site was derelict and partly flooded when first occupied. The most economical explanation is that the former economic and social status of the site had been sustained in the centuries after the collapse of Northumbria, or had perhaps been

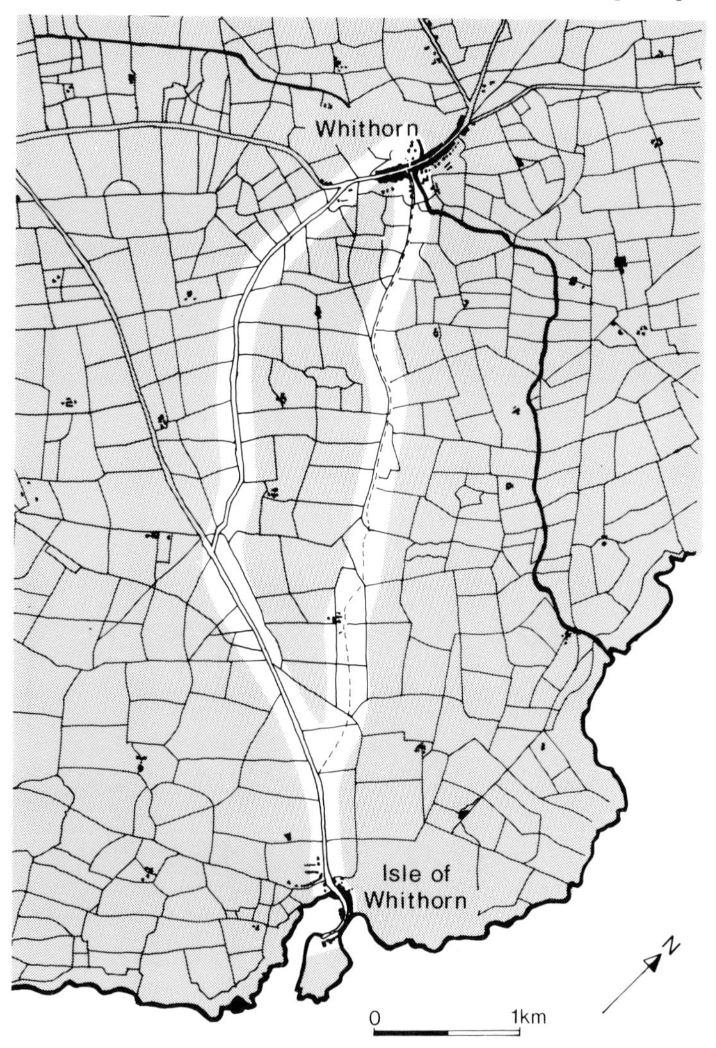

Fig.3.11 Possible routes linking Whithorn and the Isle of Whithorn.

revived under new masters. Continuing or revived ecclesiastical status is indicated by the 'Whithorn School' of sculptured crosses. Derek Craig's masterly reassessment of these and other sculptures[38] points to a parallel ecclesiastical landscape with Whithorn the centre of a new system of parishes. The phenomenon is confined to the Machars, where it embraces Northumbrian, Scandinavian and British territories.

There thus seems to have been two co-existing systems in the Machars, both focused on Whithorn. The first system, linking the polyglot, cosmopolitan peoples of Galloway in a new economic network of coastal trade, was based on former Northumbrian territories and extended throughout the Solway coast. The second is a new system of ecclesiastical organisation confined to the Machars, but disregarding linguistic and territorial boundaries. The symbiosis of these two systems means that a settlement of Hiberno-Norse artisans and traders at Whithorn can be postulated without requiring a Norse artistocracy or Norse Church leaders. An eleventh-century trading post, town or proto-town has now been identified at Whithorn, but there is no need to bring Kari Solmundarson on the tortuous trail from Berwick. We can leave him happily at Whitburgh, Berwickshire[39] and furnish Whithorn with a church, a people and an economy from the integrated study of place-names, sculptured stones and excavation evidence.

The introductory paragraphs stressed the incompleteness of the historical records of Whithorn and cautioned against the 'perilous centrality' of Whithorn to the history of Galloway. In the following pages we have attempted to fill one of the larger gaps in the historical record. The 'perilous centrality' can perhaps be redefined. I suspect that Whithorn was indeed central to the economic and social affairs of the Machars for most of the Christian era until the Reformation. It was, however, merely one of a series of centres in Galloway which reflect an enduring infrastructure of peoples and territories. The remarkable new evidence from Whithorn should be treated less as a confirmation of centrality and more as a taster for what awaits discovery at other centres.

★ ★ ★

The Whithorn Project has enjoyed the dedicated commitment of a vast and international team, and we have been enriched by discussions with numerous visiting scholars. The ideas offered here are corporate, even though the presentation is personal. I am particularly indebted to Daphne Brooke for unrestricted access to her data and for a shared enthusiasm in the early history of Whithorn.

Notes

1. Plummer, C, *Venerabilia Baedae Opera Historica,* 2 vols (Oxford, 1986); Forbes, A. P., *Lives of S Ninian and S Kentigern* (Edinburgh, 1874); MacQueen, W., 'Miracula Nynie Episcopi', *TDGAS,* 38 (1960), 21-57.

2. Rivet, A. L. F., and Smith, C. C., *The Place-Names of Roman Britain* (London, 1979), 103-47.
3. Rivet and Smith, *Place-Names,* 148-215.
4. Daphne Brooke, *Parish of Whithorn*; manuscript account of early place-name forms in Wigtownshire. I am grateful to Daphne Brooke for allowing me access to this and other unpublished studies.
5. Optimistic historiography is epitomised by the Reverend William Cumming Skinner's delightful *Candida Casa: the Apostolic Centre of Scotland* (Dundee, 1931). Optimism prevails in much of the 'mainstream' literature, notably the Whithorn volume (35, 1950) of the *Transactions of the Dumfriesshire and Galloway Natural History and Antiquarian Society,* which includes Norah Chadwick's imaginative 'St Ninian: A preliminary study of the sources', and Douglas Simpson's articulate and combative 'The Ninian controversy'. More recent works, such as Professor Charles Thomas's *Christianity in Roman Britain to AD 500* (London, 1985) are more cautious but still identify concrete evidence of the early church.
6. MacQueen, 'Miracula'.
7. Wilson, P. A., 'St Ninian and Candida Casa: Literary evidence from Ireland', *TDGAS,* 41 (1964), 156-85.
8. Dumville, D. N., 'Textual archaeology and Northumbrian history subsequent to Bede', in Metcalf, D. N., *Coinage in Ninth Century Northumbria* (British Archaeological Report 180, 1987).
9. Internal evidence of a monastery in the 'Miracula Nynie Episcopi' has been discussed by Charles Thomas in 'Ardwall Isle; the excavation of an Early Christian site of Irish type', *TDGAS,* 34 (1966), 84-116.
10. The writer shares Professor E. Cowan's disbelief in the identification of Hwitiburg with Whithorn and is dubious about the supposed visit to Whithorn of St Cuthbert's relics in the late ninth century.
11. This volume.
12. This volume.
13. Initially reported in Hill, P. H., *Excavations at Bruce Street, Whithorn 1984: interim report* SDD (A. M.), (Edinburgh, 1984). Subsequent work is summarised in Hill, P. H., *Whithorn 1: 1986 Excavations* (Whithorn Trust, 1987); Hill, P. H., *Whithorn 2: Excavations 1984-87: interim report* (Whithorn Trust, 1988); Hill, P. H., *Whithorn Supplement; 1988 Excavation* (Whithorn Trust, 1988) and Hill, P. H., *Whithorn 3: Excavations 1988-90: interim report* (Whithorn Trust, 1990).
14. Discussed briefly in Hill, *Whithorn 3.*
15. These excavations are described in Radford, C. A. R., 'Excavations at Whithorn, 1949', *TDGAS,* 27 (1950), 85-126 and Cruden, S., *The Scotsman Weekend Magazine* 4th May 1963. They are further discussed in Thomas, 'Ardwall Isle' and *Christianity in Roman Britain.*
16. Hill, *Whithorn 3.*
17. I am grateful to Miss E. J. E. Pirie for identifying and reporting upon the Northumbrian coins found in 1984-89. For the chronology of Northumbrian reigns see Lyon, S., 'Ninth century Northumbrian chronology', in Metcalf, *Coinage in Ninth Century Northumbria.*
18. Traditional dates deriving from Symeon of Durham and disputed by Lyon,

'Ninth century Northumbrian chronology' and Dumville, 'Textual archaeology'.

19. Ibid.
20. Dating proposed by Dumville, 'Textual archaeology'.
21. Ulster Annals, Annals of the Picts and Scots, discussed briefly by Smyth, A. P., *Warlords and Holymen* (London, 1984) and Crawford, B. E., *Scandinavian Scotland* (Leicester, 1987), 48-51.
22. Discussed by Professor E. Cowan, this volume.
23. The site of the former settlement was used as a graveyard divided by a ditch from new fields to the west (Hill, *Whithorn 3*).
24. Dated by coins and, to a lesser extent, radiocarbon dates from the burials. The former included two pennies of Henry III (1216-72) including one minted at Bury St. Edmunds in 1247-72. Radiocarbon assays gave four dates, calibrated and quoted at the 95% confidence level: 1045 x 1390 AD (GU-2056, 755 +/− 80 bp), 1275 x 1435 AD (GU-2051, 595 +/− 50 bp) and 1240 x 1390 AD (GU-2050 +/− 55 bp).
25. The radiocarbon date of 1015-1220 CAL AD (GU-2053, 935 +/− 50 bp) has been adapted to historical convention and is quoted at the 95% confidence level.
26. The tesserae were all recovered from a cluster of thirteenth- to fifteenth-century graves. They had, perhaps, been displaced from earlier eleventh to thirteenth century deposits.
27. Discussed in detail in Murray, H., *Viking and Early Medieval Buildings in Dublin* (British Archaeological Report 119, 1983), summarised by Wallace, P. F. and O Floinn, R., *Dublin 1000: Discovery and Excavation in Dublin, 1842-1981* (Dublin, 1988) and Edwards, N., *The Archaeology of Early Medieval Ireland* (London, 1990), 178-88.
28. Described in Hurley, M., 'Recent archaeological excavations in Waterford City', *Archaeol Ireland,* 2 pt. 1 (1988), 17-21, summarised in Edwards, *Early Medieval Ireland.*
29. Brooke, D., 'The Northumbrian settlement of Galloway and Carrick', *PSAS* 119 (forthcoming).
30. Brooke, D., 'The Deanery of Desnes Cro and the Church of Edingham', *TDGAS,* 62 (1987), 48-65.
31. Brooke, 'Galloway and Carrick'.
32. Excavation at Cruggleton has revealed what may be parts of a seventh to ninth century hall, Ewart, G., *Cruggleton Castle: Report of Excavations 1978-81* (Dumfriesshire and Galloway Natural History and Antiquarian Society Occasional Paper, Dumfries, 1985).
33. See for example Barrow, G. W. S., *The Kingdom of the Scots* (London, 1973), Chapter 1.
34. See for example Smith, I., 'Late Anglian settlement patterns in the Tweed basin', in Faull, M. L. (ed), *Studies in Late Anglo-Saxon Settlement* (Oxford, 1984).
35. This toponymic model has received remarkable archaeological support from a Northumbrian deposit at Whithorn. This deposit contained a vast quantity of animal bones apparently the debris from a great feast. The bones can be interpreted as the remains of renders in kind from a large and well-organised estate (Hill, *Whithorn 2*).

36. *Sensu lato* and *pace* Cowan. 'Negotiation' can be amicable or hostile. Various options include mercenary service (the Anglo-Saxon option), purchase, dynastic marriage or plantation by improving landlords.
37. The early forms (Biscoby, 1456 (Calendar of Papal Letters) and Byscoby, 1478 (Calendar of Papal Letters XIII)) of the place-name Bysbie which survives at the Isle of Whithorn offer tantalising hint of a Bishop's Bu in control of the economically vital harbour. It might be a Scandinavian form of an earlier Northumbrian name, a Scandinavian name in its own right, or a later formation reflecting ownership by the High to Late Medieval bishops of Whithorn.
38. This volume.
39. I am grateful to Daphne Brooke and Professor Geoffrey Barrow for suggesting this identification of Hwitiburg.

PRE-NORMAN SCULPTURE IN GALLOWAY: SOME TERRITORIAL IMPLICATIONS

D. J. Craig

The study of early medieval sculpture is often seen as an art historical backwater, and of little relevance to the wider questions of human settlement history.[1] But in Galloway in the pre-Norman period neither contemporary documents nor excavation give us very much help in recognising settlement patterns. Both these types of evidence are very thin on the ground,[2] and isolated examples assume a disproportionate importance in any assessment of the post-Roman history of the region.[3] Sculpture, on the other hand, like place-names, is fairly prolific, numbering about 170 pieces from the whole area.

The range and chronology of most of the known examples was admirably discussed by W. G. Collingwood in the 1920s,[4] and I prefer not to duplicate that work here.[5] Instead, I would like to discuss what can be learnt from an examination of the distribution of these stones and their find-spots, and how these may relate to the factors controlling their production.[6]

The partial evolution of carved stone monuments in post-Roman western Britain and Ireland,[7] and the subsequent emergence and development of sculpture in areas under Anglo-Saxon control, is primarily a phenomenon of the Christian Church and its reintroduction of Mediterranean models, whether in fashions of decoration or in the use of stone for church building.[8] As a result, it seems reasonable to suggest that there is a relationship between the distribution of sculpture and the structure of the Christian Church during this period when it was being integrated into secular society. Local groups of sculpture with similar stylistic elements in common provide a link between sites when other evidence is lacking, and thus seem to indicate networks of contemporary development. More speculatively, it may also therefore be possible to infer from such networks the influence, at the same date as the sculpture, of units of territorial organisation that only come on record at a later period.[9]

In addition to these scattered groups, concentrations of the more stylised monumental sculpture at a single site or in a limited area may be taken to indicate centres of comparative wealth, since the production of such sculpture is a matter of fashion and display as well as a skilled craft dependent on the existence of an agricultural surplus.[10] But the more simply carved, isolated monuments should probably be seen as unskilled domestic work.

The pre-Norman[11] sculpture of Galloway has been recorded piecemeal over the last hundred years,[12] with about 130 of the 170 pieces coming from Wigtownshire. There are about forty separate sites in that district and fifteen in the Stewartry. The greatest individual totals come from the

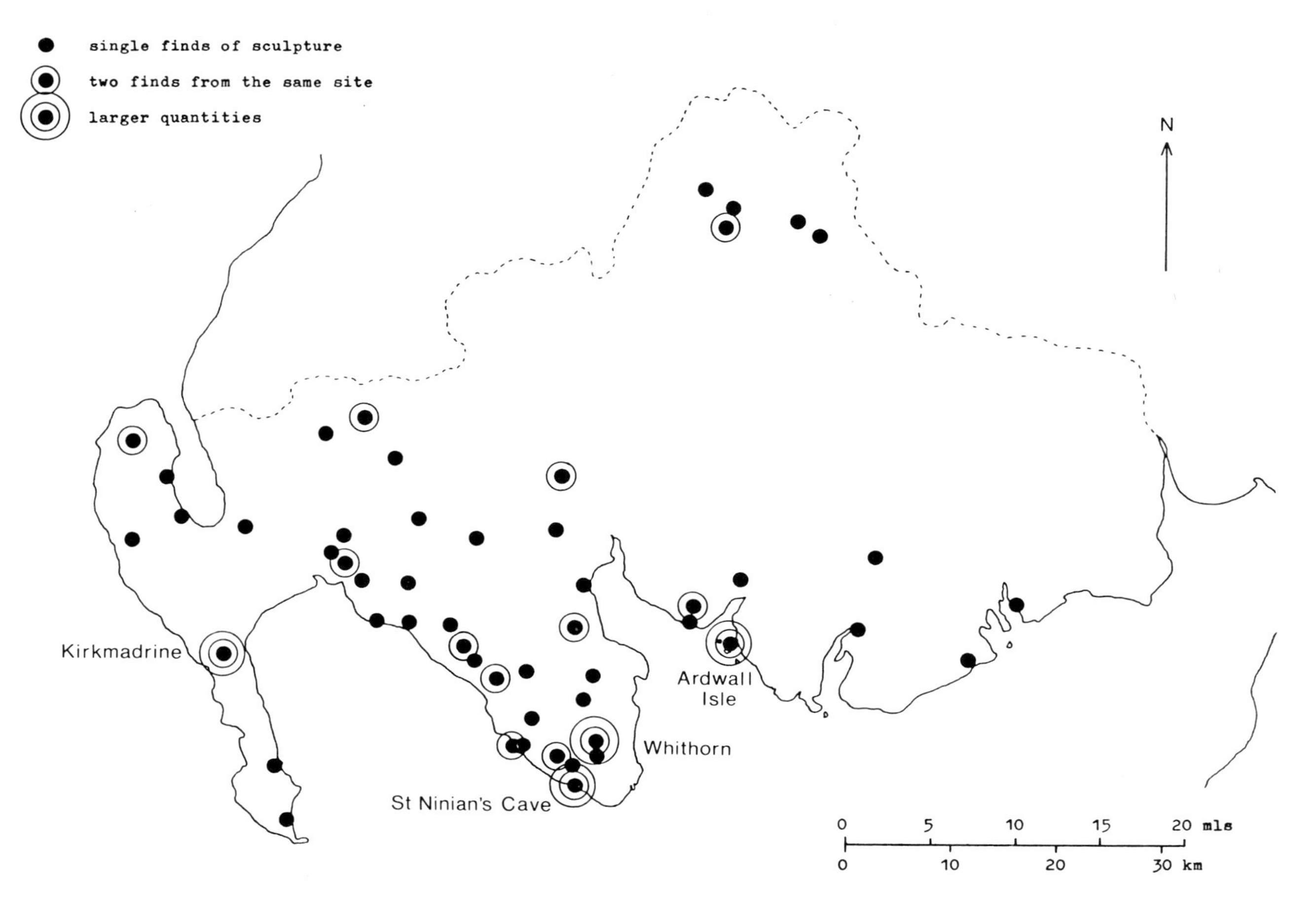

Fig.4.1 Pre-Norman sculpture in Galloway: relative totals per site.

excavated sites of Whithorn (38), St Ninian's Cave (17+7),[13] and Ardwall Island (25)[14] (Figure 4.1). Of the rest, some pieces have been dug up by chance, some have been found built into walls of comparatively recent date, and a few stand, or stood until recently, on isolated moorland sites. It might therefore be argued that the apparent distribution of these stones is largely determined by modern agricultural practice or building needs, or by their removal to modern churchyards.[15]

Against this assumption of chance survival is the pattern of clusters and blank areas[16] when the distribution of the original find-spots of these stones is plotted on a map.[17] For example, in the Stewartry these may be broken down into three main groups: one east of Kirkcudbright; another the coastal strip between Newton Stewart and Gatehouse of Fleet, with which Ardwall Island can be linked; and the third in the sparsely populated upland area around Carsphairn (Figure 4.2). But despite the growth of modern settlement between Dumfries, New Galloway and Castle Douglas, which might be expected to bring such material to light, this low-lying and fertile area[18] of the Stewartry has as yet produced no early medieval sculpture (Figure 4.2).

In addition, each of the three clusters mentioned can be defined not simply by the geographical proximity of the stones (it is also possible to

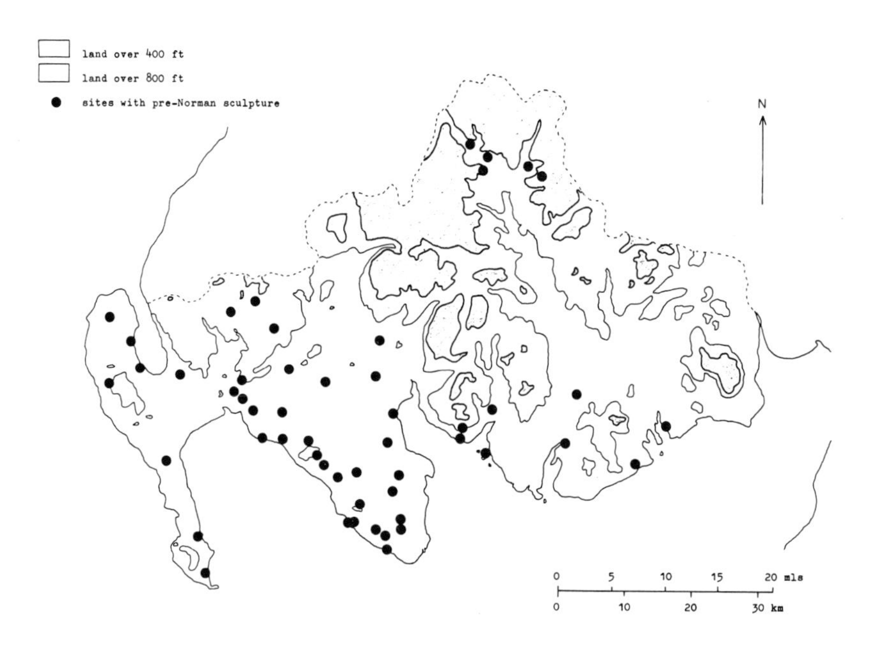

Fig.4.2 Pre-Norman sculpture in Galloway: topography.

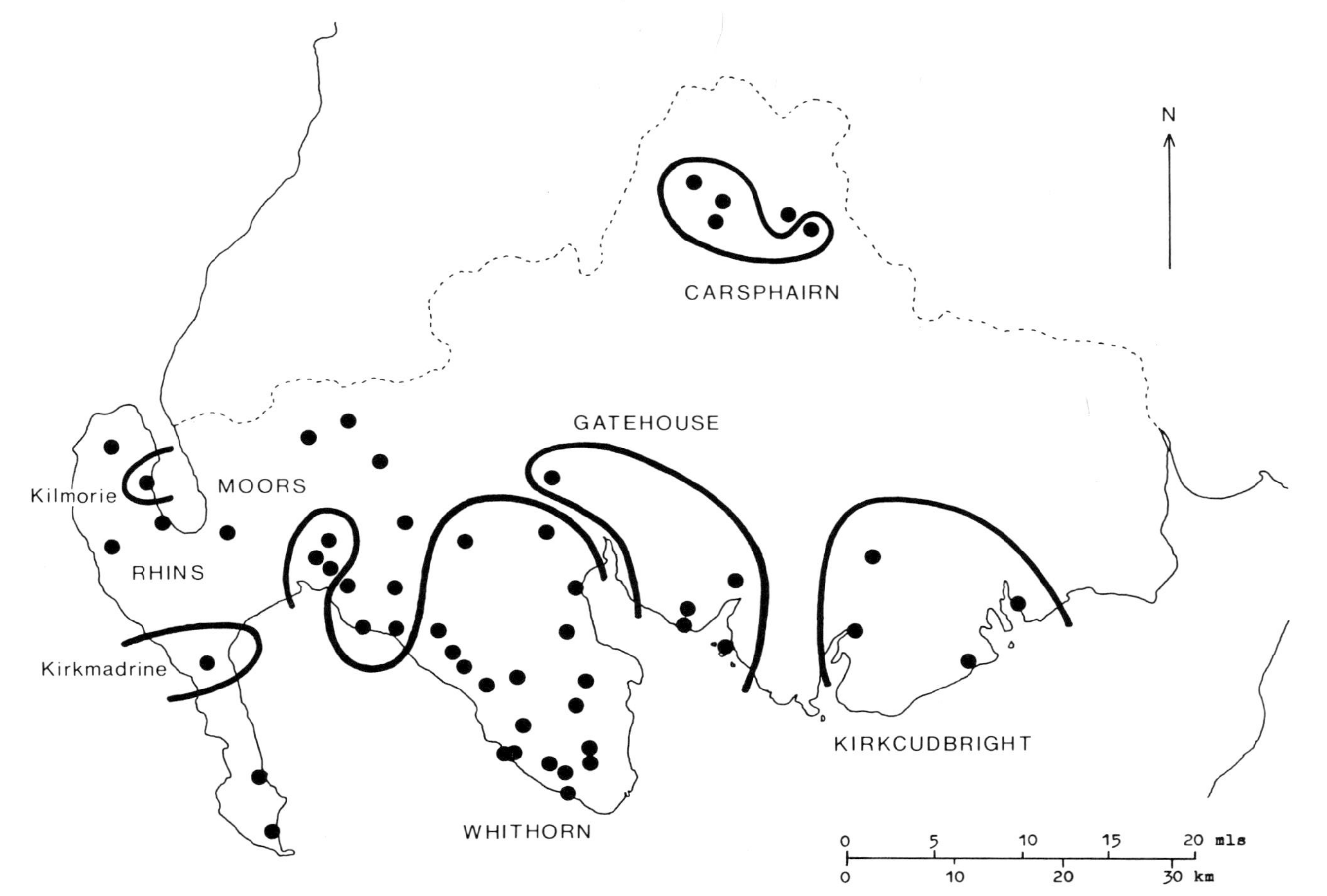

Fig.4.3 Pre-Norman sculpture in Galloway: discrete groups and clusters.

trace more wide-ranging links, i.e. between Ardwall and St Ninian's Cave), but also by broadly similar stylistic elements common to several stones in the group[19] (Figure 4.3). For instance in the group west of Gatehouse, Ardwall Island can be linked to Anwoth, Anwoth to Kirkclaugh, and Kirklaugh to Minnigaff by a chain of related features.[20] An even more limited vocabulary can be pinpointed in the stones from Daltallochan, the Cumnock Knowes ('Dalshangan'), Braidenoch Hill and Auchenshinnoch in the area of Carsphairn,[21] although their distribution makes it unlikely that they all marked a route.[22]

Comparison of these stylistic elements with material outside the region is more difficult, as many of the stones in Galloway are either very simple, very crudely carved, or follow eccentric local styles. Only in the third small group east of Kirkcudbright which relates to styles found in Dumfriesshire and northern England,[23] and in the early Christian inscribed stones from Whithorn and Kirkmadrine,[24] and the stones of the so-called 'Whithorn School',[25] solely found in the south-east peninsula of Wigtownshire (Figure 4.4), can less provincial elements be recognised.[26]

This causes certain problems. On the basis of work done on early medieval sculpture in other areas of the country, it is possible to define a range of stylistic features we might expect to find on sculpture that could attest the presence of an alien element in the population, or an awareness of a foreign decorative tradition, as well as indicating the date.[27] We might therefore hope to find material evidence for historically documented, or deduced, population movements or political takeovers.

In Galloway, the establishment of an Anglian bishopric at Whithorn, subject to the see of York, and its existence throughout the eighth century, is historically attested by Bede in his Ecclesiastical History, and by subsequent entries in the Anglo-Saxon Chronicle and elsewhere up to A.D. 802.[28] The extent of Anglian political control over the region is less clear, as is the extent of Anglian immigration into the area.[29] At Whithorn, ironically, this documented period of the Anglian bishopric is hardly represented amongst the comparatively large quantity of sculpture found at various times in the area of the priory.[30] Most of this sculpture appears to post-date the eighth century, including the two stones with Anglian runes,[31] despite the absence of further documentary evidence until 1128.[32] There is also a notable lack of standard Northumbrian forms such as free-armed cross-heads. Except for the miniature grave-marker, Ardwall no.9/16,[33] in the whole of Galloway west of Kirkcudbright, this type only occurs in the form of crosses incised in outline on a slab, and at Whithorn only on stone no.6.[34] There is a close similarity between crosses of this type from Ardwall Island and St Ninian's Cave,[35] two sites which also have simple Anglian inscriptions on other stones.[36] But classic Northumbrian plant-scroll sculpture has been found only in the east of the region, at the two sites of Argrennan[37] and Rascarrel[38] near

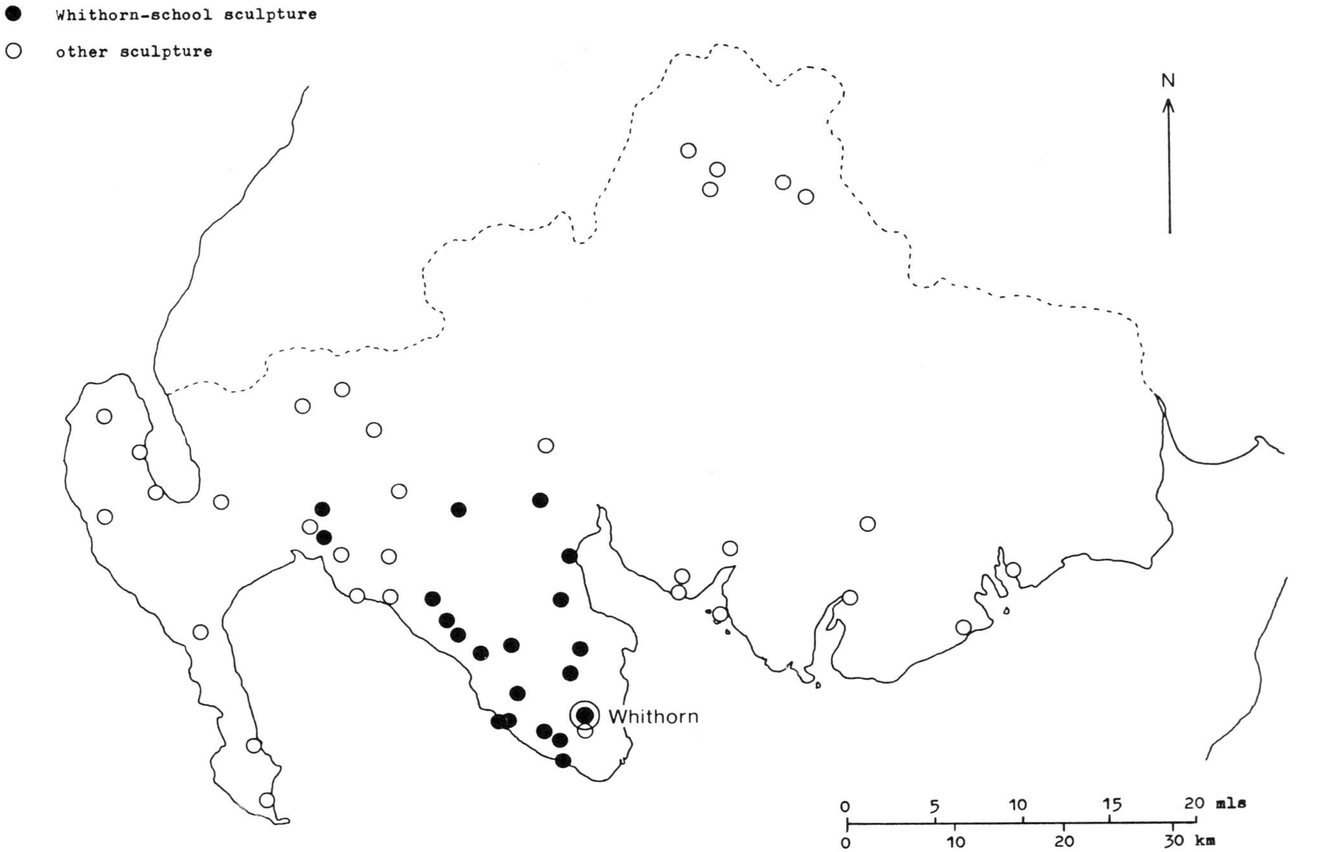

Fig.4.4 Pre-Norman sculpture in Galloway: the Whithorn School.

Kirkcudbright.[39] A piece of worn plant-scroll from the recent Whithorn excavations[40] does not appear to date from before the twelfth century. Such a small total may have been influenced by the lack of suitable sandstone in Galloway, but contrasts markedly with the evidence to the east from Dumfriesshire.[41]

Conversely, sculptural evidence has been used by a number of writers[42] to argue for an extensive, if entirely undocumented,[43] Scandinavian settlement in Galloway. There is, however, no clear-cut use in this region of the decorative elements that have been convincingly linked to Scandinavian influence elsewhere in the British Isles. For instance, there are no hogbacks,[44] although like the Isle of Man, twenty miles to the south, this may also have to do with an unsuitable geology.[45] But, unlike Man or England, nor are there any Scandinavian runic inscriptions,[46] nor scenes related to Norse mythology[47] (with one possible exception — see below), nor circle-headed crosses,[48] nor the four Scandinavian art styles[49] and the form of 'ring-chain' ornament[50] found in the Isle of Man and Cumbria.[51]

Professor Bailey has argued for a direct link between the more obviously Scandinavian-influenced sculpture of Cumbria and certain cross-slabs in western Galloway, on the basis of a decorative treatment of carved interlace known as 'stopped plait.'[52] But in Cumbria this is only found as one element of a decorative package.[53] The other elements, such as 'spiral-scroll,' do not occur on the Galloway stones with stopped plait.[54] In this region too it is just one ingredient in a very distinctive local style, and like the disc-heads also found on these 'Whithorn School' stones (see below) it seems to be a feature more indicative of the relative date of such sculpture[55] and the type of stone used, than of a Gaelic-Norse Solway province.

Only one stone from the region seems to show potential Scandinavian influence.[56] This is the remarkable slab from Kilmorie[57] (Figure 4.5), on the coast north of Stranraer (Figure 4.3), with snake-headed interlace and a hammer-headed cross[58] filled with the only example of spiral-scroll from the region.[59] On the other face is a cruely-incised Crucifixion,[60] and below it a secondary figure flanked by birds and pincers. It is possible that this represents a scene from the Sigurd legend, and such a juxtaposition of pagan and Christian elements is found on sculpture from the Scandinavian areas of northern England.[61] But here this slab is unique. The linguistic evidence for a Scandinavian takeover of Galloway was questioned by some other speakers at the conference,[62] and I can only say that this reinforced[63] my own impressions derived from working on the sculpture.[64]

It may therefore seem that we cannot use sculpture in this region to test theories derived from the historical evidence, or to attempt to bridge the undocumented period from the ninth to the eleventh century.[65] But the predominant quantity of sculpture from Whithorn appears to date from

Fig.4.5 Cross-slab from Kilmorie, Wigtownshire (from Stuart, J., Sculptured Stones of Scotland, vol. 11 (1867), pl. LXX).

this period ,[66] and unlike all other types of sculpture found in Galloway, these cross-slabs, whether found whole or as fragments, have so many characteristics in common as to appear mass-produced to a standard formula.[67] When found complete, the head is flat and circular, with a central boss and four circles near the edge, dividing the head into four segments. The shafts are very broad in proportion to their thickness,[68] and the two faces each contain a single panel of repetitive interlace carved in relief, somewhat different in design in each case but with broad flat bands, usually divided by a band down the middle, forming loops and circles arranged in vertical and horizontal columns.

About twenty-five carved stones of this type have been found at Whithorn itself (though not from the current excavations), and about twenty more, following the same formula, from other sites in the area.[69] All stones of this type, known as the Whithorn School,[70] are confined in their distribution to the triangular district sandwiched between the rivers Luce and Cree, known as the Machars (Figure 4.4). Most of the land here is below 300ft. (90m) and is nowadays, to the east of Port William, good farming country.[71] There are far more stones from this area than from any other part of Galloway. Most of these stones have been found, usually singly, on or close to known church sites. In the other cases the original position is not known, usually because the stone has been built into a post-medieval wall. But it is notable that the church sites from which stones of this tenth-century type come were the principal churches of each[72] of the later[73] medieval parishes, including such sites as Longcastle and Kirkmaiden-in-Farines where the parish was suppressed at the Reformation[74] (Figure 4.6). The geographical area of the Machars and the relevant parish church sites is also equivalent to the medieval deanery of Farines, an administrative area first recorded in the thirteenth century.[75]

Since we have a large quantity of these stones from a central place, Whithorn, recorded both earlier and later as an administrative centre,[76] and also from the surrounding dependent parishes, all showing a limited and standardised vocabulary, there appears to be evidence of some centralised control in approximately the tenth or eleventh centuries over the area equivalent to a later administrative unit.[77] This therefore suggests the continued survival of Whithorn as a regional centre in the undocumented period between 802 and 1128.

Since we have no other evidence for the development of parishes in this area before the Norman period,[78] it also raises the question why these particular sites with sculpture were later selected as parish churches. It should be noted that the distribution of the Whithorn School and the associated parish centres is confined to the area of the eastern half of the Machars nowadays classed as good arable land (classes 2-4).[79] This seems to reinforce the suggestion that the patronage of such stylised sculpture is a reflection of wealth and status,[80] especially as these stones are

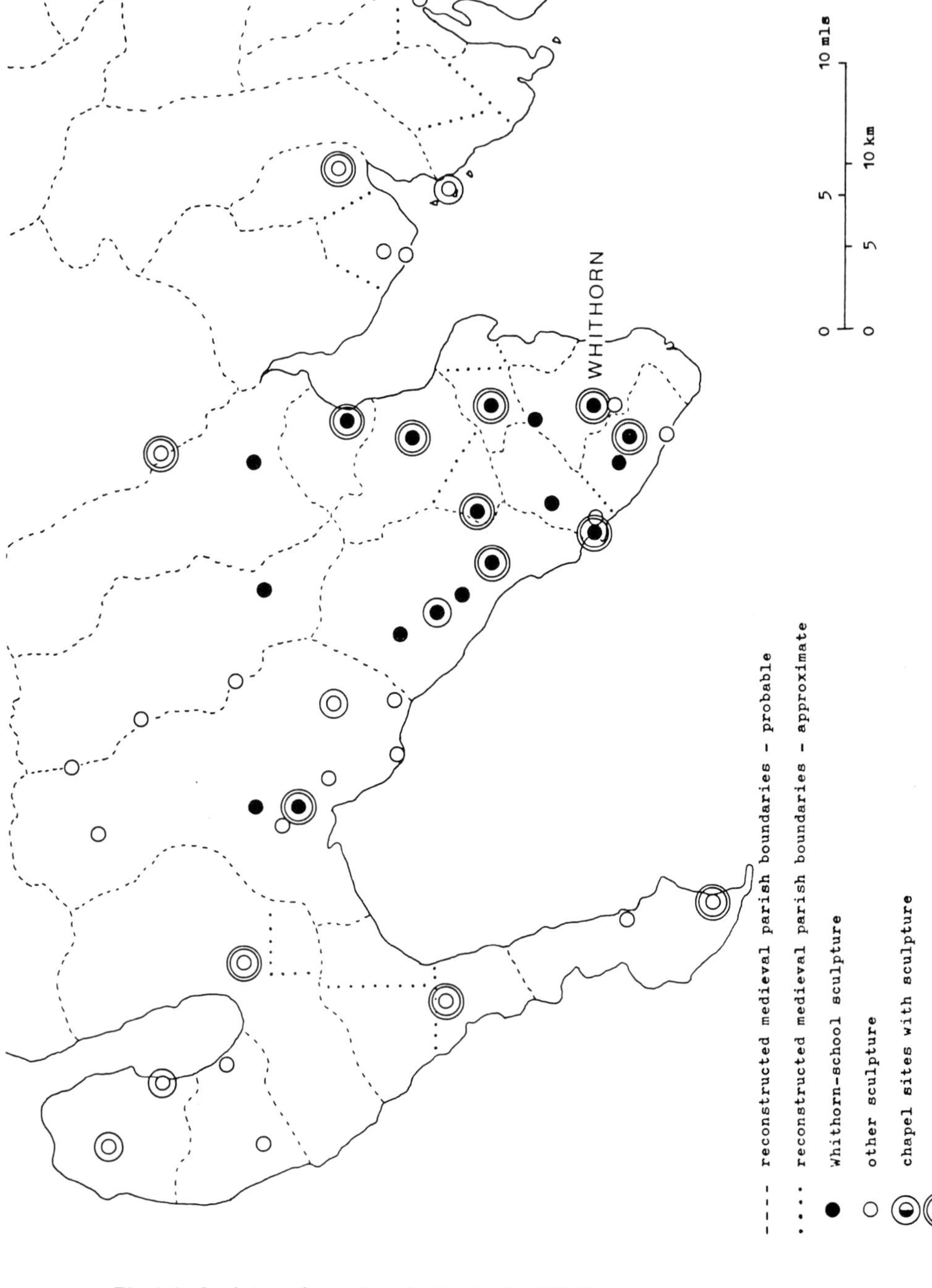

Fig.4.6 Sculpture from church sites in the Whithorn area.

imposing monuments with a comparatively large carved area, modelled in relief and with interlace constructed to a geometric formula.[81] But we also appear to have evidence of an organised professional school of carving, apparently working under the auspices of a central authority in the region. It therefore seems probable that these sites were the churches of the estate centres attached to Whithorn, possibly with rights of baptism and burial, and thus richer than any neighbouring chapels.[82] Such a network would also imply the attachment of these estates or proto-parishes to Whithorn as components of a multiple estate or collegiate minster.[83]

These deductions may be sharply contrasted with the evidence of the sculpture found outside the Whithorn area. There appears to be a clear cultural divide, both east of the River Cree (the border [84] with the Stewartry), and west of Castle Loch and the Tarf Water, with the Glenluce region as the only outlier (Figure 4.3). Beyond these boundaries almost none of the sculpture is either carved or in relief, decorated with interlace, or has a separately modelled head. The exceptions to this in the Stewartry have already been mentioned. The rare examples of relief carving and interlace in the western area include the unique, possibly Norse, cross-slab from the chapel site at Kilmorie, and several stones from Kirkmadrine Church.[85] But these show no evidence of a standardised design or a local school, despite the earlier importance of the Kirkmadrine site demonstrated by the three Early Christian stones with chi-rhos and Latin inscriptions.

The other stones in the Rhinns and the moors to the north and west of Wigtownshire are mainly unshaped, the crosses simply incised in outline on the surface of the stones, usually with fan-shaped arms and occasional subordinate crosslets.[86] The designs are often quite abstract, in comparison with the Stewartry[87] and the few incised crosses from the Whithorn area, mainly from St Ninian's Cave,[88] which follow standard forms. The stones to the west are therefore almost impossible to date, since they are primitive enough to appear either very early or very late[89] and are so provincial in style as to make comparison meaningless.

These incised stones usually come from higher altitudes and poorer land[90] than the Whithorn School and other interlace stones, and only rarely are known from church or chapel sites (Figs. 4.3 and 4.7). It is possible that there was a difference in function to the interlace sculpture, with these simply carved stones being used as route-markers or for wayside burial,[91] though this cannot be proved. There does appear to be a difference in geology, with the harder greywackes being more difficult to sculpt in relief. But the principal impression is of a lower technical and economic input, and thus a difference in status to the interlace sculpture,[92] particularly the Whithorn School, since the incised stones are generally smaller in scale and a lesser proportion of the whole surface is carved.

The difference may be between domestic and professional workmanship, but the implications of a technical break along a geographical and later

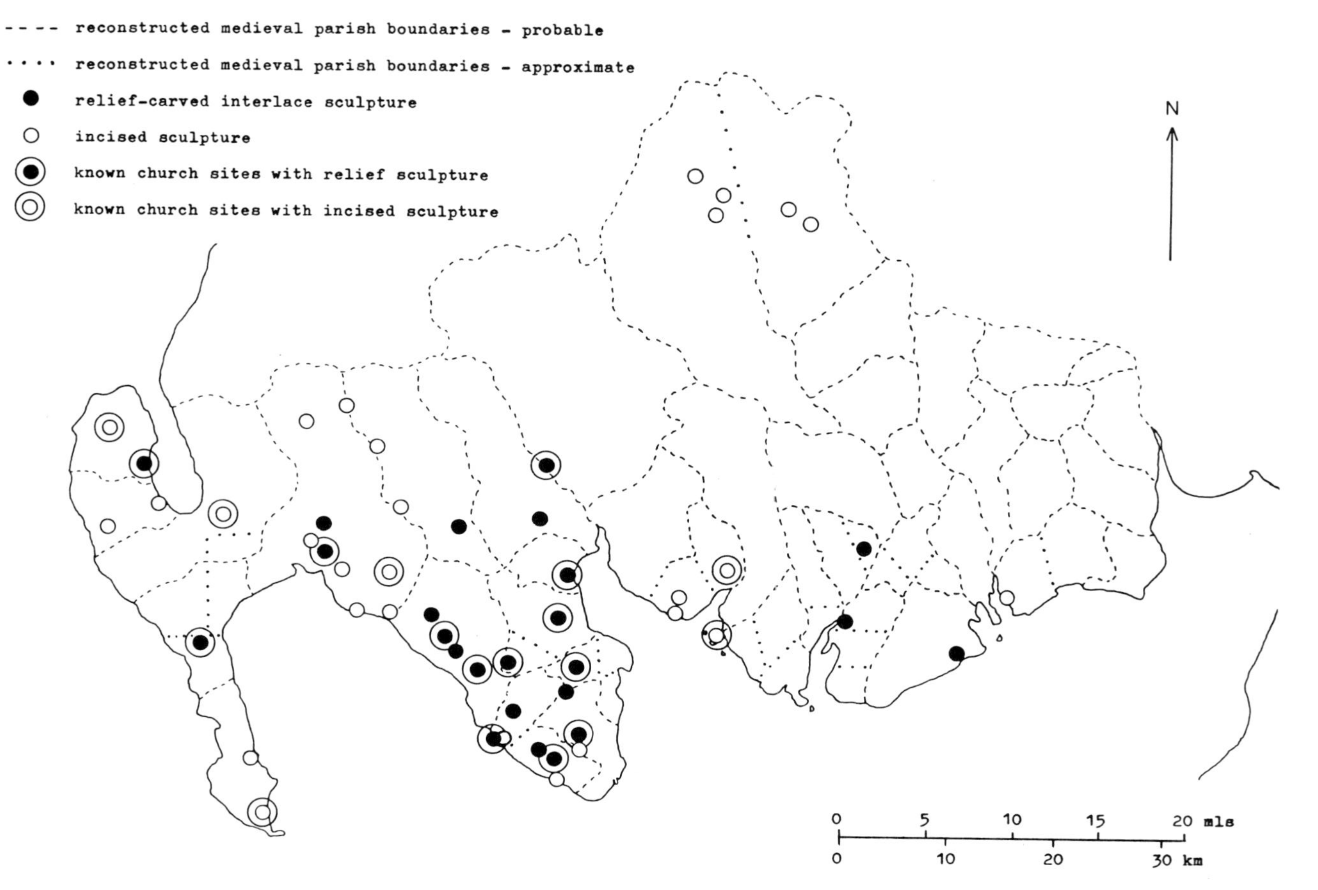

Fig.4.7 *Sculpture from church sites in Galloway.*

administrative boundary suggests that we are dealing with unintegrated cultural traditions rather than a difference in periods. This would imply that we can identify a separate Rhinns and moors territory to the west of the Whithorn territory of the Machars, in addition to the three regions of the Stewartry already discussed (Fig. 4.3). Two of these, the coastal area east of the River Cree between Newton Stewart and Gatehouse, and the upland area around Carsphairn, both use an incised technique and avoid the construction of interlace, but differ in their treatment of cross forms. The third group is the relief-carved, Northumbrian-influenced material near Kirkcudbright.

Quite apart from the limited quantity of sculpture compared with Wigtownshire, very few of these mainly incised stones from the Stewartry are associated with known chapel sites, apart from Ardwall,[93] let alone parish churches, and the link between sculpture and burials demonstrated at Ardwall Island is unique in Galloway.[94] In this eastern area few of the parishes have produced any sculpture at all, so that there appears to be no equation between sculpture and later parish churches (Figure 4.7). But this seems to emphasise the relationship between relief-carved interlace and churches[95] subsequently chosen as parish centres, despite the absence of any early architectural sculpture; it also emphasises the disproportionate quantity of the sculpture from the Whithorn area, having links with Whithorn itself and reinforces the impression that Whithorn remained a potent centre throughout the period.

Notes

1. For an example of this attitude, see Rahtz, P., 'Monasteries as settlements,' *Scottish Archaeological Forum,* 5 (1973), 130.
2. i.e. the lack of any early material in Reid, R. C., *Wigtownshire Charters*, Scottish History Society, 3rd series, LI (1960).
3. i.e. the problem of St. Ninian, and the supposed discovery of 'Candida Casa' in Dr Radford's excavations at Whithorn: discussed in Thomas, A. C., *Christianity in Roman Britain, to AD. 500,* (1981), 279-82.
4. Collingwood, W. G., 'The early crosses of Galloway,' *TDGAS*, 10 (1922-23), 205-31.
5. The pre-Norman sculpture of Galloway and Dumfriesshire is catalogued and discussed in detail in my thesis for Durham University, which also includes the detailed evidence for the conclusions reached in this paper.
6. The major proportion of the sculpture from this region appears to be tenth or eleventh century. Only certain of the stones from Whithorn, Kirkmadrine, St Ninian's Cave, Ardwall Island, the Mote of Mark, and the two plant-scroll fragments near Kirkcudbright (as well as the symbols carved on the rock at Trusty's Hill) appear to be definitely earlier than this. A few other pieces may date to the period of Norman infiltration into the region, *c.*1160-1286 (see n.11).
7. Thomas, A. C., *The Early Christian Archaeology of North Britain* (1971) , chapter 4.
8. Cramp, R. J., *Early Northumbrian Sculpture* (Jarrow Lecture 1965).

9. See O'Sullivan, D., 'Cumbria before the Vikings: a review of some 'Dark-Age' problems in North-West England,' in Baldwin and Whyte (edd.), *The Scandinavians in Cumbria*, (1985), 31.
10. See Higham, N. J., 'The Scandinavians in North Cumbria: raids and settlement in the later ninth to mid tenth centuries,' in Baldwin and Whyte, *Scandinavians in Cumbria*, 38-39.
11. i.e. predating c.1160 AD. in this region. See Barrow, G. W. S., *The Anglo-Norman Era in Scottish History* (1980), 30.
12. The early finds were catalogued by Allen, J. R., in *The Early Christian Monuments of Scotland* (1903), 476-504, and by RCAHMS *Inventories of Wigtownshire* (1912), and the *Stewartry of Kirkcudbright* (1914). Most of the known stones were illustrated and discussed in Collingwood, 'Early Crosses.' Subsequent finds have been reported mainly in *PSAS* and *TDGAS*. The sculpture from Whithorn and its neighbourhood is listed and discussed in the HMSO Official Guide by Radford, C. A. R., and Donaldson, G., *Whithorn and Kirkmadrine*, (1953). The individual references will be detailed in my thesis. I have inspected and photographed all the known stones.
13. See Radford and Donaldson, *Whithorn and Kirkmadrine*. Other stones are in the Royal Museum of Scotland at Edinburgh.
14. See Thomas, A. C., 'An Early Christian cemetery and chapel on Ardwall Isle, Kirkcudbright,' *Medieval Archaeology*, 11 (1967), 127-88.
15. e.g., see Wendy Davies, *Wales in the Early Middle Ages* (1982), 19.
16. See Cambridge, E., 'The Early Church in County Durham,' in *Journal of the British Archaeological Association*, 131 (1984), 71.
17. The earliest known position of each of the stones is analysed and discussed in the catalogue of my thesis, and forms the basis for my maps here. (N.B. It is not possible to distinguish between closely adjacent sites on maps of this scale. Nor is it feasible here to try to distinguish between the quality of the evidence in each case, for instance, between the stones built into modern walls and thus clearly no longer *in situ*, and stones dug up or still standing. Nor when the evidence for the original discovery is imprecise. But at this stage such factors are relatively insignificant).
18. Hare, F. K., Part 7, 'Kirkcudbrightshire', in Stamp, L. D., (ed.), *The Land of Britain — The Report of the Land Utilisation Survey of Britain* (1942), 355-406.
19. The maps are inevitably an oversimplification, as it is difficult in this brief paper to distinguish cartographically between different types of sculpture from the same site. And despite the work of Collingwood and others, there is insufficient evidence to say which of the unrelated groups of sculpture were contemporary. Because of this, I have not attempted here to subdivide any of the distribution maps into different periods. (But see n 6 above *re* dating).
20. See Collingwood, 'Early crosses,' 228-9, and also Collingwood, W. G., and Reid, R. C., 'Ardwall Island and its ancient cross', in *TDGAS*, 13 (1925-6), 129.
21. For the first three sites, see RCAHMS *Inventory of Kirkcudbright*, Nos. 99, 100, and 101, and for the fourth (and the quite different stone from Stroanfreggan), see Corrie, J., 'Notice of two Early Christian monuments from the parish of Dalry, Kirkcudbrightshire,' *PSAS*, 44 (1911-12).
22. As suggested by Dr Radford, See n.91.
23. See below (n.37-9 and 41).

24. Radford and Donaldson, *Whithorn and Kirkmadrine*, Whithorn 1 and 2, Kirkmadrine K. 1-3.
25. Collingwood, 'Early crosses,' 218; and see below.
26. The evidence of Mediterranean influence on the stones with the chi-rho symbol at Whithorn and Kirkmadrine may be compared with the recent evidence of contemporary imported B and E ware from the Whithorn excavations. See Hill, P. H., *Excavations at Bruce Street, Whithorn 1984, Interim Report,* 40.
27. An excellent recent example is Bailey, R. N., *Viking Age Sculpture in Northern England,* (1980).
28. See Colgrave, B., and Mynors, R. A. B., *Bede's Ecclesiastical History,* (1969), 222-3, 558-61; Whitelock, D., *English Historical Documents I c500-1042*, (2nd ed. 1979), 178-82, 267-74.
29. Laing, L., 'The Angles in Scotland and the Mote of Mark,' *TDGAS*, 50 (1973), 37-52.
30. *Contra* Collingwood, 'Early crosses,' 215-16; but see Radford, C. A. R., 'Excavations at Whithorn, First Season, 1949,' *TDGAS*, 27 (1948-9), 96. There is, however, the eighth- and ninth-century coinage from the recent excavations: see Hill, *Bruce Street, Interim Report,* 42.
31. Whithorn nos. 10 and 36: see Radford and Donaldson, *Whithorn and Kirkmadrine* (revised edition 1984), 28 and 29-30.
32. Radford, 'Excavations at Whithorn,' 102; Haddan, A. W., and Stubbs, W., *Councils and Ecclesiastical Documents Relating to Great Britain and Ireland,* Vol. II, Part I (1873), 24-5. Although there is a tantalising reference to Whithorn *c.*882 in the description of the wanderings of the Cuthbert community after the sack of Lindisfarne, in Symeon's Historia Ecclesia Dunelmensis, Book II, Chapter XII, in Arnold, T. (ed.), *Symeonis Monachi Opera Omnia*, Rolls Series no. LXXV, Part I (1882), 67.
33. Thomas, 'Ardwall Isle,' 155-7, fig. 31; Thomas, *Early Christian Archaeology of North Britain*, 121-2, fig. 59.
34. Radford and Donaldson, *Whithorn and Kirkmadrine.* See Collingwood, 'Early crosses,' fig. 10.
35. Compare the Ardwall No. 13: Thomas, 'Ardwall Isle,' 152, pl. XIXa, and the rock-cut crosses from St. Ninian's Cave, e.g. Royal Commission Inventory — *Wigtown* (1912), 4, no. 3, fig. 5.
36. Thomas, 'Ardwall Isle,' 153-5, no. 6; Radford and Donaldson, *Whithorn and Kirkmadrine*, no. C.4.
37. Williams, J. in *Discovery and Excavation in Scotland 1967*, 31.
38. See Macleod, I. F., in *Discovery and Excavation in Scotland 1970*, 29. But this piece was first recognised as plant-scroll by C. Crowe in 1985.
39. But this cluster also includes a free-armed cross-head from Kirkcudbright itself: Truckell, A. E., 'Dumfries and Galloway in the Dark Ages: Some Problems,' in *TDGAS*, 40 (1961-2), 89; and the two Anglian runic inscriptions (and interlace metal-work moulds) from the Mote of Mark excavations: Laing, 'Angles in Scotland,' 40.
40. I am grateful to P. Hill for showing me a photograph of this fragment.
41. cf. the material in Allen, *Early Christian Monuments*, 436-51, figs 458-470.
42. The primary paper is Collingwood, W. G., 'Norse influence in Dumfriesshire and Galloway,' in *TDGAS*, 7 (1919-20), 97-118; followed by Radford, 'Excavations

at Whithorn,' 97-101. It should be noted that Collingwood's argument depends initially upon the idea of the Picts in Galloway (pp. 98-9).
43. I am deliberately ignoring the evidence of the place-names here, as it is dealt with independently by other contributors to this volume. (see also n.62).
44. See Lang, J. T., 'Hogback monuments in Scotland,' in *PSAS*, 105 (1972-4), 207-9, figs. 1 and 2.
45. Bailey, *Viking Age Sculpture*, 96.
46. Ibid., 51-3.
47. Ibid., chapter 6.
48. Ibid., 70, 177-82.
49. Ibid., 53-8.
50. Ibid., 54-5.
51. Ibid., 217. And see Bailey, R. N., 'Irish Sea contacts in the Viking Period — the Sculptural Evidence,' in Fellows-Jensen, G. and Lund, N., (edd.), *Tredie Tvaerfaglige Vikingesymposium* (1980), 21.
52. Bailey, *Viking Age Sculpture*, 223-9. (But see also Bailey, 'Irish Sea Contacts,' 18-20).
53. Bailey, *Viking Age Sculpture*, 196-206.
54. The border of Whithorn no. 10 is quite different, *contra* Bailey, 'Irish Sea Contacts,' 19. See Collingwood, 'Early crosses,' fig. 14a.
55. Bailey, *Viking Age Sculpture*, 205.
56. There is not space here to argue against the Scandinavian interpretation of the swastika-bearing slab from Craignarget (Collingwood, 'Early crosses,' 229-30. It shows evidence of secondary re-cutting).
57. But for a different view, see Collingwood, 'Early crosses,' 216. Because of its present position the stone is illustrated here from Stuart, J., *Sculptured Stones of Scotland*, Vol. II (1867), plate LXX. It is 1.70 m. high.
58. Bailey, *Viking Age Sculpture*, 182-3.
59. This motif is derived from symmetrical Anglian plant-scroll, but the knotted forking of the strands at the centre of the head is a style developed in Scandinavia, not Britain. See Bailey, *Viking Age Sculpture*, 72, 206.
60. There are no other Crucifixion scenes on stones from Galloway. It is of a type relating to examples found in Yorkshire. See Coatsworth, E., *The Iconography of the Crucifixion in Pre-Conquest Sculpture in England*, (Unpublished PhD thesis, University of Durham, 1979), 133 ff.
61. See examples in Bailey, *Viking Age Sculpture*, 116-25. But Collingwood was cautious on the matter: Collingwood, W. G., *Northumbrian crosses of the Pre-Norman Age*, (1927), 92.
62. And see also Brooke, D., 'Kirk-compound place-names in Galloway and Carrick,' in *TDGAS*, 58 (1983), 56-71.
63. The presence of the refugee Cuthbert community near Whithorn *c.*882 also suggests the lack of Scandinavian settlement in the area at that date. *Symeon of Durham*, 67.
64. I suspect that most of the sculpture taken as evidence for the domination of Galloway by the *Gall-Gaidhil* should be seen as part of a Western British tradition, as it bears a general resemblance to material from Cumbria, the Isle of Man, Wales, and Cornwall, rather than Ireland or the Western Isles of Scotland.

65. Radford, 'Excavations at Whithorn,' 96-102.
66. Collingwood, 'Early crosses,' 217-27.
67. Ibid., figs. 14-37.
68. This is partly predetermined by the use of green slate in many of these carvings.
69. Most of these stones are now in the Whithorn Museum (Radford and Donaldson, *Whithorn and Kirkmadrine*), or in Edinburgh. It is impossible to list all the examples here. They will be catalogued and discussed in my thesis.
70. Collingwood, 'Early crosses,' 218.
71. Hare, F. K., Part 8, 'Wigtownshire,' in Stamp, L. D., (ed.), *The Land of Britain — The Report of the Land Utilisation Survey of Britain*, (1942), 407-22.
72. The scale of the map and the scope of this paper makes it impossible to show these relationships and to draw conclusions here without the dangers of oversimplification. The following qualifications should be noted. There are no stones from the former parishes of Eggerness or Cruggleton. A fragment has come from the recently discovered church site at Barhobble in Mochrum parish. The stones from Craiglemine and Brighouse appear to have come from lost burial-grounds in Glasserton and Whithorn parishes. The stone from Mains of Penninghame farm was found in use as a step 0.74km from the church. The stone from West Crosherie was built into a cottage 1km. from Kirkcowan Church. These are the single stones in the two northern parishes on the map.
73. Cowan, I. B., 'The development of the parochial system in medieval Scotland,' in *Scottish Historical Review*, 40 (1961), 43-55, suggests that the development of the parish system in Scotland can be dated to the twelfth century and the reign of David I. Galloway did not fall under the control of the Scottish Crown until after *c.*1160.
74. Maps no. 5 and 6 have been prepared by collating the information on the medieval parishes in Cowan, I. B., *The Parishes of Medieval Scotland*, Scottish Record Society, vol. 93 (1967), with the changes recorded in Sinclair, J. (ed.), *The Statistical Account of Scotland* (1791-9), and in Symson, A., 'A Large Description of Galloway by the Parishes in it', in *Macfarlane's Geographical Collections II*, Scottish History Society, vol LII (1907), 51-132. Boundaries between amalgamated parishes are drawn as straight dotted lines (but see n. 78).
75. See Dunlop, A. I. (ed.), 'Bagimond's Roll: Statement of the Tenths of the Kingdom of Scotland,' in *Miscellany VI*, Scottish History Society, 3rd series vol. 33 (1939), 3-77. This appears to omit parishes whose revenues were appropriated to the priory at Whithorn by *c.* 1274. I have therefore followed Cowan, *Parishes*, in deciding which parishes lay within the deanery.
76. Radford and Donaldson, *Whithorn and Kirkmadrine*
77. Barrow, G. W. S., 'The pattern of lordship and feudal settlement in Cumbria,' in *Journal of Medieval History*, 1 (1975), 126-7, figs. 4 and 5.
78. Without charter or other evidence, the boundaries themselves cannot be linked to the pre-Norman period. See also O'Sullivan, 'Cumbria Before the Vikings,' 31.
79. Brown, C. J., and Heslop, R. E. F., *The Soils of the Country Round Stranraer and Wigtown*, (1979), 287-305.
80. Higham, 'Scandinavians in North Cumbria,' 39.
81. Adcock, G., *A Study of the Types of Interlace on Northumbrian Sculpture,* (Unpublished M.Phil thesis, University of Durham, 1974), 204-6.
82. Collingwood, 'Early crosses,' 226-7.

83. See Jones, G. R. J., 'The multiple estate as a model framework for tracing the early stages in the evolution of rural settlement,' in *L'Habitat et les Paysages d'Europe*, (1971), 262, 266; and Cowan, 'Development of the parochial system.'
84. Until May 16th 1975.
85. Radford and Donaldson, *Whithorn and Kirkmadrine*, Nos. K.5, K.6, K.8; RCAHMS *Inventory of Wigtown*, 156-7, Nos. 443, 445, 446, 447.
86. See, for example, Drummore, in RCAHMS *Inventory of Kirkcudbright*, 23-4, No. 26, fig. 22.
87. Although see the two pillar-stones from High Auchenlarie, west of Gatehouse: in RCAHMS *Inventory of Kirkcudbright*, 23-4, No. 26, fig. 22.
88. RCAHMS *Inventory of Wigtown*, 3-9, No. 3.
89. Opposed positions are taken by Stevenson, R. B. K., 'The Inchyra Stone and some other unpublished Early Christian monuments,' in *PSAS*, 92 (1958-9), 50, and Curle, C., 'The chronology of the Early Christian monuments of Scotland,' in *PSAS*, 74 (1939-40), 72.
90. Brown and Heslop, *Soils Round Stranraer and Wigtown*.
91. Radford, C. A. R., 'Two unrecorded crosses found near Stranraer,' in *TDGAS*, (1948-9), 193-6.
92. In contrast to n. 80, Higham, 'Scandinavians in North Cumbria.'
93. Thomas, 'Ardwall Isle.'
94. Slabs from the excavations at Whithorn and Barhobble have been found reused in paving or walls (Hill, *Bruce Street, Interim Report*, 22; Cormack, W. F., *Barhobble Interim Report 1986*, 3-5).
95. The two interlace stones east of Kirkcudbright had been reused in modern walls.

THE VIKINGS IN GALLOWAY: A REVIEW OF THE EVIDENCE

Edward J. Cowan

Charles Hill Dick introduced his *Highways and Byways of Galloway and Carrick* by stating of the district which was the subject of his book that 'it has remained unknown to the world longer than any other part of Scotland with the possible exception of the Island of Rockall'.[1] The same could still be said of the area's history. Galloway, for reasons which are not altogether clear,[2] is comparatively poorly documented. The so-called Viking Age is virtually a blank. Indeed the period is more or less enveloped in darkness from the time of the early saints through to the emergence of the Lords of Galloway in the twelfth century.[3] The *Life of Adomnan* testifies that the traveller of 686 was as impressed as is the visitor exactly thirteen hundred years later in 1986 by the treacherous tides of the Solway.

> . . . the flood is so rapid that if the best steed in Saxonland, ridden by the best horseman, were to start from the edge of the tide when the tide begins to flow, he could only bring his rider ashore by swimming, so extensive is the strand and so impetuous the tide.[4]

The Galloway Tourist Board may have missed a bet by failing to organise annual Tide Races! This paper will argue that, despite many statements to the contrary, the Vikings would probably not have been greatly interested in competing. The inimitable Bruce Trotter wrote in his *Galloway Gossip:*

> A great Gallawa author yince remarkit, yt the authenetic traditions o' the country wus ey reliable — whun true. Deed! tae my wey o' thinking, they'r joost havers; some bigger leer nor or'nar joost maks them up an tells them, an some fules believes them an tells them again, an maybe improves them a wee, an than they get inta books.[5]

His observations could not be more accurate so far as the historical literature on Viking Galloway is concerned.

Much has been made of the supposed archaeological evidence. There are suspected boat graves at both extremes of the Galloway littoral. In 1684 Andrew Symson reported the discovery at Stranraer of a ship burial. His informants told him that the vessel was 'pretty large' and they noted that 'the boards were not joyn'd together after the usual fashion of our present ships or barks, as also that it had nails of copper',[6] a detail which suggests that the ship was certainly not Viking but may have been Roman. Daniel Wilson reported a possible boat grave at the farm of Graitney Mains at the head of the Solway.[7] Some Viking artefacts have been recovered from Kirkcudbright,[8] while Peter Hill has made some very exciting discoveries at Whithorn. To archaeology this paper will return because, Hill apart, the confident claims for a Viking administration in Galloway, based upon the slimmest of yields from the earth, seem quite untenable. Archaeologists often presume historical knowledge which quite simply does not exist. Prehistoric archaeology is undergoing some stunning revisionism, but the limitations of the hypothetical school are thrown into sharper highlights the closer one comes to the historical period. History limits archaeology, although historical sources themselves are often manipulated or ignored to suit the requirements of some archaeologists. Viking studies in Scotland have been largely taken over by archaeologists because dithering historians take longer, it seems, to analyse such slim documentation as does exist, than do their colleagues to dig up a site, report the excavation, and arrange for generalisations based upon the most restricted samples to appear in the latest archaeological synthesis.

Place-name studies are also in a state of flux, although much has been done to illuminate the value of this evidence by scholars such as Jack MacQueen, Bill Nicolaisen and, more recently, Daphne Brooke and Gillian Fellows-Jensen. Older studies by W. G. Collingwood and Herbert Maxwell are not without value. Yet the very richness of ethnic exchange and inter-relationship which the place-names of Galloway demonstrate is a problem, so far as understanding is concerned. The familiar hatching of Galloway on maps of Scandinavian place-names does not convince. Many of the preserved forms are late. With reference to onomastics George Neilson observed that 'close history is necessary of true etymology, a caveat of less forceful application, the later a name is recorded'.[9] However, answers are perhaps beginning to be found to a most sensitive and sensible question posed by the redoubtable Alfred Truckell in 1962 — 'Is there a gap in time between our two clearly separated place-name groups — the western coastal one — Southwick, Satterness, Eggerness and so on and the eastern inland group — Tinwald, Torthorwald, Tundergarth, Applegarth, etc. . . '. Should we see the coastal group 'as early and seaborne while the other was later and penetrated overland from the Danelaw?'.[10] We may eventually have to accept that some of the coastal names are also a product of secondary penetration.

Lest archaeologists and onomasticians sensibly retort that the historian is in no position to criticise, let us now turn to a review of the historical evidence, which it must be admitted, allows no opportunity for self-righteous complacency. The sources notice not one single documented Viking attack on any part of the Galloway coast. This is not, in itself, a problem. Neither are there references in British sources to attacks on such familiar Viking areas as Orkney, Caithness, Sutherland, the Dornoch Firth or Islay. Raids on Iona and Skye are well attested; in the ninth century the *Scottish Chronicle*[11] provides good evidence for attacks on east central Scotland. What is clear in the Irish Annals is that monasteries were the favoured targets. In the Celtic world the monasteries were regarded as sanctuaries where the locals deposited their valuables for protection.[12] Monastic buildings were often conveniently, and expediently, situated on the coast or on the banks of navigable rivers. Water was as important to

Celtic communications as it was to those of the Norsemen. The problem was that, so far as the speed and efficiency of sea-going vessels were concerned, the Celts (and for that matter the Saxons also) were driving Model-Ts when the Vikings arrived in their Porsches. The Nordic pilots of those sleek machines must have been barely able to credit their luck. Not only did the maritime highways of Celtic Britain provide excellent means of communication, but the natives provided the equivalent of drive-in banks conveniently sited for any marauding longships.

It would therefore be likely that Whithorn and possibly Kirkmadrine were early victims of Viking attack. Badulf, fourth and last Anglian bishop of Whithorn, was consecrated in 791 and he disappears from the record in 803, a date which might be expected to have coincided with some of the more ferocious Viking assaults.[13] Historians of Galloway in the nineteenth and twentieth centuries have tended to make much of the assertion that when the Danes attacked the north of England in 875 the relics of St Cuthbert were taken for a short time to the protection of Whithorn. Whithorn, they reason, could not have been subject to the Vikings, otherwise it would have been destroyed.[14]

Such views are based on the mistaken premisses that the Vikings were always intent upon monastic destruction, while clearly they were not. A possible explanation as to how the Irish and Scottish monasteries survived repeated attack appears in the *Life of Blathmac.* The saint achieved his desire for martyrdom in Iona in 825 only because he refused to reveal the hiding-place of the sacred reliquary holding the relics of St Columba. His *Vita* makes it pretty clear that if he had parted with the treasure, his life and his monastery would have been spared.[15] Whithorn too may have paid an early form of blackmail or Danegeld.

The only documented evidence for the Viking presence in Galloway derives from a couple of entries in the *Chronicle of Man* which have been interpreted as showing that Galloway was subject to King Magnus Barelegs of Norway (1093-1103).

In addition there are two saga references. *Orkneyinga Saga* states that Earl Thorfinn the Mighty stayed briefly in Galloway *Gaddgedlar* 'where Scotland and England meet'.[16] *Njal's Saga* relates how, after the battle of Clontari, Kari Solmundarsson visited Beruvik and Hvitsborg. The latter has often been identified with Whithorn. There Kari and his men stayed with Earl Malcolm (Melkolfr).[17] Before subjecting these entries to greater scrutiny it is instructive to examine the accounts of various local historians to ascertain how the 'havers' described by Trotter eventually 'get into books'. Most historians of Galloway are informed with a strong sense of chauvinsim and almost all are concerned to exaggerate the impact and extent of Viking influence.

The survey may usefully begin with P. H. M'Kerlie's *Galloway in Ancient and Modern Times*[18] which summarised views already published in his five-volume *Lands and their Owners in Galloway.*[19] M'Kerlie found it strange that 'occupation by the Norsemen has escaped the notice of those who have entered in Galloway history. The desire to make the Fergus line of the Lords of Galloway the ancient inheritors has blinded research'. If only the character of the people had been considered, such an omission would never have occurred.[20] It must be admitted that some avenues of research are more blind than others, not least that leading, in M'Kerlie's view, to Viking Galloway. According to him, Earl Thorfinn ruled over Galloway, administration being entrusted to Earl Malcolm who lived at Cruggleton Castle, one of several fortresses on the coast erected by Viking builders.[21] He quotes with relish the *Chronicle of Man* text which states that Godfrey Crovan, king of Man, 'brought the Scots to such subjection that if any one of them built a ship or boat, they durst not drive above three nails in it'.[22] Since the Scots who were geographically closest to the Isle of Man have been supposed to be those in Galloway, *Scoti* in this passage has been assumed to refer to the Galwegians. But the term could equally describe any of the *Scoti* in the Hebrides or the western seaboard since Godfrey not only styled himself king of the Isles, but he actually enforced his claims to distant Lewis.[23]

M'Kerlie was also impressed by the entry in the Manx chronicle stating that when Magnus Barelegs took Man in 1098 'he subdued the people of Galloway to such an extent that he compelled them to cut timber and take it to the shore for the construction of his defensive positions'.[24] This entry must imply, says M'Kerlie, that Galloway had been earlier conquered and occupied by the Vikings. However, as the previous entry indicates, the text clearly implies that the Galwegians were to transport timber to the shores of Man, not Galloway. It is a moot point whether Magnus had time for all the actions with which he is attributed. He enjoyed a crowded career, no year of which was busier than 1098 when he conquered Orkney, the Hebrides and Man, as well as attacking Wales and agreeing a treaty with the king of Scots, ceding to Norwegian rule all the islands on the west coast between which and the mainland Magnus could sail in a ship with the rudder set. As is well known, he had his galley dragged across Kintyre 'the best island in the Hebrides'.[25] Magnus, bare-legged and busy as he was, can hardly have had the time to coerce the Galwegians into cutting down trees. The chronicle entry might best be interpreted as a hollow gesture of Manx imperialism.

The Viking legend was much enbroidered by Wentworth Huyshe's *Grey Galloway.*[26] The author rejoiced that the invaders did not touch a single shrine in Galloway. 'Wigton became their chief naval arsenal. It was as protectors and allies of the Galwegians that the Norsemen occupied for centuries the Galloway coast'. To such breathtaking fiction Huyshe added the assertion that Thorfinn resided long at Gaddgedlar, a total distortion of the statement in *Orkneyinga Saga,* while his unbounded inventiveness led him to the completely untenable conclusion that Galloway constituted 'the real headquarters for practical offensive purposes of the Norse power'.[27]

W. G. Collingwood, in what remains the best account of Viking Galloway, argued that when Olaf of Dublin triumphed at the siege of Dumbarton (870-1) he set up his son Eystein as ruler of Galloway. Olaf took back to Ireland 'Angles, Britons and Picts' to peddle in the slave markets.[28] Collingwood follows Skene, who remarked that Olaf must have attacked Galloway, since only there would all three peoples have been found.[29] Both learned commentators obviously overlooked the fact that the Clyde capitals have always been emphatically cosmopolitan in character. Collingwood also suggests that Halfdan the Black may have had some impact upon Galloway after he split from the great Danish Army around 875 when he and his men put part of Northumberland under the plough.[30] Restless as ever, the ploughmen were soon intent upon further plunder. Halfdan's expeditions into Scotland are historically attested, and it is likely that he did indeed attack the south-west. The assertion that he killed Eystein Olafsson is based upon a highly dubious reading. Collingwood's other contribution was to suggest that when Harald Finehair of Norway attacked Man and the Isles in the late ninth century, Vikings already settled in those areas fled up the Solway to Dumfriesshire.[31] It is now known that Harald's expedition never took place.[32]

It remained for John F. Robertson to tie up the loose ends in what is probably the most influential book on Galloway of the last generation. According to him, Irish chronicles of the time (unspecified by him, and so far unknown to anyone else) suggest that 'the Galwegians made their peace with the Norsemen by renouncing Christianity and accepting pagan worship of the gods, Odin and Thor and the goddess Freya', thus presumably implying that Whithorn became a Viking temple at this period. In Robertson's account, Olaf of Dublin becomes a 'Norse-Galloway chieftain'. The Danes defeated a native army at the battle fought somewhere between Castle Douglas and Crossmichael. When the Danes suffered a setback in Northumbria in 944 their leader, Ronald, fled to Galloway where he established his headquarters at Craig Ronald on the shores of Loch Grannoch, this otherwise unrecorded historical episode being suggested by the place-name. During three hundred years of Norse rule the governor, or his deputy, made annual trips to collect tax, receiving board and lodgings at all the farms in the district named Bordland or Bowland, such farms being exempt from tax because of their annual hospitality to the earls. 'On the whole the Norsemen exercised a benevolent control over Galloway, permitted the local chiefs to rule over their own people and to administer their traditional laws'.[33] Needless to say, not a shred of evidence is offered in support of these statements for the very good reason that absolutely none exists. Robertson's final assertion, equally unwarranted, was to assert that Ingibjorg, widow of Earl Thorfinn the Mighty and later the wife of Malcolm Canmore, was a native of Galloway. Perhaps they had their honeymoon in Kirkcudbright!

In turning to the testimony of the spade, it is truly alarming to note the extent to which archaeologists are imprisoned in historical structures totally fabricated by local historians. Mr J. G. Scott has expertly described certain objects recovered in Kirkcudbright. These are a glass linen smoother, which he suggests comes from a settlement site, and the contents of a grave from the churchyard. The grave group consists of a sword, a ring-headed bronze pin and a blue glass bead. Nothing seems to be known about the grave itself, but it is sensibly suggested that these objects represent a pagan burial in a Christian churchyard, a phenomenon associated in particular with the Isle of Man in graves dated to the second half of the ninth century, but not without parallel in England and Scotland. So far so good. However, the social reconstructionalist in Mr Scott takes over, since most archaeologists seem to be affected by this particular virus. If the artefacts derive from the grave of a Viking warrior then burial in the churchyard implies the consent of the local population.[34] It is further suggested that 'it would be an obvious but too simplistic, an explanation to regard such burial as the imposition of pagan Viking control over a native Christian population, in an almost brutal demonstration of power', a statement which in turn seems to suggest that he favours the obvious over the simplistic, and which overlooks the pragmatic approach to burial adopted by the Norsemen. A pagan would have no qualms about being buried in consecrated ground; a convinced Christian would, on the other hand, be worried about reposing in unconsecrated soil. It has been sensibly pointed out that mobile Scandinavian raiding parties would inter their dead in Christian cemeteries for reason of security (since isolated graves would be subject to looting by a hostile population) and that such burials therefore need to have nothing to do with settlement.[35]

Mr Scott, however, wishes to go beyond 'pagan Viking control' to develop the ideas first advanced by Huyshe and Robertson. The Vikings first arrived in Galloway by agreement, 'perhaps even by invitation to act as mercenaries to protect the community against other marauding Vikings', and soon they dominated the local population. What is offered is a version of the Anglo-Saxon thesis first expounded by Gildas. The invaders are welcomed with open arms by the natives who then happily co-exist alongside them. Scott also believes that Whithorn could not have been under Viking control when St Cuthbert's relics arrived there in 875, and on this basis postulates a Viking acquisition of Wigtownshire later than that of Kirkcudbright.[36] We are even reminded that a Viking came ashore at Whithorn to spend a penny, or at least to lose one, since an Hiberno-Norse coin of that value was discovered there, to be listed along with the not very impressive finds at Talnotrie and Glenluce Sands.[37] But coins and graves do not a Viking colony make. In a valiant attempt to make sense of this evidence Mr Scott has been misled by the historians.[38]

At present the archaeological evidence, such as it is, does prove that the Vikings had some acquaintance, however fleeting, with the area under discussion. Additional evidence for a Viking presence in the ninth century does not convince. There is a late record that Alpin, father of Kenneth MacAlpin, was killed fighting in Galloway *c.*841 at what is now the Taxing Stone on the east side of Loch Ryan but which was known in the thirteenth century as Laight Alpin, more recently at Laight.[39] The greatest authority on the regnal lists, which contain this entry, is extremely cautious about the reliability of the statement.[40] Alpin's assailants are not mentioned but it is tempting to believe that if they were thought to be Vikings they would have been so designated. The king lists are not in agreement about Alpin's fate. Version K, for example, states that 'he was killed in Galloway, after he had destroyed it, by a single man who watched for him in a thick wood above the entrance to a ford of a river while Alpin rode with his men'.[41] In the midst of so much circumstantial detail one might have expected to find mention of Vikings if there was the remotest suspicion that they had been involved. It has been suggested that some Scandinavians may have found their way to Galloway during the 'Forty Years Rest' following the late 870s, at which time the invaders suffered a temporary setback in Ireland,[42] as indeed they might have done, but again there is no evidence.

Even the saga evidence, upon which slim foundation the entire notion of a Norse colony in Galloway rests, provides no firm support. *Orkneyinga Saga* which supposedly attests to Thorfinn's lengthy residence in Galloway, thus showing that it was part of his far-flung *imperium,* actually states that when Thorfinn went raiding in the Hebrides and various parts of Scotland he lay at anchor off Galloway, which is far from being the same thing. Interestingly, the passage states that Thorfinn sent some of his men south to raid the coast of England *'as the people had driven all their livestock out of his reach'* (my italics).[43] The men of Galloway were so far from acknowledging Thorfinn's superiority that they actually defended their property against his possible violent incursions; no Bordlands were available to him. The earl's schemes fared no better in England for almost all the able-bodied raiders were slaughtered, save for a few sent back to explain that thus were Vikings discouraged from raiding and looting. As Palsson and Edwards wittily phrase their translation, 'the message was put in distinctly abusive terms'.

If there is little comfort here for those seeking proof of a Norse Galloway, *Njal's Saga* is equally disappointing. Kari Solmundarsson tracked down Kol Thorsteinson, one of Njal's burners, in Wales. Kol was counting out silver when Kari's deadly sword struck at his neck. True to a typical saga motif the blow at first had no apparent effect — Kol went on counting until at 'ten' his head flew off, uttering that very numeral. Kari and his companions then sailed north to Beruvik, laid up their ship, and went on to Hvitsborg where they resided with Earl Malcolm. Hvitsborg alone connects the passage with Whithorn; the name literally means Hwitr's Castle. The place is described as *Hvitsborg i Skotlandi* and while the point is not conclusive, the sagaman could have written *Hvitsborg i Gaddgedlar* if such had been his intention. Beruvik there is none in the vicinity of Whithorn; the place has been identified on no very good grounds with Port Yerrock, a bay about a mile north of the Isle of Whithorn.[44] Just how dubious the entire passage is can be illustrated with reference to an article by the late A. B. Taylor. He thought that Beruvik should be associated with the Barbreck River which flows into Loch Craignish and he made Earl Malcolm a mormaer of Argyll. Dr Taylor's argument does not persuade. He was attempting to demonstrate that Karl Hundason of *Orkneyinga Saga* was a petty chieftain in Argyll,[45] whereas a much more likely identification is with MacBeth.[46] The conclusion is that Galloway is no more convincing than Argyll as the location of Hvitsborg and Beruvik. The sagaman's knowledge of geography became vaguer the further he ventured from Orkney; he knew that Galloway was 'where Scotland and England meet' but was possibly unaware that the places he mentioned would be more likely be found on the eastern border, far from the Solway littoral.

Bruce Trotter may preserve some folk memory when he describes local tradition about trows or trolls based on place-name evidence, such as Trowdle or Trowshouse,[47] although the 'trow' element is quite likely to be Welsh *tref,* as in Traquair and Trohoughton. In two places he refers to Galloway folk known as Fingauls. 'They're queer folk in Borgue . . . Ye see Borgue was yin o' the Fingaul settlements, and that's the wey they'r sae queer'. The Fingaul districts are listed as Southerness, Kirkcowan, Whithorn and Kirkmaiden. The folk in these parts were:

> a lot o' clever-lookin fallas . . . maistly verra lang and weel-made, wi lang faces, strecht noses and blue een, an wunnerfu feet fur size. They're maistly fair-wair't, or licht broon an the lasses is verra bonnie whun they'r young, but efter they'r twunty they get verra coorse-lookin.[48]

In recounting a tale about how the Dalziels were granted large tracts of land for assisting the king against the Danes, Trotter offered a shrewd but apposite aside — 'Thae aul' Scots kings maun a' haen an awfu account o' lan in their ain han, when they wur throwin haill glens at every stranger yt turn't up when the Danes bestit them'.[49] In no sense can *Galloway Gossip* be regarded as a reliable historical source, but its author does make at least one interesting suggestion which some future scholar may care to investigate. The Fingauls, he says, are 'the descendants o' the Norsemen, though A think the Fingaul colonies maun a' come frae the Isle o' Man, for a gey wheen o' the names o' hills an things in their districts is in Manx

Gaelic'.[50] Is it possible that some few Viking estates in Galloway were administered on behalf of superiors in Man?

The overwhelming conclusion must be that the Viking presence in Galloway was not significant. It could be objected that neither is there historical evidence for the Scandinavian settlement of the Lake District, nor was there any for the Wirral until F. T. Wainwright documented Ingemund's invasion;[51] but the place-name evidence for Galloway is nothing like as dense and voluminous as it is for north-west England. The situation is reversed for the north-east, because although Scandinavian settlement in Northumberland is attested by the *Anglo-Saxon Chronicle,* there are comparatively few matching place-names in the area.[52] Historians are a strange breed, often as contrary and confused as their sources; it is an odd contradiction that they have been as anxious to deny the existence of Picts in Galloway who are documented,[53] as they have been to emphasise the presence of Vikings who are not. At most there may have been a few pockets of Scandinavian settlement along the coast. Ideas about naval arsenals at Wigtown, or that Galloway constituted some bulwark of Norse power are ludicrous.

Why then was there so little Viking interest in Galloway? Since the major trade-routes focused on the north/south trade along the road to Ireland and the Mediterranean, the area may have been overlooked in Viking times as it is now. The Galloway coast was on the road to nowhere. Distribution maps of place-names, archaeological remains and Viking sculpture all suggest that the Norsemen regarded the southern shore of the Solway as a friendly coast. It was also on the direct route from Man or Ireland to the mouth of the Eden whose valley in all probability provided the main link between York and Dublin.[54] Another possibility is that the Galwegians were simply too strong for the Vikings. One tiny piece of evidence pointing to this conclusion shows the men of Galloway thumbing their noses at no less a warrior than Earl Thorfinn the Mighty. The Galwegians in later centuries were to have vicious reputations as particularly fierce fighters, to the point of being depicted in the more lurid English chronicles as homicidal psychopaths.[55] Far from being the benevolent rulers of Galloway, or welcome allies of the natives, or, for that matter, hired mercenaries, there is a real possibility that the Vikings were only allowed to settle on native terms. Even if a few chiefs did force themselves upon the population, there is no reason to suppose that the Galwegians paid any more attention to them than they do to the 'white settlers' today who have an illusory and exaggerated influence upon the community, because they tend to make more noise and cause more fuss than do the locals. It is to be fervently hoped that further Viking artefacts will be unearthed at Whithorn, but they will not transform Galloway into a Viking colony.

Perhaps, in conclusion, one further murky puddle might be added to the quagmire of speculation and hypothesis which currently represents the early medieval history of Galloway. Elsewhere in this volume Daphne Brooke convincingly argues that the time is perhaps appropriate to sunder the Gall-Gaidhil from Galloway. The twelfth-century poem 'The Owl and the Nightingale' seems to reinforce the idea of some link between Scandinavia and Galloway in the couplet.

Hwi nultu fare to Noreweie
An singin men of Galeweie[56]

The connection may have been demanded by nothing more than the rhyme scheme but the passage does suggest a useful analogy. If Norwegia or Norvidia means the way to the north, Galweia or Gallovidia should mean the way to the Galls, the foreigners or strangers viewed from an Irish perspective. Such foreigners would originally have been Britons and, later, Angles. A Gall-Gaidhil, a foreign Gael was clearly a foreigner who spoke Gaelic; no other explanation makes sense. The first such persons probably appeared as the result of the Irish migrations to Galloway in the fifth century at the same time as Fergus Mor led his kindreds into Argyll. Thus, in the pre-Viking period the term would have embraced Brittonic-Gaels and Anglo-Gaels. It was used with specific reference to people of Norse-Celtic blood by Irish annalists for a short time in the ninth century; it was then revived by Irish and English writers in the twelfth century, at which period it is most often applied to the Galwegians. Although, sadly, it appears to be human nature to attribute undesirable qualities to hybrid peoples, the Gall-Gaidhil in a ninth-century context do not deserve the unenviable reputation which was later conferred upon them. In all but one reference to the Gall-Gaidhil of Ireland (they are nowhere associated with Galloway), they are found assisting Irish kings against the Scandinavians. By the twelfth century Galloway must have been regarded as an area *par excellence* for people of mixed blood, which would explain why Gall-Gaidhil gradually became reserved for the inhabitants of that area. The fierce reputation of the Galloway warriors, earned at least in part through holding the Viking threat at bay, could have contributed to the savage semantic load of the term Gall-Gaidhil. They were a hardy breed, those men of the Rhinns and the Machars. They were tough, independent and wary of outsiders, but it is the final submission of this paper that Vikings they were not.

Notes

1. Dick, C. H., *Highways and Byways in Galloway and Carrick* (London, 1916), vii.
2. The conclusion of the late Kathleen Hughes that little history was written down in the early Scottish Church is acceptable, but possibly unduly pessimistic: Hughes, K., 'Celtic Britain in the early Middle Ages. Studies in the Scottish and Welsh sources', in Dumville, D. (ed.), *Studies in Celtic History* II (Woodbridge, 1980), 20.

3. Galloway is barely mentioned in the most recent survey of this period in Scottish history: Smyth, A. P., *Warlords and Holy Men. Scotland AD 80 to 1000* (London, 1984).
4. Neilson, G., *Annals of the Solway until AD 1307* (reprinted, Beckermet, 1974), 27.
5. Trotter, R. de B., *Galloway Gossip or the Southern Albanich 80 Years Ago* (Dumfries, 1901), 255.
6. Dick, *Highways and Byways,* 294.
7. Neilson, *Annals,* 29.
8. Scott, J. G., 'A note on Viking settlement in Galloway', *TDGAS,* 58 (1983), 52-55.
9. Neilson, *Annals,* 29.
10. Truckell, A. E., 'Dumfries and Galloway in the Dark Ages: Some problems,' *TDGAS,* 40 (1962), 96.
11. Cowan, E. J., 'The Scottish Chronicle in the Poppleton MS', *Innes Review,* 32 (1979), 3-21.
12. Lucas, A. T., 'Irish-Norse relations: Time for a reappraisal?', *JCHAS,* (1966), 62.
13. Chadwick, N. K., 'St Ninian: A preliminary study of the sources', *TDGAS,* 9-53 at 20.
14. e.g. Huyshe, W., *Grey Galloway. Its Lords and Its Saints* (Edinburgh, 1914), 94; Scott, 'Viking Settlement', 54.
15. Anderson, A. O., *Early Sources of Scottish History AD 500 to 1286* (Edinburgh, 1922), i 263-5.
16. *Orkneyinga Saga. A New Translation with Introduction and Notes,* Taylor, A. B. (Edinburgh, 1938), c.23; *Orkneyinga Saga. The History of the Earls of Orkney,* (trans.) Palsson, H. and Edwards, P. (London, 1978); *Orkneyinga Saga,* (ed.) Gudmundsson, F., Islenzk Fornrit 34 (Reykjavik, 1965).
17. *Njal's Saga,* (trans.) Magnusson, M. and Palsson, H. (Harmondsworth, 1960), c.158; *Brennu-Njals Saga,* (ed.) Sveinsson, E. O., Islenzk Fornrit 12 (Reykjavik, 1954).
18. M'Kerlie, P. H., *Galloway in Ancient and Modern Times* (Edinburgh, 1891).
19. M'Kerlie, P. H., *The History of the Lands and Their Owners in Galloway* (Edinburgh, 1870-79).
20. M'Kerlie, *Galloway Ancient and Modern,* 121.
21. There is no mention of 'Viking' levels in Ewart, G., *Cruggleton Castle. Report of Excavations 1978-81* (Dumfries and Galloway Natural History and Antiquarian Society, Dumfries, 1985).
22. Anderson, *Early Sources,* i. 45; *Chronicles of the Kings of Man and the Isles,* (ed. and trans.) Broderick, G., and Stowell, B. (Edinburgh, 1973), 8.
23. *Chron.Man,* 8.
24. *Chron.Man,* 10; Anderson, *Early Sources,* ii, 103.
25. *Orkneyinga Saga,* c.41.
26. Huyshe, *Grey Galloway.*
27. Ibid., 94-105.
28. Anderson, *Early Sources,* i., 301-3.
29. Skene, W. F., *Celtic Scotland. A history of Ancient Alban* 3 vols (Edinburgh, 1876), i, 324-5.

30. Anderson, A. O., *Scottish Annals from English Chroniclers AD 500-1286* (London, 1908), 62.
31. Collingwood, W. G., 'Norse influence in Dumfries and Galloway', *TDGAS,* 7 (1920), 98-117.
32. Sawyer, P. H., 'Harald Fairhair and the British Isles', in Boyer, R. (ed.), *Les Vikings et leur civilisation. Problèmes actuels* (Paris, 1976), 105-9.
33. Robertson, J. F., *The Story of Galloway* (Castle Douglas, 1963), 37-9.
34. Scott, 'Viking settlement', 53.
35. Higham, N., 'The Scandinavians in North Cumbria. Raids and settlements in the late ninth and tenth centuries', in Baldwin, J. R., and Whyte, I. D. (eds.), *The Scandinavians in Cumbria* (Edinburgh, 1985), 43; Higham, N., *A Regional History of England. The Northern Counties to AD 1000* (London, 1986), 322.
36. Scott, 'Viking settlement', 54.
37. Dolley, R. H. M., and Cormack, W. F., 'A Hiberno-Norse Penny of Dublin found in Wigtownshire', *TDGAS,* 44 (1967), 122-5.
38. I have no wish to challenge Mr Scott to single combat; he is simply the most recent respected authority to discuss this subject. He is more considered in his approach than Stephen, W. L., 'The Scoto-Norse period in Dumfriesshire', *TDGAS,* 2nd series 19 (1905-7), or Radford, C. A. R., 'Excavations at Whithorn. First Season', *TDGAS,* 27 (1949). Mr Scott discussed these points with me at the Gatehouse Conference and presented me with a copy of his paper.
39. Watson, W. J., *The History of the Celtic Place-Names of Scotland* (Edinburgh, 1926), 198.
40. Anderson, M. O., *Kings and Kingship in Early Ireland* (Edinburgh, 1978), 195-6.
41. Anderson, *Early Sources,* i, 270n.
42. Ibid., i, 405n.
43. *Orkneyinga Saga,* c.xxiii.
44. Huyshe, *Grey Galloway,* 104.
45. Taylor, A. B., 'Karl Hundason King of Scots', *PSAS,* 71 (1937), 340-1.
46. Cowan, E. J., 'Caithness and the Sagas', in Baldwin, J. R. (ed.), *Caithness. A Cultural Crossroads* (Edinburgh, 1982), 33.
47. Trotter, *Galloway Gossip,* 182-3.
48. Ibid., 129, 181.
49. Ibid., 281.
50. Ibid., 181.
51. Wainwright, F. T., 'Ingimund's Invasion', *EHR,* 63 (1948), 145-69.
52. Mawer, A., 'The Scandinavian Kingdom of Northumbria', in Quiggin, E. C. (ed.), *Essays and Studies Presented to William Ridgeway* (Cambridge, 1913), 306-14.
53. The presence of the Picts in Galloway remains a matter of contention. Jack MacQueen has argued that the Picts and the Gall-Gaidhil were one and the same: 'The Picts in Galloway', *TDGAS,* 39 (1962), 127-43. Nor does there appear to be any consensus as to whether the Pictish symbol on Trusty's Hill, Gatehouse, is genuine.
54. I am indebted to Michael Vance for allowing me consult two unpublished

papers: 'Does Viking Age sculpture reflect traditional or Scandinavian patterns in Cumbria, or links along the York-Dublin axis? (1984) and *Aspects of Viking Age Sculpture in the British Isles, with particular reference to settlement history* (unpublished MA dissertation, University of York, 1985).

55. Cowan, E. J., 'Myth and identity in Early Medieval Scotland', *SHR,* 63 (1984), 132.
56. *The Owl and the Nightingale,* (ed. and trans.) Stanley, E. G. (Edinburgh, 1960), 75.

Port Logan Harbour: general view.

SCANDINAVIANS IN DUMFRIESSHIRE AND GALLOWAY: THE PLACE-NAME EVIDENCE

Gillian Fellows-Jensen

THE KINGDOM OF RHEGED

In the sixth century Dumfriesshire and most of Galloway formed part of the British kingdom of Rheged. The exact extent of this kingdom is not known but it certainly embraced Carlisle, while the place-name Dunragit in Wigtownshire, meaning 'fort of Rheged', suggests that this settlement may have been a western outpost of Rheged and that the Rhinns may not have formed part of the kingdom. It also seems likely that Rheged included the Eden valley as far as the crest of the Pennines, and its territory may even have spread beyond Rey Cross into Yorkshire.[1]

That the language spoken by the inhabitants of Rheged was the Brittonic form of Celtic, sometimes referred to as Cumbric, can be deduced from the place-name evidence. A good indication of the area in which Cumbric was spoken is provided by the distribution of place-names containing the generic *cair* 'fort'. There are hardly any instances north of the Forth-Clyde line, and the distribution-pattern of the names probably reflects the extent of the two British kingdoms of Rheged and Strathclyde.[2] There are a few *cair*-names in Dumfriesshire but none in Galloway and Carrick, and it is therefore tempting to accept Watson's suggestion that the generic may have become confused with, or replaced by, Gaelic elements as the Gaelic language became dominant in the area and Gaelic names and elements were superimposed upon the earlier stratum of Cumbric names.[3]

A Cumbric habitative generic which has a wider distribution than *cair* in south-west Scotland is *tref* 'homestead, village'. There are several *tref*-names in Dumfriesshire and Kirkcudbrightshire. Since the only place-name containing *tref* to be found between Triermain in Cumberland and the many in Wales is Treales in Lancashire, however, many of the *tref*-names in south-west Scotland may reflect the close relationship between Wales and Strathclyde in the period after the Border counties had passed under English rule, and did not derive from the period of the flourishing of Rheged.[4]

The inhabitants of the kingdom of Rheged would seem to have been Christian. Christianity certainly flourished in the Carlisle area in the fourth century and it may have survived there throughout the fifth and sixth centuries, while traces of fifth- and sixth-century Christian activity have been noted in the Dumfriesshire plain east of the Nith, and at Whithorn and Kirkmadrine in Galloway.[5] In the period between 450 and 650 the ecclesiastical establishment at Whithorn would seem to have kept in touch with the developments in the Irish church and to have expanded into a monastic centre. The expansion of Whithorn and the arrival of Gaelic-speaking settlers in Galloway at this period are unlikely to have taken place completely independent of each other.[6]

EARLY GAELIC SETTLEMENT

The Gaelic settlement cannot be dated particularly closely but a study of the distribution-patterns of certain Gaelic generics in various parts of Scotland in relation to the generics introduced by settlers speaking other languages has made it possible for a number of tentative conclusions to be drawn. It would seem that the distribution of the generic *sliabh* 'mountain' in Scottish place-names, mostly in hill-names but also in a number of settlement-names, marks a very early stage in Gaelic settlement, perhaps going back as far as the late fifth or early sixth century. Such names are particularly common in the Rhinns of Galloway and in Islay and Jura, and there are altogether about three dozen instances in Galloway.[7]

A study of the place-names containing Gaelic *baile,* the most widespread Gaelic habitative generic and also the one with the most general significance, shows that such names are of particulary common occurence in southern Ayrshire, Wigtownshire and to a lesser extent in Kirkcudbrightshire.[8] On the basis of their distribution Bill Nicolaisen has divided southern Scotland into four zones: Galloway, Dumfriesshire west of the Nith, and Carrick lie in Zone 1, where it is assumed that there was a full-scale and long-lasting settlement of Gaelic-speakers; the rest of Dumfriesshire falls into Zone 2, where Gaelic settlement would seem to have been rather more short-lived and less intense.

A third generic of interest for the study of Gaelic immigration into south-west Scotland is *cill* 'hermit's cell', later 'church'. Bill Nicholaisen has pointed out that in areas with many Gaelic names for churches or many chapels dedicated to Gaelic saints there must have been a substantial Gaelic-speaking population and not merely a few Gaelic missionaries preaching to a predominantly Christian population. South of the Forth-Clyde line *cill*-names are practically restricted to the counties bordering on either the Firth of Clyde or the Solway Firth, and they are commonest in Ayrshire and Wigtownshire. The almost complete absence of such names from Caithness and Sutherland, to which Gaelic-speakers penetrated in the ninth century, has suggested that the distribution-pattern of the *cill*-names represents the spread of Irish ecclesiastical influence within a Gaelic-speaking context in pre-Norse times.[9] The thriving ecclesiastical establishment at Whithorn would probably have contributed to the density of *cill*-names in Wigtownshire. The possibility that there may once have been a good many more names in *cill* in south-west Scotland than survive to the present day in that form is one to which I shall return later.

ANGLIAN SETTLEMENT

In the course of the sixth and seventh centuries the Angles of Northumbria extended their kingdom westwards across the Pennines and they must have reached Dumfriesshire and Galloway at some time towards the end of the seventh century, that is, after their conversion to Christianity in about 630.[10] By 731 Whithorn had become the seat of an English bishopric and there is evidence for the influence of Northumbrian Christianity in the region in the form of carved stone crosses, which are found mostly in Dumfriesshire but also in Whithorn. It has been pointed out that the most likely source of inspiration for the details of the Ruthwell DMF cross is to be found at Jarrow DRH, that much of the scroll-work on the Bewcastle CMB cross would seem to be based on work at Hexham NTB and that the rosette and vine-scroll on a cross at Hoddom DMF has close parallels in crosses from Kirkby Stephen WML and Wycliffe YON.[11] These resemblances probably reflect both the political unity of the area between the Forth and the Humber, and the wide flung contacts between monasteries in this early period.

How intense was the Anglian settlement of Dumfriesshire and Galloway and how long did it last? English place-names of an early type are rare. Instances include *Edyngaheym c.*1124, which may be identified with either Edingham KCB or with the lost *Ednemland* DMF, two certain *hams,* Smallholm DMF and Penninghame WIG, and one possible *hom,* Twynholm KCB, and two *botls,* Buittle KCB and *Arsbotl.*[12] The element *tun,* which is by far the commonest habitative generic in place-names in England, occurs quite frequently in south-west Scotland, too. The problem with names in *-tun,* however, is that, since they continued to be coined for several centuries, there is no way of knowing how many of the names in Dumfriesshire and Galloway were actually coined in the early period of Anglian settlement. It seems likely, however, that distribution-maps of names in *-tun* present a good general picture of the areas settled by the English in the pre-Norse period. In Dumfriesshire the *tuns* are mostly found in the coastal plain, Liddesdale and Annandale. Twenty-five of the forty *tun*-names have as their specific a personal name or surname and most of these would probably not have assumed their present form until after the arrival of the Normans. In Galloway there are concentrations of *tun*-names in the lowlands of Kirkcudbrightshire and in the Machars of Wigtownshire. A few of these names, too, may contain the names of tenants from the post-Norse period. The place-names alone cannot reveal how long the Anglian settlement survived in south-west Scotland. The information they yield has to be compared with information from other sources. The last known Anglian bishop of Whithorn was consecrated in 791 and is not mentioned after 803.[13] The bishopric simply disappears from the records but it seems likely that the church itself survived. The fact that a high proportion of the Anglian settlement names survived to become the names of parishes in the twelfth-century parochial organisation probably also points to a continuing Anglian presence,[14] although it should be remembered that in the Danelaw Viking settlers are known to have adopted and continued to use many place-names of English origin.

SCANDINAVIAN SETTLEMENT

There is no written record of the settlement of south-west Scotland by Scandinavians but an entry in the Anglo-Saxon Chronicle for 875 records that while wintering on the Tyne, the Danish leader Halfdan and his men made frequent raids against the Picts and the Strathclyde Britons. These raids must have taken him across the Carlisle plain and Dumfriesshire. There is no suggestion that any Danes settled in these areas at the time, and the fact that the community of St. Cuthbert was seeking refuge near Whithorn as late as about 880 may imply that the Vikings had not yet settled here.[15] By the beginning of the tenth century, however, conditions west of the Pennines had clearly become unsettled, for at that time Abbot Tilred of Haversham was making preparations to become a member of the community of St Cuthbert and abbot of Norham in Northumberland, and a nobleman called Alfred fled over the mountains to the east, expressly to escape from pirates.[16] By 927, when King Athelstan made a covenant of peace with the king of Scots and the king of Strathclyde at Eamont Bridge in Westmorland, the Strathclyde Britons would seem to have been able to reoccupy south-west Scotland and northern Cumberland, probably as a result of the disruption caused in Northumbria by the Scandinavian invasions. The place-names of northern Cumberland certainly provide evidence that some of the Scandinavian names must have been coined before this British ingression.[17] It would seem, therefore, that the Scandinavian settlement of south-west Scotland must have taken place in the period between about 880 and 920.

THE GALL-GAIDHIL

Who were these Scandinavians who settled in Galloway and Dumfriesshire? The generally accepted view has been that they, like the Vikings who had begun to settle in the Northern and Western Isles about a hundred years earlier, were mainly of Norwegian extraction, while the marked Goidelic characteristics betrayed by some of the Scandinavian place-names in south-west Scotland have been taken as an indication that the settlers were in fact Norwegians who had lived for some time in one of the Norwegian colonies in the Western Isles or Argyll. It has also been assumed that these were the people known as the *Gall-Gaidhil* or 'foreign Gaels'. The information about the *Gall-Gaidhil* has been discussed in detail by Daphne Brooke and I would merely add that the sparseness of the place-name evidence for a Scandinavian presence in Galloway does not suggest a high degree of linguistic scandinavianisation in the *Gall-Gaidhil* who settled in Galloway.

Another early assumption that ought probably to be abandoned is that the Scandinavian settlement in Cumbria, which also produced a number of place-names betraying Goidelic influence, was the work of a different group of Norse-Goidelic settlers from those who settled in south-west Scotland, namely, settlers whose immediate place of origin was Ireland.[18] My recent study of the place-names of Cumbria has suggested that the Goidelic influence reflected in the names is rather to be ascribed to settlers arriving from the Western Isles or from Galloway and western Dumfriesshire.[19]

SCANDINAVIAN TOPOGRAPHICAL NAMES

Do the Scandinavian names in Galloway, Dumfriesshire and Cumbria bear any resemblance to the place-names coined by Norwegian settlers in the Northern and Western Isles? Very little, in fact. Of the habitative generics which occur most frequently in the Isles, *stadir, setr* and *bolstadr,* there is not a single certain occurrence. Many individual settlements in the Northern and Western Isles have Scandinavian names that must originally have denoted topographical features, names with generics such as *-nes, -dalr, -holmr* and *-gill.* Such generics do certainly occur in settlement names in south-west Scotland. For example, there are Eggerness WIG and Almornes KCB, Kidsdale WIG, Kirkdale KCB and Dryfesdale DMF, Hestan *(holmr)* KCB and Lyneholm DMF, Gategill KCB and Carlesgill DMF. There are three names which might be thought to contain Scandinavian *vik:* Rerwick, Senwick and Southwick; but early recorded forms of these names, none of which show any trace of a *v* or *w* in the second element, suggest that they are more likely to be names in Scandinavian *eik* f. 'oak-tree' or the collective *eiki* n. 'oak-trees'.

I have noted altogether forty-one instances of Scandinavian names functioning as settlement names in Dumfriesshire and thirteen in Galloway. Such names are of even more frequent occurrence in north-west England, however, with 195 instances in Cumberland, 130 in Westmorland and 191 in Lancashire.[20] Such names are also of frequent occurrence to the east of the Pennines, notably in Yorkshire[21] but also to a lesser but not inconsiderable extent in the East Midlands.[22] The topographical names in south-west Scotland can therefore just as well have been coined by Danes as by Norwegians.

The distribution-pattern of names in *-fell* might at first sight seem to provide evidence for the introduction of this element by Norwegians to Wigtownshire, with subsequent dissemination eastwards and southwards to Dumfriesshire and Cumbria. The pattern is deceptive, however.[23] There are a few settlement names in *-fell* in the Lake District[24] but there is not a single instance in Dumfriesshire or Galloway, in spite of the hilly nature of much of these counties. It is as hill-names that names in *-fell* are common in south-west Scotland, particularly in Wigtownshire. Very few, if any, of these names are likely to have been coined by the Scandinavian settlers themselves. The first element of the names is often the name of another geographical feature, in many cases a name of English or Gaelic origin, and what the *fell*-names in fact reflect is the adoption of the Scandinavian term as a loan-word in both English and Lowland Scots. The names in south-west Scotland are unlikely to date from the period after which Lowland Scots began to displace Gaelic as the local language and they cannot be used as evidence of a Norwegian origin for the Scandinavian settlers in the region.

The element *bekkr* 'stream' occurs frequently in place-names in both Norway and Denmark, but there is reason to think that this generic might be able to provide some information about the nationality of the Scandinavian settlers in England and Scotland. This is because, while it is very common in the Danelaw, it is of relative infrequent occurrence in most of the areas which are known to have been settled by Norwegians. There is only one instance, *Kviabekkr,* among the Icelandic names recorded in *Landnámábok,* and no instances are recorded in the six most northerly of the Faroe islands. It is of rare occurrence in Shetland and apparently not recorded in Orkney or the Hebrides. Two doubtful instances have been

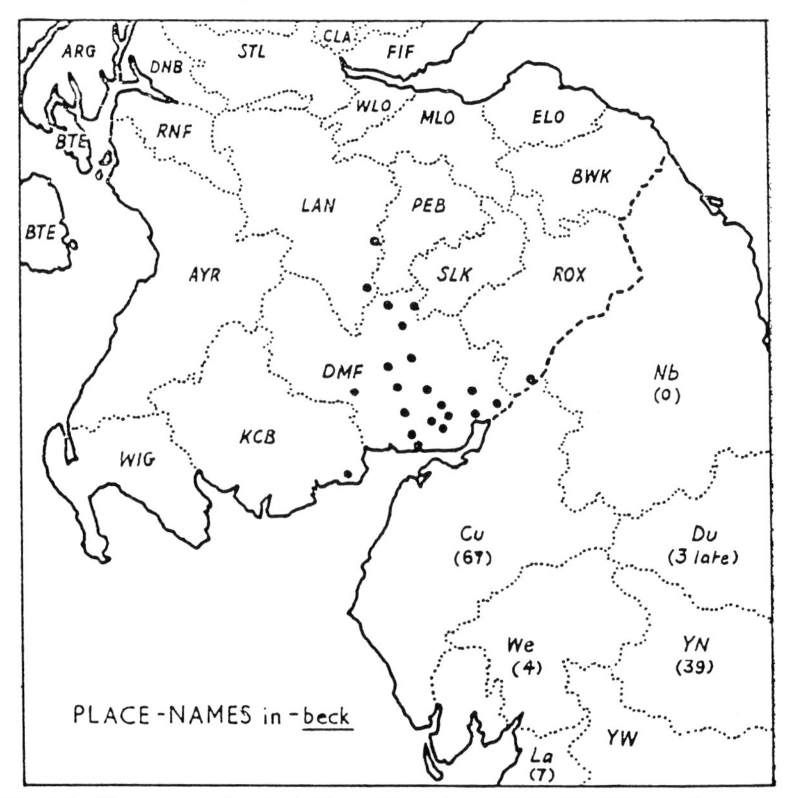

Fig.6.1 Place-names in -beck (from Nicolaisen, W. F. H., 'Norse place-names in south-west Scotland', Scottish Studies, 4 (1960), Fig. 1).

noted in the Isle of Man.[25] In Scotland the names containing *bekkr* cluster in Dumfriesshire, with a few instances in neighbouring counties, and Bill Nicolaisen considers that the element was introduced into Dumfriesshire from north-west England, where it is also of common occurrence.[26] The word *bekkr* was adopted into the dialects of northern and eastern England and became for a time the normal word for denoting 'running water smaller than a river' in the areas that had been subject to Norse influence.

It is therefore possible that the use of *beck* to coin names did not spread into Dumfriesshire until post-Scandinavian times, but there are three factors which argue against this. Firstly, a few of the Dumfriesshire names in *bekkr* are purely Scandinavian compounds with a Scandinavian specific, for example Allerbeck and Elbeck, both containing the collective *elri* 'alder-trees', and very possibly Fishbeck and Greenbeck. Secondly, five of the names are borne by settlements. Thirdly, neither the *Dictionary of the Older Scottish Tongue* nor the *Scottish National Dictionary* records a word *beck* meaning 'stream' so the word can hardly have become firmly established in the south-west Scottish dialect. The only recorded instance of *bekkr* in Galloway is Beck Burn KCB, the name of a small stream which flows into the Southwick Water. Nicolaisen sees the addition of tautological Scots burn to the originally simplex name as an indication that the name was created by English rather than Scandinavian speakers, but to me the more likely explanation would seem to be that the stream was called **bekkr* by the Scandinavian settlers and that the epexegetic *burn* was not added until the Scandinavian language had dropped out of use in the area. The name Beck Burn, in fact, is evidence that *beck* did not enter the local dialect in south-west Scotland. I would argue that the names in *-bekkr* can be taken to reflect Danish influence on the nomenclature of Dumfriesshire.

NAMES IN -BÝ

The Scandinavian habitative generic which occurs most frequently in south-west Scotland is -bie, representing either Old Danish *by* or Old East Norwegian *býr.* This generic was used in Scandinavia and the Danelaw of almost any kind of settlement from a single farm to a thriving town. There are twenty-three instances of names in *-bý* in Dumfriesshire, and three each in Kirkcudbrightshire and Wigtownshire. These figures pale into insignificance in comparison with the seventy-six instances in Cumberland and the hundreds of names in Yorkshire and Lincolnshire. The names recorded in south-west Scotland, however, resemble in type the *bý*-names of the Danelaw and Denmark much more closely than the *boer*-names of the Northern and Western Isles. In the Isles there are at least ten simplex names and five Husabys, for example, but not a single simplex name or a Husaby occurs in south-west Scotland or England. There is one *bý*-compound which occurs twice in the Hebrides, twice in Argyll and is of frequent occurrence in Norway and Iceland and which also occurs in south-west Scotland, namely **saur-boer* or *-bý*. There are Sorbies in both Wigtownshire and Dumfriesshire (as well as one in Ayrshire and one in Fife), but since there are also two Sowerbys in Lancashire, two in Cumberland, two in Westmorland and four in Yorkshire, and the name occurs three times in Denmark, the south-west Scottish instances do not necessarily reflect Norwegian influence.

As long ago as 1894 Sir Herbert Maxwell noted that *bý* in Scottish place-names is supposed to mark occupation by the Danes rather than the Norwegians[27] and the distribution of names in *-bý* in south-west Scotland suggests that Dumfriesshire was settled by Scandinavians coming from south and south-east of the Solway and from across the English border rather than from across the Irish Sea,[28] while the *bý*-names in the lowlands of Kirkcudbrightshire and Wigtownshire would seem to mark an extension westwards. It is significant that five of the seven *bý*-names in Galloway have exact parallels in England. Bagbie KCB has a parallel in Bagby YON, Bombie KCB has parallels in Bombie and Bombay DMF as well as in Bomby WML and Bonby LIN, Applebie WIG has parallels in Applebys in WML, LIN and LEI and in Eppleby YON, Corsby WIG has parallels in Crosby in CMB (3), WML (2) and LNC, while Sorbie WIG, as mentioned above, has many parallels in both England and Scotland. The two remaining *bý*-names probably have personal appellatives as their specifics. Mabie KCB would seem to contain Scandinavian *mey(ja)* or *máer* 'maiden, kinswoman' or the related OE *maege,* while the specific or Bysbie

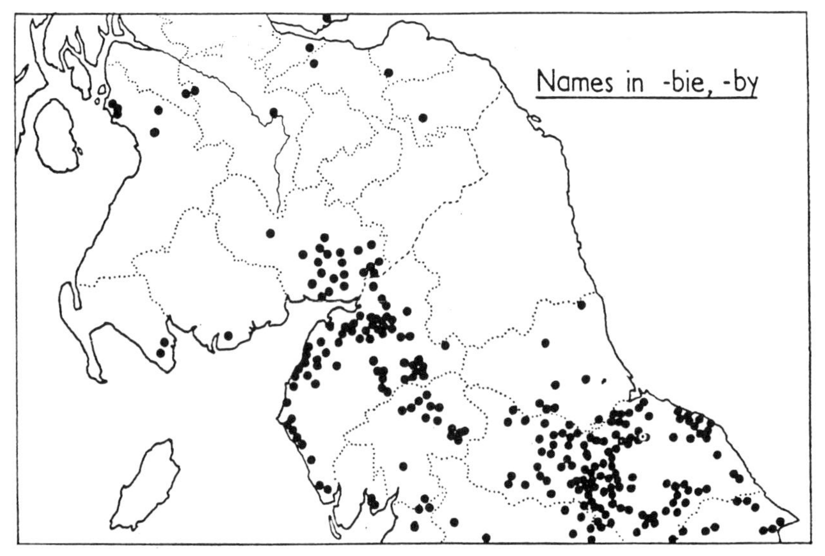

Fig.6.2 Place-names in -bie, -by (from Nicolaisen, W. F. H.).

WIG is Scandinavian *biskup* or a scandinavianised form of cognate OE *biscop* 'bishop'.

In light of the similarity in type between the *bý*-names in Dumfriesshire and Galloway and those in the Danelaw, it seems reasonable to assess the significance of the names in south-west Scotland in the context of the *bý*-names in England. I have argued elsewhere that in the Danelaw most of the *bý*-names date from the period after 900 and reflect the takeover and fragmentation of old estates rather than the exploitation of virgin land.[29] The names with appellatival specifics would largely seem to have been bestowed upon pre-existing English settlements, while the names with personal names as specifics may reflect the original agricultural units into which the old English estates had been broken up. In the English counties of the north-west, Lancashire, Cheshire and Westmorland, where *bý*-names are quite common, there are no certain instances of names having personal names as specifics, probably because these counties were only under Scandinavian rule for a comparatively short period of time, so that there would have been little opportunity for fragmentation of the old estates there by Viking settlers.

In Cumberland and Dumfriesshire, on the other hand, the picture is very different. There are thirteen names in *-bý* in Cumberland and one, Ouseby, in Dumfriesshire whose specific is a Scandinavian personal name, while in the Carlisle area, the coastal plain of Cumberland and in eastern Dumfriesshire, mainly in Annandale, there are no less than twenty-eight *býs* whose specific is a Norman personal name. In my opinion the *býs* containing Scandinavian personal names reflect the granting of small territorial units to individual Scandinavians, while the hybrid names containing continental personal names reflects the taking over by Normans and Flemings in the later eleventh and twelfth centuries of settlement which, at the time of the takeover, had had Scandinavian names in *-bý*. For the original specifics of these names the new tenants would seem to have substituted their own personal names, for example, *Puncun* and *Richard* in Ponsonby and Rickerby CMB, *Lochard* and *Godefrid* in Lockerbie and Gotterbie DMF. As they penetrated further up the Annan valley, the Normans would seem to have come upon a settlement with an English name in *-tun*. After its takeover by a Norman called John, this was referred to as Johnstone and not as *Johnbie.[30] Geoffrey Barrow has argued that in southern Scotland the settlement names formed in the twelfth century and consisting of a personal name plus *-bý* or *-tun* do not imply wholly new units of settlement[31] and the same must surely apply to the names in Cumberland which consist of the name of an eleventh- or twelfth-century tenant plus *-bý*. I would argue that there is no certain evidence for the use of the generic *bý* to coin new place-names in England or Scotland after the Norman Conquest and that the vast majority of the *bý*-names had been coined as such by the middle of the tenth century. What took place in the eleventh and twelfth centuries was simply a partial re-shaping of the place-names to incorporate the forenames or surnames of the new tenants.

HYBRID PLACE-NAMES IN -TUN

None of the *býs* in Galloway has a personal name as its specific, and this suggests that in Galloway, as in Lancashire, Cheshire and Westmorland, Scandinavian rule might have been comparatively short-lived, leaving little time or opportunity for the fragmentation of the old estates by Viking settlers. Of the Galloway *tuns,* however, one, Gelston, would seem to have received a Scandinavian personal name as its specific. It is apparently identical with Gelston LIN and both names would seem to contain a Scandinavian personal name *Gjofull,* an original by-name meaning 'generous, munificent'.[32] It has been argued that such names as Gelston in the Danelaw represent English settlements taken over and partly renamed by the Vikings. The same probably applies to Gelston KCB. Takeovers with subsequent partial renaming in the Norman period may be represented by Galloway names such as Corbieton KCB and Gordonston KCB. Corbieton is said to have been granted to Robert Corbet by David I in the first quarter of the twelfth century[33] and the Gordons have also been traced to a continental home.[34] Arkleton DMF is a name of the same type as Gelston KCB and must reflect the takeover of an English settlement by a Viking called *Arnkell.*[35] There are also a number of *tuns* in Dumfriesshire and Galloway whose appellatival specifics betray Scandinavian interference. Three Carletons WIG (2), KCB are scandinavianised forms of an Old English name **ceorla-tun,* 'the settlement of the free peasants',[36] two Keltons KCB, DMF probably contain either Scandinavian *kjolr* m. 'keel' or Danish *kael* 'wedge-shaped piece of land'.[37] Myrton WIG and Merton WIG may contain Scandinavian *myrr* f. 'wet, swampy ground, boggy place', perhaps in one name merely influencing the form of an OE *mere* 'lake', for Myrton Castle stands beside the White Loch of Myrton, while close to Merton Hall is Merton Hall Moss.[38] Finally, Beckton DMF probably contains the Scandinavian appellative *bekkr* m. 'stream'.[39]

PLACE-NAMES IN THVEIT

The generic *thveit* 'clearing', which is very common in both Norway and Denmark, is normally classified as a topographical one, but in fact it would seem to have had a quasi-habitative significance from the very beginning.[40] It occurs in place-names in the Northern Isles, the Danelaw and Normandy. Apart from the isolated instance of Moorfoot in Midlothian, however, the only county on the Scottish mainland in which the generic *thveit* occurs in place-names is Dumfriesshire, where there are ten Scandinavian compounds and nine hybrid names. In England, too, *thveit* has a much less general distribution than the exclusively habitative generic *-bý.* It is particularly common in Cumberland, Westmorland, northern Lancashire and the North and West Ridings of Yorkshire, while it is of comparatively rare occurrence in southern Lancashire, Cheshire, the East Riding of Yorkshire and the East Midlands.[41] Naturally enough, the *thveits* tend to occur in wooded areas and in Cumbria they are mostly found in the valleys within the mountain dome. I have argued elsewhere that settlement names in *-thveit* mark secondary settlements founded after the initial Scandinavian settlements established by the Vikings on hitherto unoccupied land in north-west England are to be found in Annandale.[42] Most of the nineteen *thveits* in Dumfriesshire are also situated in the hill valleys, although there is a cluster along the lower reaches of the Annan. There is not a single *thveit* in Galloway, a fact which suggests that the Scandinavian settlement there was not long-lasting enough or dense enough to lead to the establishment of new settlements on cleared land.

TINWALD

The place-name evidence I have considered so far — the Scandinavian topographical names functioning as settlement names, the names in *bekkr,* and the names in *-bý* and *-thveit* — has pointed to a settlement of eastern Dumfriesshire, of a fairly large area west and north of Kirkcudbright, and of a smaller area in the Whithorn district of Wigtownshire by Scandinavians whose immediate place of origin was probably the Danelaw. There has been nothing to suggest an origin for the settlers in Norway or the Northern and Western Isles. There is, however, one name which points in the direction of the Norwegian colonies. This is Tinwald DMF, which is related to Tingvoll in Norway and Thingvellir in Iceland, the meeting-place of the Icelandic *thing* or legislative assembly, and which has parallels in Tingwalls in Orkney and Shetland, Dingwall on the Cromarty Firth, Tynwald in the Isle of Man, but also in Thingwalls in Lancashire and Cheshire and a lost *Thingwala* in the North Riding of Yorkshire.[43] The Danish equivalent of Norwegian Tingvoll is Tinghoj, and this name occurs in the North Riding of Yorkshire, Lincolnshire, Leicestershire and Suffolk. It seems likely that the Tinwald-type names were borne by Scandinavian administrative centres and the location of Tinwald DMF in an area where Scandinavian place-names are comparatively rare is rather strange. It must be significant that Tinwald is not far from the county town of Dumfries.

I have suggested elsewhere that the Tingwalls in Lancashire and Cheshire may have been named by settlers who had become familiar with both the name and the concept in the Isle of Man, since there is other evidence pointing to a movement from Man to the coast of north-west England.[44] The exact site of *Thingwala* in Yorkshire is not known but it would seem to have lain within the township of Whitby. This shows that the name could occur in an area of predominantly Danish settlement, but it nevertheless seems reasonable to look upon Tinwald DMF as a name reflecting the influence of settlers from Norway or from one of the Norwegian island colonies.

INVERSION COMPOUNDS

There is another group of names which points very markedly in the direction of the Norwegian settlements in the Gaelic-speaking areas. These are so-called inversion compounds, in which the generic precedes the specific in younger Celtic word order. In the areas of Scandinavian settlement in England such names are found only in the north-west, principally in Cumberland and Westmorland. There are three purely Scandinavian instances in Lancashire (all now lost) and one purely Gaelic one, Noctorum, in Cheshire which was probably coined by settlers from Ireland or the Isle of Man.[45] In Cumberland there are no less than twenty-four instances, in which at least one of the elements is of Scandinavian origin and thirteen of purely Gaelic compounds, while Westmorland has ten partially Scandinavian compounds and two purely Gaelic ones. The purely Gaelic inversion compounds were probably coined at the time of the tenth-century Strathclyde reoccupation of south-west Scotland, northern Cumberland, and Westmorland east of the Eden. They form a natural extension eastwards and southwards of the many names of the type in western Dumfriesshire.

The names in which at least one of the elements is of Scandinavian origin need examining more closely. The possibility exists that the Scandinavian element in question had been adopted into the local vocabulary. Richard Bailey has drawn my attention to the fact that if the inversion compounds involving familiar elements such as *kirk* are omitted from the map, then the distribution- pattern of inversion compounds in Cumberland is more limited and hardly extends north of a line running from the Ellen to Penrith. Bailey argues that the spread northwards of the Celtic compounds probably represents an extension of this type outside its original area at some time after the period of the first Scandinavian settlements. If the *Kirk*-names are omitted from the map, then the distribution in Cumbria of inversion compounds correspond fairly closely with that of names containing the Gaelic loan-word in Scandinavian *aergi* 'shieling', that is, mainly in the coastal lowlands and in the Kent valley. It may well be that the inversion compounds and the *aergi*-names in these areas reflect an influx of settlers of mixed Norse-Gaelic origin, an influx that in the Kent valley would seem to have led to economic upheaval, since there is no Viking period stone sculpture at Kendal and Haversham, where Anglian period sculpture is found, although two-thirds of the sites with Anglian period sculpture in the north-west also have Viking-period sculpture.[46]

Against Bailey's hypothesis of a late expansion northwards from southern Cumberland of the partially Scandinavian compounds, can be ranged Alfred Smyth's suggestion that the distribution of Celtic-type compounds in Cumbria represents an eastwards and southwards extension of the concentration of such names in Galloway.[47] Of particular significance for this theory are the many names whose generic is Kirk- from Scandinavian *kirkja* and whose specific is the name of the saint to which the church was dedicated, for example, Kirkbride.

NAMES IN KIRK-

Kirkbride-type names are characteristic of the south-west of Scotland, being found, apart from six names in Cumberland and a few outliers, only in Dumfriesshire, Galloway and Carrick.[48] Apart from a few dedications to Christ, St Michael and St Andrew, three to St Cuthbert and two to St Oswald, all the dedications in Scotland are to saints of the Irish church, some of which are very obscure.[49] John MacQueen examined the Kirkbride-type names in Galloway in the light of Gaelic names in which *cill* is combined with a saint's name to give names of the Kilbride-type. He argued that the Gaelic language must have been established in Galloway before the Norse settlement there, and that some at least of the Galloway compounds in Kirk- must be partial scandinavianisations of older Gaelic compounds in Kil-. On the other hand, the presence in Galloway of names such as Kirkoswald and Kirkcudbright suggested to Bill Nicolaisen that in some names Kirk- supplanted Kil- not in Scandinavian but in Anglian mouths. Recently, Daphne Brooke has argued that the names are merely

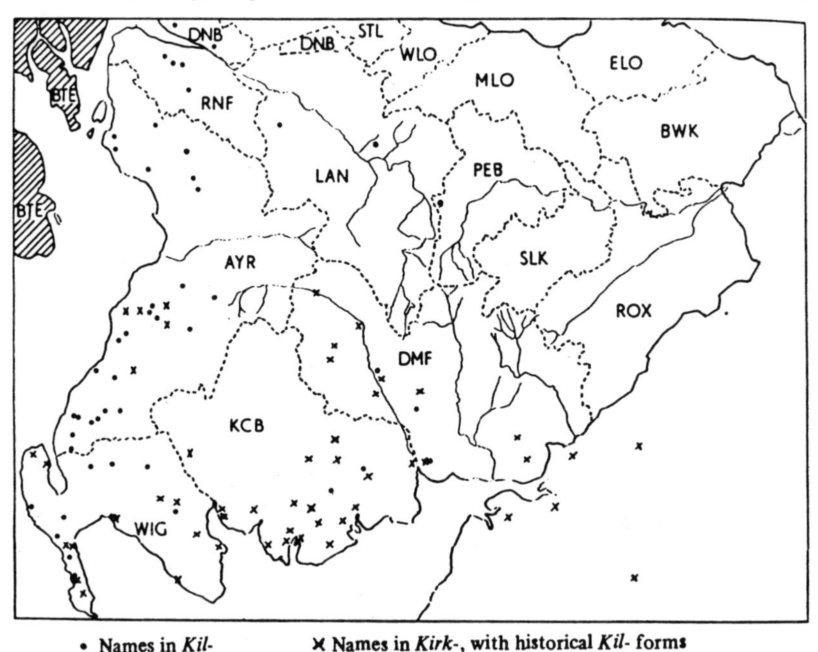

• Names in *Kil-*
× Names in *Kirk-*
× Names in *Kirk-*, with historical *Kil-* forms

Fig.6.3 Names in Kil- and Kirk- in Southern Scotland (from Nicolaisen, W. F. H., Scottish Place-Names (1976), Fig. 13).

'the response of a multi-lingual society to the advent of a strictly territorial parish system' in the twelfth century. She is unwilling to associate the Kirkbride-type names with Scandinavian settlement in south-west Scotland. One of her arguments is cogent. She points out that the geographical distribution of the Kirk-compounds within the region is far too wide to allow of any significant correspondence between these names and Scandinavian settlement. Such place-names as undoubtedly do point to Scandinavian settlement in Galloway, for example, the *býs* and the originally topographical names, have much more restricted distributions, being more or less concentrated around Whithorn and Kirkcudbright.

I would nevertheless argue that it is Scandinavian rather than Anglian influence that is reflected in the Kirkbride-type names. Kirksanton CMB is recorded as early as in Domesday Book (DB) of 1086 in the form *Santacherche.* Arguing that the spelling in *-cherche* must reflect OE *cirice* rather than Scandinavian *kirkja,* Brooke has taken the Domesday spelling as an indication that the element *kirk* in this name, and in others which have early forms in *cherche* or *chirche,* derived from Anglian rather than Scandinavian speech.[50] In DB, however, the voiceless stop (k) was normally represented before *e* and *i* by *ch*[51] and on the basis of a comparative study of Domesday manuscripts Peter Sawyer has argued convincingly that this was a very generally accepted Anglo-Norman convention.[52] For the pronunciation (k) before *e* and *i* the spelling *ch* predominated in the earliest post-Conquest manuscripts and was gradually superseded in the course of the twelfth century by *k.* [53] No significance can therefore be attached to spellings with *ch* in Anglo-Norman manuscripts in the eleventh century as evidence for an English origin for the element *kirk.*

The possibility cannot, nevertheless, be dismissed that *kirkja* has replaced OE *cirice* in some of the names in our area, as it did in the Northamptonshire place-name Peakirk.[54] How likely is this possibility? In England the type of name in which OE *cirice* is combined with a saint's name is extremely rare outside the area subject to Welsh or Cornish influence, where they can sometimes be proved to be translations of a Celtic name.[55] It is probably significant that most of the Oswaldkirk-type names are found in north-west England or the North Riding of Yorkshire, areas not too far removed from the sphere of Celtic influence. It is nevertheless possible that *kirk* may have replaced *cirice* in some of the place-names of Cumberland and south-west Scotland in which the name either of an Anglo-Saxon saint, or of a saint popular among the British, or of one of the biblical saints favoured by the Northumbrian church, is now combined with Kirk- in younger Celtic word order: Kirkoswald, Kirkbrynnock and two Kirkandrews in Cumberland, Kirkcudbright and Kirkmichael in Dumfriesshire, Kirkcarsewell (Oswald), Kirkcudbright and the three Kirkandrews in Galloway, and Kirkoswald, Kirkcudbright and Kirkmichael in Carrick. The absence of Kirkbride-type names from the Border counties and the Lothians, however, argues against an Anglian origin for the majority of the names in Kirk- in south-west Scotland.

As far as the Kirk-names containing Irish saint's names are concerned, it seems most likely that these reflect the replacement of Kil- by Kirk-. The distribution of the Kirkbride-type names corresponds reasonably closely with that of the Kilbride-type names in southern Scotland, except that the Kirkbride-type names do not extend as far north as the Firth of Clyde and that they cluster more thickly around the Solway Firth. This suggests very strongly that the Kilbride-type name lies behind the Kirkbride-type one, and that the Kirkbride-type name has spread out from the heavily scandinavianised areas of Cumberland and eastern Dumfriesshire into Galloway and Carrick.

I should like to suggest a possible source of inspiration for the replacement of Kil- by Kirk- in so many names. In all the areas of England in which place-names of Scandinavian origin point to Scandinavian settlement in the Viking period there are **kirkju-bý* place-names, forty-six instances in all. At least forty-two of these names would appear to have been given by Scandinavian settlers to old-established English settlements in which they found a church on their arrival. In comparison with these forty-six Kir(k)bys, the nine names consisting of a saint's name plus *kirkja* are comparatively few and they have a much more restricted distribution. The situation in Cumberland is interesting. Here there are three Kir(k)bys and Bridekirk and Islekirk, containing the name of St Hild. It is significant that there are recorded forms of all three Cumberland Kir(k)bys which incorporate the name of the saint to which the church is dedicated.[56] St Bees is first recorded as *Cherchebi c.*1125, but it has one run of forms such as *Kirkebibeccoch* (1188x98) 1308, and another run of forms such as *Bechockirke c.*1210. *Beghoc* is an Irish diminutive form of the saint's name *Bega.* The now-lost *Kirkeby crossan* is recorded in this form in the middle of the thirteenth century, while other more or less contemporary documents have the forms *kirkecrossan* and *Kyrcros. Cros(s)an* has been explained as an Irish personal name. The name *Kirkebi Johannis* which did not survive, was given to a new borough in 1305, the year after a church dedicated to St John had been licensed there.[57] Kirkby Stephen in the neighbouring county of Westmorland is first recorded in the form *Cherkaby Stephan* 1090x97 and the affix probably refers to the dedication of the church. In no other counties of England are Kir(k)by names distinguished by the addition of a saint's name, and it therefore seems likely that these four Kir(k)bys in Cumbria represent a compromise between the Kir(k)by-names of the Danelaw and the Kilbride-type names of south-west Scotland. I would argue that it was the confrontation of the Kilbride-type names with the Kir(k)by-names in areas of dense Scandinavian settlement that inspired the replacement of Kil- by Kirk- in some Kilbride-type names and the inversion of the order of the elements in some of the Bridekirk-type names. I would also argue that the south-west Scottish parish names of the Kirkbride-type were the inspiration for the same type of name in the Isle of Man.[58] Finally, it must be acknowledged that the parochial reorganisation of the Anglo-Norman church in the twelfth century was probably responsible for the creation of several of the younger parish-names of the Kirkbride-type.[59]

CONCLUSION

In conclusion, then, it would seem to be advisable to omit the Kirkbride-type names from the list of names pointing directly to Scandinavian settlement in Dumfriesshire and Galloway. This leaves us with concentrations of Scandinavian place-names in eastern Dumfriesshire and smaller groupings around Kirkcudbright and Whithorn. Scandinavian settlement in Dumfriesshire would seem to mark a natural extension of the land route across the Carlisle plain of the settlement in Cumberland and Westmorland. The settlers in Dumfriesshire took over old-established settlements from their Anglian predecessors and would also seem to have split up some old estates into small independent units that were given names in *-bý*, units which at a later date were taken over and partially renamed by Flemish and Norman settlers. The Viking settlers in Dumfriesshire would also seem to have cleared woodland in order to establish new settlements on virgin land — the *thveits*.

The settlers around Kirkcudbright may well have come by land from Dumfriesshire but it is also possible that they had crossed the Solway Firth from Cumberland. The sea route is perhaps the more likely one to have been taken by the settlers around Whithorn. Richard Bailey has pointed to evidence for artistic contact in the Viking period between this area and the coastal plain of Cumberland, a contact which by-passes the Carlisle plain, Dumfriesshire and Kirkcudbrightshire.[60]

The settlers in Galloway cannot have been anywhere near as numerous as those in Dumfriesshire. There is no place-name evidence for fragmentation of large estates into *býs*, or for the clearing of woodland in order to establish *thveits*. There is, however, evidence that many of the settlements with Scandinavian names were among the more important settlements in the region. John MacQueen has pointed out that almost half of the Galloway parishes have names which are either Scandinavian or show Scandinavian influence.[61] The fourteen parish-names of the Kirkbride-type cannot, of course, be taken as direct evidence for the administrative power wielded by the Scandinavians, but there are five parishes with purely Scandinavian names: Sorbie WIG, Stoneykirk WIG, Borgue KCB, Rerwick KCB and Senwick KCB (plus the additional now-defunct Southwick KCB), while Kelton KCB is a scandinavianised name. These names point to a takeover by Scandinavians of well-established settlements. It would seem that in Galloway, as argued by John MacQueen, Scandinavian influence was felt most strongly at the centres of local government.

Acknowledgements:

I am greatly indebted to Daphne Brooke for generously supplying me with early forms of many Galloway place-names and to Richard Oram for conducting me on tours of the landscape and monuments of south-west Scotland.

Abbreviations:

CMB — Cumberland	LIE — Leicestershire	WIG — Wigtownshire
DMF — Dumfriesshire	LIN — Lincolnshire	WWL — Westmorland
DRH — Durham	LNC — Lancashire	YON — Yorkshire (North Riding)
KCB — Kirkcudbright	NTB — Northumberland	

Notes

1. Watson, W. J., *The History of the Celtic Place-Names of Scotland* (Edinburgh, 1926), 156; Jackson, K. H., 'The Britons in Southern Scotland', *Antiquity,* 29 (1955), 77-88 at 82.
2. Nicolaisen, W. F. H., *Scottish Place-Names* (London, 1976), 160-2 and map 19.
3. Watson, *Celtic Place-Names,* 366.
4. Nicolaisen, *Scottish Place-Names,* 168 and map 21.
5. Thomas, A. C., 'The evidence for north Britain', in Barley, M. W., and Hanson, R. P. C. (edd.), *Christianity in Britain 300-700* (Leicester, 1968), 93-121; Thomas, A. C., *Christianity in Roman Britain to AD 500* (London, 1981), 282-5.
6. MacQueen, J., 'The Gaelic speakers of Galloway and Carrick', *Scottish Studies,* 17 (1973), 17-33 at 17; Thomas, *Christianity in Roman Britain,* 279.
7. Nicolaisen, *Scottish Place-Names,* 42-45, 122 and map 1.
8. Ibid., 123-7 and map 11.
9. Ibid., 128-30, 143 and map 16.
10. Jackson, K. H., *Language and History in Early Britain* (Edinburgh, 1953), 218.
11. Bailey, R. N., *Viking Age Sculpture in Northern England* (London, 1980), 83.
12. Nicolaisen, *Scottish Place-Names,* 71-8.
13. Smyth, A. P., *Warlords and Holy Men: Scotland AD 80-1000* (London, 1984), 29.
14. Brooke, D., 'Kirk-Compound place-names in Galloway and Carrick', *TDGAS,* 58 (1983), 56-71 at 67.
15. Radford, C. A. R., 'From Prehistory to History', in Piggott, S. (ed.), *The Prehistoric Peoples of Scotland* (London, 1962), 125-54 at 127.
16. Fellows-Jensen, G., *Scandinavian Settlement Names in the North-West* (Copenhagen, 1985), 2-3.
17. Jackson, K. H., 'Angles and Britons in Northumbria and Cumbria', in Lewis, H. (ed.), *Angles and Britons* (Cardiff, 1963), 60-84 at 81-3.
18. e.g. Jackson, 'Britons in Southern Scotland', 86; 'Angles and Britons', 72.
19. Fellows-Jensen, *Settlement Names in the North-West,* 319-20.
20. Ibid., 297-30, and maps 12a and b.

21. Fellows-Jensen, G., *Scandinavian Settlement Names in Yorkshire* (Copenhagen, 1972), 181-3, and map 6.
22. Fellows-Jensen, G., *Scandinavian Settlement Names in the East Midlands* (Copenhagen, 1978), 257, and map 9.
23. Nicolaisen, W. F. H., 'Norse place-names in south-west Scotland', *Scottish Studies,* 4 (1960), 49-70 at 59-61 and fig 3.
24. Fellows-Jensen, *Settlement Names in the North-West,* 79.
25. Fellows-Jensen, G., 'Danish Lake- and River-names in England', in Dalberg, V., and Fellows-Jensen, G., *Mange baekke sma. Til John Kousgard Sorense pa tresarsdagen 6.12.1985* (Copenhagen, 1986), 59-74.
26. Nicolaisen, 'Norse place-names', 52-5 and fig.1.
27. Maxwell, H., *Scottish Land-Names* (Edinburgh, 1894), 91.
28. Nicolaisen, 'Norse place-names', 55-7 and fig.2; cf. Nicolaisen, *Scottish Place-Names,* 112.
29. Fellows-Jensen, G., 'Place-names and settlements: some problems of dating as exemplified by place-names in *by', Nomina,* 8 (1984), 29-39 at 35.
30. Barrow, G. W. S., *The Anglo-Norman Era in Scottish History* (Oxford, 1980), 40, 47.
31. Ibid., 40 n.37.
32. Fellows-Jensen, *Settlement Names in the East Midlands,* 191.
33. Maxwell, H., *The Place-Names of Galloway* (Glasgow, 1930), 76; Black, G. F., *The Surnames of Scotland* (New York, 1946), 170.
34. Black, *Surnames,* 319.
35. Johnson-Ferguson, E., *The Place-Names of Dumfriesshire* (Dumfries, 1935), 40.
36. Maxwell, *Place-Names of Galloway,* 59.
37. Fellows-Jensen, *Settlement Names in the North-West,* 187.
38. But see Maxwell, *Place-Names of Galloway,* 210, 216.
39. Fellows-Jensen, *Settlement Names in the North-West,* 185.
40. Ibid., 301.
41. Nicolaisen, 'Norse place-names', 57-8; Fellows-Jensen, *Settlement Names in the North-West,* 298-302 and map 13.
42. Fellows-Jensen, *Settlement Names in the North-West,* 415-16.
43. Nicolaisen, *Scottish Place-Names,* 119-20; Fellows-Jensen, *Settlement Names in the North-West,* 168-9, 312; Smith, A. H., *English Place-Name Elements* 2 (Cambridge, 1956), 204.
44. Fellows-Jensen, *Settlement Names in the North-West,* 312.
45. Ibid., 303, 320, 373.
46. Bailey, *Viking Age Sculpture,* 80.
47. Smyth, A. P., *Scandinavian York and Dublin* 1 (Dublin, 1975), 81.
48. Nicolaisen, *Scottish Place-Names,* 108-10, and map 10.
49. MacQueen, J., 'Kirk- and -Kil in Galloway place-names', *Archivum Linguisticum,* 8 (1956), 135-49 at 137-9; Brooke, 'Kirk-compound place-names', 68-71.
50. Brooke, 'Kirk-compound place-names', 58.
51. Feilitzen, O von, *The Pre-Conquest Personal Names of Domesday Book* (Uppsala, 1937), 107.

52. Sawyer, P. H., 'The place-names of the Domesday manuscripts', *BJRL,* 38 (1956), 483-506 at 495.
53. Zachrison, R. E., 'A contribution to the study of Anglo-Norman influence on English place-names', *Lunds Universitets Arsskrift.* (Lund, 1909), N. F. Afd. 1. Bd.4. Nr.3, 35.
54. Fellows-Jensen, *Settlement Names in the East Midlands,* 214.
55. Gelling, M., 'The word 'Church' in English place-names', *Bulletin of the CBA Churches Committee,* 15 (1984), 4-9 at 6-7.
56. Fellows-Jensen, *Settlement Names in the North-West,* 34.
57. Pevsner, N., *The Buildings of England. Cumberland and Westmorland* (Harmondsworth, 1967), 170.
58. Fellows-Jensen, G., 'The Vikings' relationship with Christianity in the British Isles: the evidence of the place-names containing the element *kirkja', Proceedings of the Tenth Viking Congress* (Oslo, 1986).
59. Brooke, 'Kirk-compound place-names', 66.
60. Bailey, *Viking Age Sculpture,* 223-9; Bailey, R. N., 'Irish Sea contacts in the Viking period — the sculptural evidence' in Fellows-Jensen, G., and Lund, N., (edd.), *Tredie tvaerfaglige Vikingesymposium* (Hojbjerg, 1984), 6-36 at 18-19.
61. MacQueen, 'Kirk- and Kil-', 147.

Sweetheart Abbey; general view of east end and crossing from the south-east.

GALL-GAIDHIL AND GALLOWAY

Daphne Brooke

> During the latter years of Kenneth's reign (AD 844-60) a people appear in close association with the Norwegian pirates joining their plundering and expeditions, who are termed Gallgaidhel. This name was formed by the combination of the word gall, a stranger, a foreigner, and Gaidhel, the national name of the Celtic race. It was certainly first applied to Galloway and the proper name of the province, Galwethia, is formed from Galwyddel, the Welsh equivalent of Gallgaidhel.
>
> W. F. Skene *Celtic Scotland*

The hypothesis that the Gall-Gaidhil settled and ruled Galloway and gave its name has dominated the historical thinking about the region for nearly a century. A generation after Skene wrote the passage just quoted it received added authority from W. J. Watson and has been accepted ever since.[1] Yet the acceptance has become increasingly uneasy. Not only is the logic of the Gall-Gaidhil story as argued from the Irish annals difficult in places to follow, but any critical study of the Scottish and English medieval documentation suggests inferences which are scarcely compatible with the Gall-Gaidhil thesis at all. A fresh look at both bodies of evidence is needed and the Conference of the Scottish Society for Northern Studies, at which this paper was presented, provided an admirable opportunity to initiate that reappraisal.

Skene's first interpretation of the Irish annals was that Gall-Gaidhil originally signified the inhabitants of Galloway, the Gael under foreign (Northumbrian) rule. His second thoughts were that the term first applied to the men of the Isles and afterwards to Galloway. Watson seems to have regarded it as meaning Gael of mixed (Scandinavian) blood, which applied to the Islesmen and men of Kintyre, and subsequently 'settled down to mean Galloway.' Professor MacQueen explains the term as applying to the Galwegians: 'Some of these Gall-Gaidhel may have been descendants of early Irish settlers in Galloway who, in the ninth and tenth centuries were won or forced over to the Norse way of life. Others were certainly incomers from Ireland or the Hebrides. The Gall-Gaidhel, it is clear, are the people who created the great majority of the Gaelic place-names in Galloway.'[2] D. P. Kirby puts the proposition a little differently by saying that Galloway takes its name from 'a particular kind of Gaelic-speaking incomer from Ireland — the Gallgaidhel — who were apparently renegade Irish associates of the pagan Norse and Danes.'[3] We return to the interpretation of the term Gall-Gaidhil later. It commonly seems to be seen as implying Gaelic-speakers of Hiberno-Scandinavian stock.

The inferences to be drawn from the Scottish and English medieval charters are at odds with the Gall-Gaidhil story, whether it is told in terms of a small ruling elite or an influx of population. The twelfth- and thirteenth- century documents reveal a mixed society in which Gaelic had only recently become a dominant language. They imply for the preceding undocumented centuries an alternation of power by Cumbric and Anglian aristocracies over what may have been a Gaelic-speaking peasantry. This shows itself in the place-names and settlement pattern discernible from the charters, as well as the survival of an older administrative structure. Despite the probability of some Gaelic-speakers being established in Galloway by the ninth century, the majority of the Gaelic place-names are, as Watson commented, of a common and late type.[4] The names of the more important places such as the parishes and great estates were rarely Gaelic, and point to a long history of occupation by the Cymry and Angle.

Professor Geoffrey Barrow describes the essentially Cumbric sub-structure:

> Galloway continued throughout our period (1000-1306) to show traces of its earlier history as Cumbria or Strathclyde, a Celtic land using the Cumbric variant of Brittonic speech, organised on the basis of the kindred (Welsh *pencenedl*), and divided into districts which in size and physical character resembled the cantreds or historical divisions of Wales. As late as the second half of the thirteenth century the senior member of the Kennedys (the chief family in Carrick) was formally recognised as the 'head of the kindred' in a document using the Gaelic form *ceann cineil* of the Welsh *pencenedl*. In 1296 a conquering Edward I took the fealty of the chief men of the lineage of Clan Afren in Galloway, just as he would have done their counter-part in Wales.[5]

The inconsistency which this analysis suggests, put alongside the Gall-Gaidhil thesis, is reflected in the findings of other disciplines. Place-name scholars have attempted to find a class of place-name that could be recognised as evidence of Gall-Gaidhil settlement and power, notably the *Kirk*-compounds.[6] MacQueen remarked in this context that these place-names appeared to be the only evidence of the Gall-Gaidhil to be found. I have tried to demonstrate elsewhere the difficulties in the way of associating these place-names with the Gall-Gaidhil. The historical development of these names, the names mainly of parishes, is well documented. It suggests that the *Kirk*-compounds, often replacing older names, were the product of the emergent territorial parish system of the Anglo-Norman church.[7] A subsequent study of the place-names relating to the pennylands and quarterlands, units of taxation in an old naval levy, have similarly been shown not to derive from the Gall-Gaidhil. The levy existed in Scottish Dalriada in the seventh century.[8]

The Christian sculptures of the tenth and eleventh centuries, and in particular the Whithorn school of crosses, testify both to the continuation of a settled church in Galloway and the persistence of an unmistakably Northumbrian style. Professor Bailey has recently posited a close relationship between some Wigtownshire crosses and some in southern Cumbria. He has also plotted the distribution in northern England of a form of sculpture associated with the Hiberno-Scandinavian settlements there — the hog-back.[9] T. F. Lang has done similar work in Scotland, and reveals that the hog-back is totally absent in Galloway. This would have been the kind of evidence to be expected from a region settled by the Gall-Gaidhil.

The history of the Gall-Gaidhil derives exclusively from the Irish sources, the annals and some martyrologies. Extracts from the most relevant of these are given in Appendix A. They divide into three phases. First, certain late texts of the martyrologies. Extracts from the most relevant of these are given in Appendix A. They divide into three phases. First, certain late texts of the martyrologies record the deaths of St Donnan and St Blaan in the seventh century as taking place in the islands of Eigg and Bute respectively 'among the Gall-Gaidhil'. There is no other mention of the Gall-Gaidhil before the ninth century, and the apparent anachronism represents late interpolation. Both Skene and Watson regarded the earliest authentic references to the Gall-Gaidhil as the ninth-century entries in the Annals of Ulster.

In the middle of the ninth century the Gall-Gaidhil are recorded as a war band or band fighting both at sea and on land in Ireland for Aed of Ailech, and for a force of Scandinavians in Munster. Aed was then engaged in a three-cornered contest for supremacy in Ireland against another native prince, Maelsechlaind on the one hand, and the Scandinavians on the other. Thus, in Meath in 856 the Gall-Gaidhil were fighting against the Scandinavians, and in Munster alongside them. Watson described the Gall-Gaidhil as mercenaries. In ninth-century terms this would mean that they were freelance fighters at the disposal of any chief whose activities offered adequate plunder.

Of the sources of this part of the story the Annals of Ulster form the oldest and most reliable, and Duald MacFirbis among the latest and least trustworthy. The Annals of Ulster excepted, none of the accounts predates the twelfth century, and MacFirbis was one of the hereditary historians of Ireland who died in the seventeenth century. It is significant that the much-quoted description of the Gall-Gaidhil (Appendix A, para. 9) should be his. As evidence it is valueless; and all that can be concluded so far is that in the ninth century there was a fighting force or forces in Ireland called the Gall-Gaidhil. Why and where they came from remain matters for speculation.

The obit of Suibne 'King of the Gall-Gaidhil' (or a king of the Gall-Gaidhil) recorded in the Annals of Ulster in 1034 has every appearance of authenticity. Watson associated Suibne withe Castle Sween and Loch Sween in Knapdale. He figures in the traditional genealogies of the MacSween family, who were among the most distinguished of the families of Kintyre ruined by the Wars of Independence. Dubhgall MacSween was lord of Kintyre in 1262.[10] The chronology of the genealogies is somewhat at odds with other written evidence but the family claimed descent from the kings of Ailech for whom the Gall-Gaidhil were fighting in the ninth century. Either as kin or clients the connection with Ailech seems well established.[11]

The Annals of the Four Masters has an account against the year 1154 how the Cenel Eoghain (again the tribe of the kings of Ailech) hired the Gall-Gaidhil to fight at sea for them. The fleet was commanded by MacScelling. The Four Masters is a late compilation and the story would be of little account for our purposes if it were not that Robert I's charter confirming the properites of Whithorn Priory records that the church of Columcille in Kintyre had been given to the priory by Patrick MacScilling and his wife, Finlach. Together, these two references establish another connection between the Gall-Gaidhil and Kintyre.

The Irish sources are consistent in pointing to the coast and islands of southern Argyll as 'among the Gall-Gaidhil', though how far the term became territorialised is doubtful. It nevertheless comes as a shock after reading the Annals so far to find suddenly Roland of Galloway (who died 1199-1200) and later Alan (d. 1234) accorded the title 'King of the Gall-Gaidhil.' Records of Alan of Galloway's fleet of ships, his dubious activities at sea, and the 'Viking' behaviour of his natural son, Thomas, suggest that Alan, and probably his father Roland, were quite literally Gall-Gaidhil chiefs, so long as the term is taken to mean 'sea-raider, pirate' rather than implying territory. Alan's mercenaries were employed by King John of England in the conquest of Ireland. Two other explanations have been given. One is that Argyll and Galloway were both known as Gall-Gaidhil territory; the other is that the Gall-Gaidhil shifted ground between 1034 and 1136 when Fergus, Roland's grandfather, appears first in records as 'Fergus de Galweia.' The first explanation may be considered by reviewing the historical background of the two regions. Geographically close, and no doubt in constant contact, Knapdale-Kintyre and Galloway belonged, between the ninth and the twelfth centuries, to two totally different cultural and political groupings.

Dr John Bannerman has traced how Kintyre, originally at the centre of primary settlement, was relegated in the ninth century to a peripheral position in the kingdom of Dalriada. In 849 the relics of St Columba were translated from Iona to Dunkeld, a shift of the religious centre which reflected the movement of the political hub with the uniting of the kingdom of Dalriada and the kingdom of the Picts.[12] The coastlands were already being penetrated by Scandinavian settlers; sometime before 853 Kenneth macAlpin had created a lordship of the Isles and had conferred it upon the Irish king of Airgialla, Godfrey, son of Fergus.

Scandinavian settlement of these coasts had begun, according to Sellar, around AD 800. He pictures a rapid and easy absorption of the newcomers, and their conversion to Christianity.[13] Already, then, by the mid-ninth century the term Gall-Gaidhil, with the meaning Scandinavian-Scot, would have been applicable, and since the life of the coasts was essentially sea-going, very likely 'Viking-Scot' as well. By the early eleventh century, the time of Suibne, Kintyre and Knapdale were part of this culture, based on mixed Scandinavian-Scottish settlement and maritime adventure. By the last quarter of the century Godfrey Crovan of Man had established power over Kintyre and the Isles. Later, the Norse lords of the Isles, owing allegiance to Norway, established Scandinavian power and cultural influence. To this extent, the inhabitants became, in Skene's phrase, 'Gael under foreign rule.'

Meantime Galloway had seen the end of the Northumbrian supremacy and the resurgence of the kingdom of Cumbria (Strathclyde). The Cymry extended their territory southwards into the Eden valley as far as the Stanemore Pass. Professor Jackson has demonstrated that for a time this represented a political and cultural ascendancy of some power.[14] By the early eleventh century, under the combined pressure of the kings of Scots and of Wessex, that power was broken. A fragmented and demoralised Cumbria passed into the hands of the kings of Scots, a process well on its way to completion by the time of Owen the Bald's death in 1018, with no heirs surviving. Barrow has described the final disintegration of Cumbria into what became a dozen or so Anglo-Norman fiefs: Annandale, Liddesdale, Nithsdale, Carrick, Kyle, Clydesdale, Eskdale etc.[15] In so far as the whole retained an identity, it was known to contemporaries as Galloway.

The charters of the period refer, as Barrow points out, both to a greater and a lesser Galloway.

> In its widest sense Galloway denoted the whole of Scotland south and west of Clydesdale and Teviotdale . . . At various dates between 1138 and 1249, the Irvine valley . . . lands in mid-Kyle, in the valley of the Doon and even in Annandale could be described as 'in Galloway.' But neither the lordship nor the bishopric of Galloway covered so wide an area. There is no evidence that Fergus of Galloway had any control over Carrick in the west, while on the east Dunegal, lord of Strathnith or Nithsdale, and his sons Ralph and Donald, ruled independently of Fergus and his dynasty. Moreover, Nithsdale and Carrick formed rural deaneries of the diocese of Glasgow.[16]

On the one hand, then, Galloway consisted of the Stewartry and the Shire, and on the other, of almost all the erstwhile kingdom of Cumbria shorn only of the territory which shortly after the accession of Henry II became finally and irretrieveably English. Extensive as this greater Galloway was, it could not by any stretch of the imagination be held to have included Kintyre. Could two such disparate territories qualify for the same descriptive term 'among the Gall-Gaidhil'?

Perhaps when all is said, this is a land-lubber's question, which fails to take into account the unity to the seafarer of the islands and peninsulas of the west. Perhaps the rapid change of political alignments was bound to lead to a certain casualness in making such identifications among onlookers such as the Irish. Generations of scholars, faced with these difficulties, have taken the logical alternative and concluded that the people, that is the Gall-Gaidhil, moved from A to B. Suppressing our legitimate doubts, we have all tried to picture the Gall-Gaidhil taking ship and making land-fall in Galloway like a second division Norman Conquest, to seize land and political power. Kirby envisages this happening in the ninth century, MacQueen in the tenth. They do not necessarily agree upon the point of embarkation but they are in accord in positing their arrival. Did it really happen? Significantly, the MacSweens and the MacScillings remained in Kintyre and the Isles.

This is as far as we need take the Irish evidence. The medieval documentation from Scottish, English and Galwegian sources has now to be considered. I propose first to review the etymology of the place-name Galloway as revealed by the charters. The conclusions will raise the questions whether it is possible to dispense altogether with the Gall-Gaidhil hypothesis and still take account of the rapid change in eleventh-century Galloway from Cumbric to Gaelic speech, and questions concerning the origins of Fergus of Galloway. The evidence of the strongholds and demesne land of the lords of Galloway will be explained, and finally a possible alternative derivation of Galloway as a place-name be offered for consideration.

Appendix B contains thirty-three of the earliest records of the name of Galloway, drawn mainly from Scottish and English charter and literary sources. The latest date, 1234, is the date of the death of Alan, last of the hereditary lords of Galloway. In Appendix C nine forms of the name given to the people of Galloway start somewhat earlier, and include Fergus's own description of his people — Galwitenses or Galwits.[17] With only a very few exceptions, all forty-two forms come from Latin documents and the names have been Latinised by the addition of the first declension feminine ending *-ia* as applied to the place-names, and the third declension masculine plural *-enses* as applied to the people.

One more item should be added to Appendix B. South of Lancaster is a village called Galgate. Ekwall described it as named from 'the ancient road running past Kendal called Galwaithgate (1190), Galwathegate (*c*.1210)'.[18] He comments: 'the name means the Galway road and is said to refer to the road having been used by cattle drovers from Galway.' Ekwall's informants were mistaken. Galway is in the far west of Ireland and its place-name forms are different. Galwaithgate clearly refers to Galloway.

A striking feature of these forty-four forms is the consistency with which the first element appears as Gal- and not Gall-; and how *w* or its equivalents begin the second element. Watson explained the *w* by saying: 'it has been thought to indicate the influence of the Welsh form Galwyddel, and this may be so, but the supposition is hardly necessary; and the *o* in Galloway represents an indeterminate vowel developed in Gaelic between the two parts of the compound (Galla-Gaidhil) and after this the vowel *gh* would readily become *w*'. We shall come back to the indeterminate vowel later. Watson goes on: 'other forms are Galwegia, where the *g* represents *dh*; Galwithia, Galweia, where the *dh* has disappeared. All these are practically the same.'[19] Watson's command of the laws of Gaelic mutation is beyond question; and it has already been established that Gall-Gaidhil meant Galloway in Ireland in the twelfth and thirteenth centuries. What can and should be questioned is the assumption made by Watson and others that Gall-Gaidhil was a Gaelic adaptation of an already existing name.

At least thirty-six out of the forty-four names before us divide into two distinct groups, each with the first element Gal- except where the l is dropped, but displaying differentiated second elements. Ten belong to the group containing the second element *-wit*, *-with*, *-wyth*, or *-weth*. Twenty-six take the second element *-weg*, *-wei*, *-wey*, or *-way*. The first group Watson ascribed to Cumbric influence, positing the derivation from Galwyddel, the Cumbric equivalent of Gall-Gaidhil. It is not necessary at this point to assume that a translation of the Gaelic Gall-Gaidhil is the root of the Cumbric form. It is enough to note that a Cumbric form is recognised. The second group (*-weg*, *-wei*, *-wey*) looks like another adaptation — the Anglian version of the Celtic name. The progression *-weg*, *-wei*, *-way* is commonly found in the development of English place-names deriving from the OE *weg* (road), and marks the change from Old English through Middle English to the modern language. Ekwall lists Broadway (three times, Holloway, Radway, Stantway, Stanway, and Stowey.[20]

The element *weg* in English place-names often signified a Roman road. The importance of the Roman road in opening up Ayrshire to early Anglian settlement may explain why *weg* replaced the Cumbric *wid* in the mouths of English-speakers. It is conspicuous that six out of seven appearances of the indeterminate vowel occur in the early forms followed by *-weg*, *-wei*, *-way*. It may be argued that this measure of anglicisation was the work of Anglo-Norman scribes; but is this really tenable? Anglicised forms, including the OE *weg*, occur ten times before 1150.

A third group with the second element *-wad*, *-wath*, *-wal*, and *-wall* come nearer to the Irish Gall-Gaidhil. Let us look at a few authentic Irish examples:

Gall Gaidhil	9th century	Annals of Ulster
Gallgaedelaib	9th century	Martyrology of Tallacht
Gallgedelu (accusative)	*c*.1150	Book of Leinster
Gallaedelaib	*c*.1150	Book of Leinster
Galgaidhel	1234	Annals of Ulster
Gallgaidelaib	14th century	Martyrology of Oengus (Franciscan)

Probably derivative from the Irish forms is Gaddgedlar of the thirteenth-century composition known as Orkneyinga Saga.

The most important discovery emerging is that the existence in the twelfth century of more than one adaptation of the name Galloway points to it already having been an ancient name. It is the mark of a name that has survived the ascendancy of more than one people. The classic example of such a name is the English city of York as described by Professor Reaney:

> The ancient city of York bears a name which conceals centuries of its history. The name is first mentioned in 150AD by the Greek geographer Ptolomey in the form 'Eborakon.' In AD79 Agricola made it the headquarters of a Roman legion and it became the military centre from which the north was controlled. The name was latinised Eburacum and Eboracum. It had long been recognised as Celtic, and is found in the ninth century Welsh sources as Cair Ebrauc, from the Old British Eboracon either from a British personal name Eburos or from *eburos* (yew) from which the name was derived. By the end of the Romano-British period *b* had come to be pronounced very much like *v*. The Angles who controlled the city in the seventh and eighth centuries adopted the name and spelled it Eforwic (*c*.897) and Evorwic (*c*.1150), replacing the meaningless *ac* by the common OE *wic* (village, town). The first element, too, was assimilated to their own speech habits and associated with the common *eofor* (boar), Eoforwic (1053-66), which made sense of a sort, 'Boar Village.' In 865 York was captured by the Scandinavians and in 875 became a Danish kingdom under Halfdan, and in the tenth century an Irish-Viking kingdom under Raegnald. Like their predecessors, these Scandinavians adopted the name, pronouncing it in their own fashion, and spelling it Iovik (962) which later became Iork, Zeork, Zork, and finally York in the thirteenth century.[21]

York, a strategic and economic centre confined within walls, was the subject of successive military conquests, and the place-name followed a unilateral development, each people stamping their own adaptation of the name over that of their predecessors. In Galloway a different course of history produced a different result. For Galloway was a rural society dispersed over a heavily wooded countryside. The overlords to whom tribute and sometimes military service was due, had alternated over the centuries between the native Cumbric chiefs and Northumbrian thanes, and finally power had passed by the reign of Malcolm III at the latest, to the king of Scots. The multi-lingual society, assimilating its newcomers with ample space between the settlements, continued its traditional life. From time to time that life may have been lawless, violent and fraught with feuding. In the long term it maintained something, which allowing for an imperfect world, looks like toleration between people of different language and stock. Hence the name of Galloway developed more than one adaptation in parallel.

By the twelfth century, as Appendices B and C demonstrate, the current forms of the place-name reflected the mixed society which produced them. This process had taken time. The chronological order which I would suggest puts the Cumbric form as antedating the Anglian and the Irish adaptation — Gall-Gaidhil — if it was current in Galloway at all, as last-comer. In my submission, 'Gall-Gaidhil' as applied to Galloway originally had no more meaning that the English 'Boar Village' had as a description of the sub-Roman city of York. If, as the evidence suggests, the term Gall-Gaidhil came into existence in Ireland in the eighth or ninth century as an attempt to transpose into Gaelic phonetics the sounds 'Galwit-Galweg', it had no specific meaning of its own. As we have seen in relation to York, the phonetic adaptation comes first, and secondly acquires a meaning in the adapter's tongue. Once the Irish version became invested with Gaelic meaning as Gall-Gaidhil (Foreign Gael), the name became applicable to the settlers of southern Argyll, part-Scot and part-Scandinavian.

Between the ninth and eleventh centuries the term appears to have been very loosely applied. It has been suggested that in Ireland the element 'Gall-' had come to mean 'mercenary' as well as 'foreigner', and might have been applied to any people on the eastern littoral of the Irish Sea whose warbands would fight in Ireland.[22] By the twelfth century the situation had changed. The Islesmen had come to be known as the Innsegall, and Galloway had become largely Gaelic-speaking. The irony and wit of Gall-Gaidhil as applied to it is very much in the Irish fashion.

Insofar as Gall-Gaidhil was understood to mean 'stranger-Gael' it was a term which no one would apply to himself. So it remained the Irish name for the people of Galloway and thence of Galloway itself. Apart from a handful of forms in Appendix B there is not a scrap of evidence that the Gaelic-speakers of Galloway used this version of the name, or that it was used in Scotland at large. The Gall-Gaidhil of the ninth century may have been Galwegians, but the Galwegians of succeeding centuries were not Gall-Gaidhil insofar as the term implied newcomers. Those pantomime pirates were the first and last inhabitants of cloud-cuckooland.

This claim raises the following questions: without invasion by the Gall-Gaidhil, how did it happen that a society, admittedly of mixed peoples, yet traditionally Cumbric in institutions, abandoned Cumbric speech and turned so quickly and comprehensively Gaelic? How can the dynasty of Fergus, so long represented as their descendants, be called as witnesses against the Gall-Gaidhil? And finally, if Gall-Gaidhil was not the derivation of the name Galloway, in what direction are we to look for an authentic derivation?

The main evidence usually advanced for the change from Cumbric to Gaelic speech in the eleventh century is the proliferation of Gaelic place-names on the modern map. Some of these were already current in the charters of the Middle Ages. It may be helpful to look at a random sample of the place-names recorded before 1500. A collection of roughly 700 names from the Shire and Stewartry constitutes all but a complete list of the place-names of Galloway of which documentation has been preserved.[23]

Centres of strategic, administrative and economic importance, such as the parishes and great estates, preserved either Cumbric or Anglian names with remarkable consistency. This is demonstrated later in relation to the strongholds and demesne lands of the lords of Galloway. Further, between the Cumbric and Gaelic settlement names there is a marked distinction. The Cumbric names were either for the most part habitation names containing elements signifying a homestead (tref) or court (llys), or else an assembly-place marked by a standing-stone (men).

In contrast, the Gaelic settlement names are mainly compounded from the names of natural features, and contained such elements as: *ard* (height), *barr* (round hill), *blar* (plain), *carn* (heap of stones, tumulus), *cnoc* (hill), *creag* (back of a hillside), *loch* (lake). The total number of place-names containing these elements amounts to 35% of the Gaelic place-names collected. Names implying landholding such as *earann* (portion, acre), *ceathramh* (quarterland), *peighinn* (pennyland), *achadh* (ploughland), and the habitation name *baile*, total roughly another 9%. Of the *baile* names several are demonstrably of fourteenth- or fifteenth-century coinage. Exceptions are Barncrosh (Balencros), and Balmaghie (Balemakethe), recorded in the twelfth and thirteenth centuries respectively.

Who makes a place-name: the indweller or the stranger, the heir or the incomer, the lord or the peasant? The answers must be many and various; but the character and meaning of the Gaelic names reviewed argue, surely, that they were the product of the peasantry.

The Gaelic personal names of the twelfth-century Galwegians were discussed at the conference. The charter witness-lists represent the cultural mix as it then was and give a glimpse of the process of change from one Celtic language to the other, as well as the assertion of Anglo-Norman supremacy then taking place. Among the patronymics prefixed by the Gaelic *Mac* and the Cumbric *Ap* or *A'* which appear in the same document, are names forwarded from the Gaelic *Gille-* (disciple, servant) plus a saint's name. Gillecuthbert and Gilloswald represent the Anglian tradition, and there are Cumbric forms like Gillecatfarch and Gillegunnin.

These *Gille*-names were popular throughout Scotland in the eleventh and twelfth centuries but a list of sixty drawn from Black's *Surnames of Scotland* show a marked distribution pattern.[24] The major concentration, more than half, were associated with the greater Galloway, with another significant cluster in Lennox and smaller groups in Fife and Moray — all districts in which Brythonic speech had given way, or was in the process of giving way to Gaelic. This, and the occasional appearance of names prefixed by *Cos-* or *Gos-*, suggests that at least some of these names were replacing the parallel Cumbric form *Gwas-* followed by a saint's name, most familiar in the name Gospatric.

It has been demonstrated that some Gaelic-speakers had settled in Galloway before the ninth century, leaving their mark in the place-names given to moors and hills.[25] Jackson infers that in the tenth century there were Gaelic-speakers among the men of Strathclyde who penetrated the lands of Cumbria south of the Solway. The presence of their counterparts in Galloway at this time therefore needs no arguing. Indeed, so near to Ireland, Galloway must have attracted an inconspicuous but steady infiltration of Irish settlers throughout the ages at any period of scarcity in Ireland. Our problem, therefore, is to account not so much for Gaelic-speaking in Galloway as the ascent of Gaelic speech on the social scale, and the aristocracy's conversion from Cumbric to Gaelic speech. The explanation seems to lie in the collapse of the power of the ancient kingdom of Cumbria (Strathclyde) at the beginning of the eleventh century and in the confidence and vitality of the kingdom of Scots.

In the eleventh century the kingdom of Cumbria, with traditions dating back to the Roman period, was engulfed by the Scots, much as the Pictish kingdom had been earlier. Cumbria is now more familiar by the name the Scots gave it — Strathclyde. The all-conquering capacity of the Gaelic language at that period reflected the Scottish mood. With Pictland assimilated, and Strathclyde open to them, Northumbria ruined and cut off from the rest of England by Scandinavian settlements, Scotia seemed at last to be able to cast covetous eyes to the rich lands of Lothian and greater Galloway. This coincided with the succession of able and relatively long-lived kings from Macbeth to the Margaretsons.

Over the next two hundred years the kingdom of Scots was to be troubled by discord in the north, and the presence of Scandinavian power in Caithness and the Hebrides. In relations with the south it experienced repeated military failures. Yet this period was one of rare and subtle achievement. For the disparate elements — Scot, Pict, Cymry, Angle, Viking, and later, Anglo-Norman — were gradually gathered into a community with an exceptionally well-developed sense of common identity. Some of the buoyancy and self-assurance that went into the making of the thirteenth-century community of the realm can be seen two hundred years earlier in the exuberance of the Gaelic language in relation to Cumbric in the west, and even Anglian-speaking Lothian in the east. This strength took political form in Malcolm III's ability to muster detachments of Galwegians in his war host invading Northumbria in 1079.[26]

The king of Scots' ascendancy over Galloway may well have been precarious and intermittent, but it provided the motivation for the swing from Cumbric to Gaelic-speaking. In its last phase, Cumbric may have been largely an aristocratic language. Once it was politically advantageous to speak Gaelic, this not only gave opportunities to Gaelic-speakers, hitherto of minor significance in Galloway, but also a new generation of Cymry can be pictured as learning Gaelic as a social accomplishment, in place of picking it up from their inferiors as their fathers had done.

The revolution may not have been entirely cultural, nor wholly bloodless. That the old kingdom of Cumbria was left entirely leaderless tells its own story; the king of Scots, or their heirs the princes of Cumbria, manoeuvered into positions of power in the south-west men they felt able to control. This brings us to the question: who was Fergus of Galloway? His origin and identity are obscure. In his one surviving charter he proclaimed himself king of the Galwits using the Cumbric form of the name. Henry II acknowledged kinship with his sons, Uhtred and Gilbert.[27] We know very little more.

The descent from Fergus of his heirs and successors was regularly rehearsed in charters, but all genealogy stopped with Fergus. He was a man without pedigree.[28] One source of information about the line of Fergus remains available to us, and that consists of the disposition of their strongholds and personal estates. When the power of the ninth earl of Douglas was finally broken in 1455, the estates he held as lord of Galloway were confiscated and annexed to the Crown. By the harvest of 1456 the Exchequer had taken possession of the lands and were collecting rents and leasing the holdings to local proprietors. Although this large and scattered estate must have lost and gained individual lands over the centuries, the detailed survey recorded in 1456 left a general profile of the demesne estate which can be taken as representing an ancient inheritance.[29] For the present purpose, however, a review of the principal castles and supporting estates will suffice.

In Wigtownshire the traditional stronghold was Cruggleton Castle. Recent excavations have traced the existence of a timber hall of eleventh-century date. This will have been the predecessor of the thirteenth-century stone castle topping the high cliffs overlooking Wigtown Bay. Behind the narrow coastal strip and headland, which constitutes the medieval parishes of Cruggleton and Eggerness, lay the larger and agriculturally rich lands of Carnmoel (Kirkinner) which were concentrated in the lord of Galloway's hands. In Glasserton to the south lay outlying estates which after 1456 became royal manors. To the north of Cruggleton the parish of Kirkcowan stretched to the Carrick border. Much of it was demesne.[30] Cruggleton seems to have been the lord of Galloway's main holding in Wigtownshire, but the castle of Lochnaw may have been another.[31]

In the Stewartry the lord of Galloway held two castles, both surrounded by very large estates. One lay in the coastal belt commanding the estuaries of the river Urr, and later the Dee. The other, or possibly more than one, was in the Glenkens, controlling the valley of the upper Dee and Ken, where the route to Ayr lies through an easy pass.

Buittle was first recorded in *c.*.1251.[32] The OE place-name *botl* (homestead, hall) has been established as an early Anglian settlement name, dating probably from the Northumbrian overlordship.[33] Its unqualified form suggests that the rulers of Galloway occupied the site from the seventh or eighth century. The medieval stone castle was dismantled after the wars of Edward Balliol, and once the Douglases became lords of Galloway (1369) they appear to have established themselves on an apparently ancient site at Threave on an island in the Dee. Margaret of Touraine's charters are the earliest to survive dated there, beginning *c.*1424.

About four miles higher up the Dee from Threave lay the second stronghold in the district of the Glenkens. The castle is commonly believed to have been Kenmure. How old Kenmure was, and whether the lord of Galloway ever held it is not clear. It is not documented before the reign of David II, when it was held by Gilbert of Carrick, and afterwards passed to the Gordons. Earlston,[34] strategically placed some miles to the north in a narrow part of the Glen, did belong to the lords of Galloway; but whether its name implied its foundation by the earls of Douglas, or by a Northumbrian earl is unknown. The most certainly ancient stronghold in the Glenkens was *mea castra de insula arsa*, to quote Edward Balliol's charter of 1352[35] — Burned Island in the Ken itself. By 1456 the castle was gone, but the lands were still demesne lands and their name was then revealed as having the same claim to antiquity as the castle of Buittle, for it was Erysbutil or Arsbutil.[36].

All the strongholds held by the lords of Galloway, with the exception of the two doubtfuls, Lochnaw and Kenmure, had either Cumbric or Anglian names. Cruggleton, appearing as Crugeldum in 1448-52,[37] appears to be a hybrid tautology similar to Cricklewood and Crichel Down in England, where the Cumbric *cruc* (hill) is followed by the OE *hyll* and *dun* (both meaning hill). Both Buittle and Burned Island preserve the OE *botl.* Earlston is clearly Anglian, though of uncertain date. Threave, recorded as Trefe in 1430,[38] is the unqualified Cumbric *tref*, its modern spelling and pronunciation indicating the use of the definite article with consequent mutation — *y Dref* (the Homestead). The strongholds of the lords of Galloway preserved traditional names from the Northumbrian supremacy, and the reassertion of Cumbric power that followed.

The main concentrations of demesne land repeat this pattern. With the possible exception of Eggerness, the most important estates attaching to Cruggleton were Carnmoel,[39] later Kirkinner; Athelgalwyn or Awengalteway,[40] later Kirkcowan; and Manhincon, later Craighlaw.[41] Leswalt and Menybrig, both Cumbric names, surrounded Lochnaw. In the Stewartry, Buittle lies near the centre of a chain of Anglian parish names. In the Glenkens the fifteenth-century parish name of Balmaclellan conceals the older Cumbric name, Trevercarcou.

An influx of Gall-Gaidhil colonists might have been expected to stamp their identity upon newly-won demesne and castles, just as the conquerors of the city of York had done. We might expect that at least some of the Old English and Cumbric names would have been changed or translated into Gaelic. In some places a change of site might be anticipated. Nothing of the kind appears. Fergus, whoever he was, seems to have taken control of the lands and residences of his predecessors without either shifting ground or occasioning any change in local toponymy. This evidence does not provide a conclusive argument; but the case against the Gall-Gaidhil is cumulative. Whatever test is applied, whatever evidence is assembled and analysed, the result is the same. The Gall-Gaidhil leave no footprints. Their credibility has depended for a generation or more on the supposed derivation of the name Galloway. The evidence presented here suggests that the name is much older that the tenth- or eleventh-century coinage that this would imply; and surely, casts considerable doubt on a Gaelic derivation.

Bede, writing in 731, had no name for the region in which Whithorn lies. He referred to is as part of Bernicia; but then he was making a political statement. In total, the apparent age of the name, Bede's silence, the existence in the twelfth century of the greater and the lesser Galloway, add up to the conclusion that the name Galloway was neither an ethnic nor a political name but a topographical one. Considering the terrain of the greater Galloway, the name is not likely to have been derived from a river or a mountain range; but it could have been a forest. Great tracts of the terrain were heavily wooded in the Middle Ages, as the charters and place-names both testify. For these reasons, in looking for an alternative derivation of the name Galloway, I would plead that the place-name scholars should consider again the controversial matter of *Coid Celidon*.

Over the past fifty years this has been the occasion of two sharp differences of opinion between scholars of reputation. Dispute has turned on where *Coid Celidon* was, and whether the middle vowel in the word *Celidon* and its derivation Caledonia or Caledones was a short *i* or a long *e*. The forest has been located according to whether the evidence of Ptolomey's map or Welsh medieval tradition was given greater weight. O. G. S. Crawford was apparently the first to locate the *Coid Celidon* of Nennius in south-western Scotland,[42] and in this he has been followed by most modern scholars concerned with the Welsh tradition. The linguists take a different view. Both Jackson and Professor Rivet identify the site with *drumos Kalidonios* of Ptolomey in the Great Glen. There is general agreement, nevertheless, that the term Caledonia was often used in classical times in a very vague and general sense.

A voluminous literature has collected around the question whether the medial vowel of the name and its adjectival form was long or short. Jackson and Watson before him insist that the short *i* was the correct form. Rivet agrees, but says:

> The e/i variation in recorded Latin forms is probably of little account: this applies not only to the present name of the region but also the personal and ethnic names and the adjectival forms. It is

> noteworthy that Pliny has -i- 'correctly' . . . the other first mentions in the 1st century are all in verse; it is likely that *Caledius* has the -e- in order to fit the hexameter . . . and that such was the authority of verse that the name tended to settle down in Latin — but not exclusively — in this form. The same e/i variation is in any case recorded on coins and in personal names.

He concludes that Caledonia has the better authority.[43]

This seems to establish that, although not wholly correct, the long *e* was current at the same time as the short *i.* We are concerned with a place-name here, which is what people say, rather than with linguistic purity. The critical nature here of the long *e* or short *i* is put succinctly by Watson:

> The old Welsh form of Caledones is seen in *coit Celidon*, the 'wood of the Caledonians', later *coed Celyddon* . . . this cannot represent an early Caledon- for e (ei) yield, wy in Welsh, i.e. Caledon- would become Calwyddon. Further the change of Cal- to Cel- indicates that the vowel of the next syllable must have been i.[44]

If one accepts the guidance of the medieval Latin that the Cumbric name Galwit-, Galwydd- was feminine, then prefaced by the definite article Calwyddon would become y Galwyddon. This coincidence is too striking to be ignored.

The currency of the Welsh Celyddon is not an insurmountable objection. It argues only the preservation of the more correct medial i form in northern literature preserved in Wales, and does not rule out parallel use of the medial e form in the vernacular of Strathclyde. In the same way the Gaelic form of the term Caledonian which emerged for instance with Dun Caillen[45] would not affect what was still a largely Brittonic-speaking region until the eleventh century.[46] Where the Caledonian forest was, and the correct etymology of the name leave room for honest difference of opinion.[47]

It is not necessary to press the suggestion further. Right or wrong, it does not affect the general conclusions reached in this study of the Gall-Gaidhil. These can now be summarised. The general hypothesis that the Gall-Gaidhil settled and ruled Galloway represents an interpretation of the Irish evidence to which there is a viable alternative. The Gaelic place-names of Galloway are demonstrably the product of the peasantry and not of its political masters. The Gaelic personal names of the twelfth-century charter witnesses illustrate a general change to Gaelic speech after the collapse of the kingdom of Strathclyde, which can be satisfactorily explained without positing an influx of new settlers. What is known of Fergus and his dynasty is too slight to clinch the argument either way, except insofar as their strongholds and demesne estates can be identified as of ancient standing, and of Northumbrian and Cumbrian foundation. Analysis of the medieval forms of the place-name Galloway prompts the question whether the term Gall-Gaidhil was the derivation of Galloway at all or a Gaelic adaptation current mainly in Ireland, of a very old topographical name.

The more advances are made in Galloway studies the plainer it becomes that the Gall-Gaidhil hypothesis fits neither the documentary evidence nor that supplied by place-name study and archaeology. The question before the conference, therefore, is whether the settlement and rule of Galloway by incomers known as the Gall-Gaidhil in the ninth, tenth or eleventh century, is any longer tenable as a working hypothesis?

Appendix A

Main references to the Gall-Gaidhil in Irish Annals and martyrologies, as translated by A. O. Anderson *Early Sources of Scottish History.*

1. 618 the burning of Donnan of Eigg. *Annals of Ulster*
2. Donnan of chilly Eigg with his followers. *Martyrology of Oengus*
   Whitley Stokes, editor of the Martyrology, added a note in his 1905 edition taken from the *Lebar Brecc* 'this Donnan is he who went to Columcille to take him for his confessor . . . Donnan went after that among the Gall-Gaidhil and took up his abode there . . .' Only the sentence that says Donnan died in Eigg is in Latin. 'The rest,' reports Anderson, 'in Irish, is from a different account and fabulous.'
3. The *Book of Leinster* refers to the death of Donnan, and a note inserted between the lines by the compiler located Eigg a 'rock between Gellgedelu and Cendtiri.'
4. 659 died fair Blaan of Kingarth (Cendgaradh) *Martyrology of Oengus*
   In the Franciscan MS is a note reproduced in the 1905 edition by Whitley Stokes 'a bishop of Kingarth . . . and he was from Kingarth in n Gallgaidhelaib.' The *Martyrology of Tallacht* and the *Book of Leinster* have 'Kingarth in Gallgaedelaib' and (Kelly's text) 'in Gallghaelaigh Udnochtan.'
5. 856 . . . a great war between the gentiles and Maelsechlaind with the Gall-Gaidhil . . . a great victory by Aed, Niall's son over the Gall-Gaidhil in Glenelly. *Annals of Ulster*
   Four Masters
6. 857 a victory gained by Ivar and Olaf over Ketil the White with the Gall-Gaidhil in the lands of Munster. *Annals of Ulster*
7. 858 Cerbaill, King of Ossory defeated the Gall-Gaidhil in Tyrone.
8. 858 a rout of the (Cenel) Giachach and the Gall-Gaidhil of Cond's half . . . *Chronicon Scottorum*
9. 858 Maelsechlaind went into Munster . . . he ought to have come to kill those whom he killed there of the Gall-Gaidhil; because these were men who had forsaken their baptism; and they were called Northmen because they had the Northmen's manners and had been fostered by them; and though the original Northmen did evil to the churches these did far worse i.e. this people (the Gall-Gaidhil) wherever they were in Ireland. *Duald MacFirbis*

10. A similar vote by MacFirbis for 859 in which he refers to the 'fleet of the Gall-Gaidhil.'
11. 1034 Suibne, Kenneth's son, King of the Gall-Gaidhil died. *Annals of Ulster*
12. 1200 Roland, son of Uhtred, a King of the Gall-Gaidhil, reposed in peace. *Annals of Ulster*
13. 1234 Alan . . . King of the Gall-Gaidhil died. *Annals of Ulster*

Appendix B

Forms of the name Galloway recorded in miscellaneous Scottish and English documentary sources before 1234:

Galweia	1109-35	*Melrose Liber.*
Walweithia	*c.*1125	*William of Malmesbury.*
Galwegia	*c.*1130	*CDS*, i.
Galewegia	*c.*1138	*John of Hexham.*
Galweia	1139-41	*Glasgow Registrum.*
Galweia	*c.*1159	*RRS*, i.
Galwathea	1161-64	Edgar, *Dumfries.*
Galwidia	1161-74	*St Bees Register.*
Galweia	1161-64	*Holyrood Liber.*
Galuweth	1161-64	*Holyrood Liber.*
Galwadia	*c.*1170	Walter Daniel, *Life of Ailred.*
Galeweia	1185	*CDS*, i.
Galeweia	1192	SRO GD 90/i/ii.
Galweia	1196-1200	*Melrose Liber.*
Galweithia	12th cent.	*Jocelin of Furness.*
Galewei	1200	*Owl and the Nightingale.*
Galuuethia	1200	*Reginald of Durham.*
Galweia	1200	*Symeon of Durham.*
Galweth	1200-6	*Holyrood Liber.*
Galweya	1207	*CDS*, i.
Galwaithe	1208	*CDS*, i.
Gaweia	1212	*CDS*, i.
Galwidia	*ante* 1214	*Melrose Liber.*
Galweia	*ante* 1214	*Holyrood Liber.*
Galeweya	1214-15	*CDS*, i.
Galweia	1223	*Melrose Liber.*
Galweye	1225-6	*CDS*, i.
Galweth	1200-34	*St Bees Register.*
Galwithia	1200-34	*Dryburgh Register.*
Galeweia	1200-34	*Melrose Liber.*
Galwythia	1200-34	*Glasgow Registrum.*
Galwaith	1200-34	*Holm Cultram Register.*
Galuuath	*ante* 1234	*CDS*, i.

Appendix C

Forms of the name given to the people of Galloway in Scottish and English documents before 1200 (nominative forms in brackets).

Galweiensium (Galweienses)	1130	*CDS*, i.
Galwensibus (Galwenses)	1138	*CDS*, i.
Gawensibus (Gawenses)	1139-41	Anderson, *Early Sources.*
Galwensibus (Galwenses)	1143-4	*Melrose Liber.*
Galweensibus (Galweenses)	1147-53	*Anderson, Early Sources.*
Gawenses	1150	*Dryburgh Liber.*
Gallowidenses	1151-2	*Dryburgh Liber.*
Galwitensium (Galwitenses)	*c.*1160	Dugdale, *Monasticon Anglicanum.*
Gawensibus (Gawenses)	*a.*1165	*RRS*, i.
Galuensibus (Galuenses)		
Galguensibus (Galguenses)	*c.*1170	*TDGAS,* Wragge.
Galwalenses	*c.*1188	*Med Latin Word List.*

Notes

1. Watson, W. J., *A History of the Celtic Place-Names of Scotland* (Edinburgh, 1926).
2. MacQueen, J., 'Gaelic speakers of Galloway and Carrick,' *Scottish Studies*, 17 (1973) 172-3.
3. Kirby, D. P., 'Galloway prior to *c.*1100,' in MacNeill, P., and Nicholson, R., (edd.), *Historical Atlas of Scotland* (St. Andrews, 1975), 22.
4. Watson, *Celtic Place-Names.*
5. Barrow, G. W. S., *Kingship and Unity. Scotland c.1100 to 1306* (London, 1981), 11-12.
6. MacQueen, J., 'Kirk- and Kil- in Galloway Place-Names,' *Archivum Linguisticum*, 8 (1956), 135-49; Nicolaisen, W. F. H., 'Norse Place-Names in South-West Scotland,' *Scottish Studies*, 4 (1960), 49-70.
7. Brooke, D., 'Kirk- compound place-names in Galloway and Carrick. The historical evidence,' *TDGAS*, (1983), 56-71.
8. MacQueen, J., 'Pennyland and Davoch in South-West Scotland,' *Scottish Studies*, 23 (1979), 69-74; Megaw, B., 'A note on pennyland and davoch in south-west Scotland,' *Scottish Studies*, 23 (1979), 77-9.
9. Bailey, R., *Viking Age Sculpture in Northern England* (London, 1980); Lang, J. T., 'Hogback monuments in Scotland,' *PSAS*, 105 (1973-4), 206-35.
10. *Registrum Monasterii de Passelet* (Maitland Club, Edinburgh, 1832), 120-21.
11. Sellar, W. D. H., 'Family origins in Cowal and Knapdale,' *Scottish Studies*, 15 (1971), 21-37.
12. Bannerman, J., 'The Scots of Dalriada,' in *Historical Atlas of Scotland*, 13-15.
13. Sellar, W. D. H., 'The Western Isles *c.*800-1095,' in *Historical Atlas of Scotland*, 23-4.
14. Jackson, K. H., 'Sources for the Life of St. Kentigern,' in Chadwick, N. K. (ed.), *Studies in the Early British Church* (Cambridge, 1958), 277-9; Jackson, K. H., *Language and History in Early Britain* (1955), 9-10, 219.
15. *Regesta Regum Scotorum*, Barrow, G. W. S. (ed.), (Edinburgh, 1960), i, 38-9.

16. *RRS,* i.
17. The 'Galwit' of the Fergus charter is echoed recognisably in 'Galuvet', a term of abuse in Dumfries in 1259, *CDS*, i, No. 2176.
18. Ekwall, E., *Concise Oxford Dictionary of English Place-Names* (Oxford, 1960). A stretch of road between Dumfries and Kirkpatrick Durham used to be called the Galgate (MacFarlane MS appended to MacKenzie, W., *History of Galloway from the Earliest Period to the Present Time* (Kirkcudbright, 1841)).
19. Watson, *Celtic Place-Names*, 174.
20. Ekwall, *English Place-Names.*
21. Reaney, P. H., *The Origins of English Place-Names* (1980), 24-6.
22. Megaw, B., 'Norseman and native in the kingdom of the Isles,' *Scottish Studies*, 20 (1976).
23. Brooke, D., *The Place-Names of Galloway* (Forthcoming).
24. Black, G., *The Surnames of Scotland* (New York, 1946).
25. Nicolaisen, W. F. H., 'Slew- and Sliabh', *Scottish Studies*, 9 (1965), 91-106.
26. 'Ailred of Rievaulx's Saints of Hexham,' in *The Priory of Hexham* (Surtees Society, 44, 1863), 79-80. The Galwegian presence was recorded by Ailred decades after the event; but he was a Hexham man, and the tradition of the Galwegians' descent on the town may have been alive in his youth. What Wallace did there is remembered today.
27. Henry II called them 'cousins,' an imprecise term. The story that Fergus married an illegitimate daughter of Henry I may be wrong, deriving in error from Chalmers' *Caledonia.* His authority, Sandford, quotes Ordericus Vitalis as saying that Elizabeth, youngest natural daughter of Henry I, married the king of Scots. We know her as Sybilla, who married Alexander I.
28. cf. Oram, 'Fergus, Galloway and the Scots', this volume.
29. *Exchequer Rolls*, 6, 191-210.
30. See Brooke, 'Kirk- compound place-names.'
31. The Sibbald MS appended to MacKenzie's *History of Galloway* speaks of the loch of Lochnaw '. . . wherein the kings of old had ane house.' Margaret of Touraine, lady of Galloway, appointed a constable, which implies that the castle was hers.
32. Salter, H. E., *The Oxford Deeds of Balliol College* (Oxford, 1913).
33. Nicolaisen, W. F. H., 'Celts and Anglo-Saxons in the Scottish Border Counties', *Scottish Studies*, 8 (1964), 141-71.
34. *Exchequer Rolls*, 6, 192.
35. SRO, RH/1/1.
36. *Exchequer Rolls*, 6, 200; Wyntoun says of this castle:

    Bot in Karryk John Kennedy
    Warrayid Gallwey sturdaly
    He and Alane Stewart tha twa
    Oft dyd Galways mekill wa
    Yhit the Balioll all that quhill
    In Gallwa wes at the Brynt-yle.
37. *St. Bernard's Life of St. Malachy of Armagh*, Lawlor, H. C. (ed.), (London, 1920), 76-9.
38. SRO, GD 72.

39. 'Bagimond's Roll: Statement of the Tenths of the Kingdom of Scotland,' Dunlop, A. I. (ed.), *Miscellany of the Scottish History Society*, 6 (1939), 74-5.
40. 'Bagimond's Roll,' 74-5.
41. See Brooke, 'Kirk- compound place-names.'
42. Crawford, O. G. S., 'Arthur and his battles,' *Antiquity*, 10 (1935), 177-91.
43. Jackson, K. H., 'Calidon and the Caledonian Forest', *BBCS*, 23 (1969), 199-200; Rivet, A. L. F., and Smith, C., *Place-Names of Roman Britain* (London, 1979), 289-91.
44. Watson, *Celtic Place-Names*.
45. *Annals of Ulster*, Hennessy, W. M. (ed.), (4 vols, Rolls Series, 1887-1901), 1, 481.
46. Jackson, K. H., 'Two early Scottish names,' *SHS*, 33 (1954), 14-15.
47. Merthyn, according to the Welsh tradition, wandered and lived rough in *Coed Celyddon* after the battle of Arthuret. One can scarcely imagine him travelling to the north of Scotland after the battle before going mad and taking to the woods. (See Dillon, M., and Chadwick, N. K., *The Celtic Realms* (1967)). The disappearance of *Coed Celyddon* reinforces my thesis. The forest has not gone away — it assumed camouflage colouring!

FERGUS, GALLOWAY AND THE SCOTS

Richard D. Oram

From the early twelfth century until 1234, the country lying west of the Nith and south of the watershed of the western Southern Uplands lay under the governance of one family: the lords of Galloway of the House of Fergus. As a political unit, the lordship was to be one of the longest-lived of the subdivisions of medieval Scotland, surviving as a distinct entity until 1455 when, with other forfeited Douglas lands, it was absorbed into the properties of the crown. Down to 1234, its rulers commanded positions of power and influence in both Scotland and England, and intervened actively in the affairs of the kingdom of Man and the Isles. The last of the male line, Alan, had a reputation as a warrior which reached as far as the Norwegian court. Despite these facts, however, little is known of the circumstances whereby this vast agglomeration of territory was fused into a cohesive political entity; even less is known about the origins and ancestry of the founder of the ruling dynasty. It is the aim of this paper to examine the evidence for the formation of the lordship, and to assess the part played in that process by members of the Canmore dynasty.

Despite arguments advanced in favour of Earl Malcolm and Suibne Mac Cinaedh,[1] there is no evidence for any independent power in the south-west before the emergence in the 1130s of Fergus of Galloway. The ancestry of this man, and the source of his powers in the lordship have, since the nineteenth century, been the subjects of much scholarly conjecture. In view of the evidence for military service being performed by Galwegians in the armies of Malcolm Canmore in the later eleventh century,[2] it was regarded as clear that the south-west had been subject to Scottish overlordship, probably derived from Scottish acquisition of the lands and rights of the former rulers of Strathclyde. As a result, Fergus came to be viewed either as an upstart who had carved a position for himself in a region where royal power was weak, or as a protégé of the Scots, established in Galloway as a vassal of the crown.[3] To writers such as M'Kerlie, he was no more than a foreign governor, a non-Galwegian imposed by an unprincipled king upon a people left leaderless by the death of its rulers at the battle of the Standard.[4] His lack of a patronymic fuelled this view, implying that there may be some truth in the belief that he was a mere *parvenu,* the first of his line.

More elaborate traditions developed out of these initial observations. Fergus has come to be depicted as a boyhood friend of the future David I, sharing with him an upbringing at the court of Henry I of England. According to Huyshe, it was there that he met and fell in love with his future bride, Henry's illegitimate daughter, Elizabeth.[5] As a close friend and confidant of David, and son-in-law of the English king, Fergus was destined for greatness. This supposed upbringing at the Anglo-Norman

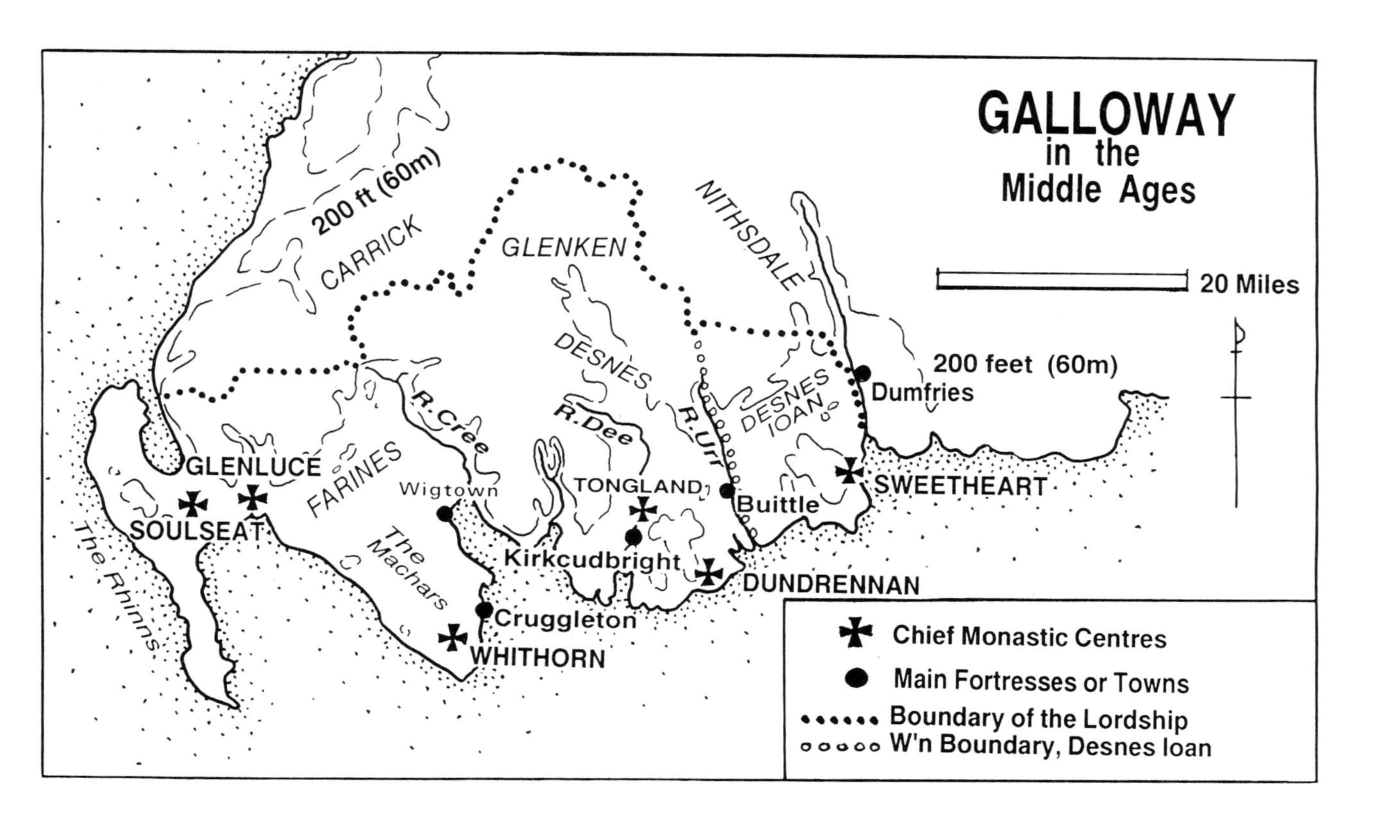

Fig.8.1 Galloway in the Middle Ages.

court is a mere echo of M'Kerlie's belief in Fergus's non-Galwegian origins. There is, however, little about Fergus to suggest an Anglo-Norman background. Indeed, his association with the conservative earls in the 1159-60 rebellion against Malcolm IV[6] may indicate a marked antipathy towards the new social and cultural trends being introduced by the Canmore kings. Moreover, the supposed childhood spent at the English court appears to be pure fabrication, invented by nineteen-century writers who were seeking to find suitable circumstances for Fergus to have met his future bride. That such a marriage took place is now generally accepted,[7] but it is unlikely to have been the love-match proposed by Huyshe. Instead, it was probably a politically-motivated union, a simple act of English foreign policy designed to draw a powerful regional lord into the orbit of the English crown. This marriage was to have serious political repercussions later in the twelfth century.

The proposal that Fergus was a 'creation' of David I may have a more substantial basis in fact, and does not rely upon the spurious claims of childhood friendship to give it foundation. Several factors appear to combine to support the contention that Fergus was installed in his lordship by the king of Scots, but there are still serious weaknesses within this thesis. The main arguments focus on the question of his antecedents. Certain aspects of the landed properties pertaining to the lordship seem to indicate that Fergus had predecessors in Galloway, but whether these men were ancestors or not is an altogether different matter. The lack of any patronymic, where he appears it is simply as 'Fergus of Galloway',[8] and the manner in which the pedigrees of his successors are rehearsed in their charters back to Fergus and no further,[9] have been seized upon as proof that he was an upstart. If, though, he was not of Galwegian stock, what were his antecedents and why was he to become established in Galloway?

At this point, some students of Galwegian history would brandish the 'evidence' of the *Roman de Fergus,*[10] and seek to identify the hero of the romantic poem with the historical lord of Galloway. The hero of the poem is described as the youngest son of a certain Somerled, whom the poet depicts as a boorish peasant, elevated through a good marriage to a position of wealth and higher social status. Somerled's name has been seized upon subsequently as direct evidence for a link between the dynasties of Galloway and Argyll,[11] with several members of the latter being advanced as Fergus's progenitor. Various theories have been put forward to explain how a member of the Argyll dynasty could have gained control of Galloway.[12]

There are serious chronological problems with most of the proposals made upon the basis of the romance, most of these stemming from the difficulty of finding a Somerled of the right generation to be the father of Fergus. The almost frenzied efforts of partisans of the Fergus-Somerled thesis to find a viable alternative when valid objections are raised about their previous submissions have largely discredited the value of the poem as a source. There is, moreover, no general consensus about the circumstances of the composition.[13] It has been interpreted by literary historians as either a panegyric composed for Alan of Galloway, a glorification of the founder of his dynasty, written at the time of his marriage to a niece of the Scottish king,[14] or as a work of propaganda produced later in the thirteenth century for Devorgilla Balliol in support of her ambitions for her family.[15] In both cases, the bad light in which Somerled is portrayed, and the clear references to his inferior background, can have been of little credit to the supposed patron of the work. The Devorgilla thesis, where the romance is supposedly a work designed to cast lustre on her family, and aid them in their aspirations to the Scottish throne, is particularly untenable. Firstly, she would have had to have possessed clairvoyant abilities to know that her youngest son was to be a contender for the throne in 1290-1. Secondly, advertising that your family was descended from peasant stock would surely have been suicidal in this context. With success dependent upon the support of the aristocracy, it would have been a serious blunder to focus attention on the lowly origins of your dynasty, irrespective of its status by that date.

There are further objections which cast serious doubts upon the genealogical value of the romance, and call into question the whole issue of its connection with the Galloway dynasty. Most notable amongst these is the question of the specific aim of the author of the work. If, as has been proposed by Owen,[16] the poet was composing a near parody of the conventional romance genre, as represented by the work of Chrétien of Troyes, what value should be attached to names and locations used in his poem? Many obscure allusions, lost to us, may have been instantly recognisable to connoisseurs of the fashionable romances of the thirteenth century. It should be noted, moreover, that the poet, a Picard clerk named Guillaume, possessed only a very sketchy knowledge of the geography of western Britain, and more particularly of Galloway and the Isles.[17] This deficiency is difficult to explain if Guillaume is to be identified with Alan of Galloway's clerk, William, prior of St Mary's Isle.[18] Similar objections can be raised regarding the composer's supposed attachment to Devorgilla's household. In view of these internal factors, therefore, the *Roman de Fergus* cannot be accepted as an authoritative source concerned with the origins of the historical Fergus.

One element of the numerous hypotheses surrounding the *Roman* which was apparently supported by independent tradition is that which proposes some link between the dynasties of Argyll and Galloway. It should be stressed that no factual basis for this argument was ever established, but a number of circumstantial factors appeared to combine to make it a proposition worthy of consideration. The origins of this tradition appear to stem from the genealogical claims advanced for the MacDowells,[19] a family prominent in Galwegian politics from the late thirteenth century onwards. They, on no clear authority other than the dubious grounds of heraldry, have been represented as descendants of some unknown scion of the main Galloway dynasty. Past observers have accepted this supposed link without comment, although the MacDowells themselves appear never to have voiced claims to such illustrious ancestry. The family's rise to prominence after 1296 stemmed from their exploitation of the power vacuum in the lordship following the deposition of John Balliol, not from any kinship association with the former ruling house. Such objections were generally overlooked, attention instead focusing upon the patronymic MacDowell (and its variants MacDowall and MacDouall) and its clear etymological relationship with MacDougal. Despite obvious chronological impossibility, this developed into a theory that the MacDowells (and, by extension, the main branch of the Galloway dynasty), sprang from the senior line of the descendants of Somerled. While it is by no means impossible that the MacDowells *did* share some kindred link with the lords of Lorne, the fact that Fergus was a contemporary of the father of the eponymous Dugald of the MacDougals renders it definite that the Galloway dynasty did not.

Although a direct line of descent from the main branch of the Argyll dynasty must be ruled out, the activities of Fergus and his thirteenth-century successors in Man and the Isles indicate some long-term and deep-seated interest in these areas. The alliance which Fergus forged with the Manx dynasty, through the marriage of his daughter, Affreca, to Olaf Godredsson,[20] forms the most obvious source for this long-lived involvement, but the roots may lie deeper. Other speakers at the Conference pointed to the reported activities of Magnus Barelegs in the Solway region in the late eleventh century. When taken in conjunction with the evidence for the limited settlement of Scandinavian colonists in the southern Machars and the country around the Dee estuary, it is perhaps possible that there was a movement of settlers into Galloway from Man, or from parts of the Hebrides under Manx influence. No-one has suggested that this settlement represented a conquest, but the material evidence from the excavations at Whithorn suggests that the cultural and economic implications were considerable.[21] Significantly, the areas of densest Scandinavian settlement coincide with the two chief foci of lordship power in the twelfth and thirteenth centuries, based on Cruggleton and Kirkcudbright. Is it possible that an initially economic dominance of Galloway by settlers from Man or the Norse-Celtic colonies of the Hebrides was transformed into political mastery as the colonists became more entrenched in Galwegian society? The development of the European colonial empires in the Far East in the eighteenth and nineteenth centuries suggest that it is.

Of the various origins proposed for Fergus, descent from a Norse-Celtic family, probably intermarried with native Galwegian elements, forms the most viable of the options at our disposal.[22] The evidence is still tenuous, but does not rely upon the complicated genealogies which enmesh most of the alternatives. Certainly, the traditional outlook of the Galwegians, away from Scotland towards the powers of the Irish Sea and Hebrides, suggests that it was from those areas that Fergus's predecessors were drawn. The disposition of the family estates, concentrated predominantly in the lower Dee valley and the coastal region around Whithorn,[23] associates him closely with the areas of principal Scandinavian settlement along the north shore of the Solway. Such general observations form only a skeletal framework, but they are as specific as the surviving sources will allow. To attempt to add flesh to these bare bones would be only to indulge in unwarranted conjecture.

The question of Fergus's antecedents settles only in part the issue of whether he was a protégé of the Scottish crown installed in Galloway as a governor, or a native ruler exercising his powers independently of the king. That he was probably of south-western stock does not rule out the possibility that he had been established in authority over his compatriots by the Scots, although such an action is not characteristic of what is known of David I's policies regarding the introduction of royal vassals into areas where royal influence was thinly stretched. In any case, it is unclear to what extent David possessed the ability to influence the affairs of Galloway, whether he was in fact capable of installing one of his own creatures into a position of power in a region which lay on the periphery of his sphere of authority. The question of the degree and extent of David's power prior to his accession to the throne in 1124 has never been addressed satisfactorily, despite its obvious implications regarding the formation of the pattern of secular lordship in the south-west.

From 1107 until 1124, David had exercised rule over a substantial portion of southern Scotland (excluding Lothian), which had been bequeathed to him by his elder brother, King Edgar. During this phase of his career, he is most commonly referred to as 'Earl David',[24] a title held in recognition of his possession of the Midlands earldoms of the St Liz family, but on occasion he is described as 'prince of Cumbria' (or some variant of that formula),[25] a title specifically associated with his domain in southern Scotland. The full extent of this 'principality' is still a matter of debate, but there is general consensus regarding the core of its territory. David's title associates him clearly with the Brythonic peoples of the central Southern Uplands, Clydesdale, Tweeddale and the valleys around the head of the Solway. The bulk of this territory fell beneath the episcopal authority of the bishops of Glasgow, and it is clear from many of David's later acts that there was a marked correspondence between the sphere of jurisdiction of the prince and that of the bishops. The latter are acknowledged as the successors of the 'tribal' bishops of Strathclyde,[26] whose see corresponded in territorial terms with the lands controlled by the kings of Strathclyde, expanding and contracting with the fortunes of the kingdom.

Recognition of the correspondence between David's territories and the lands of the see of Glasgow raised awkward questions of early students of Galwegian history. The most problematical of these concerned the inclusion of the easternmost subdivision of the lordship, Desnes Ioan, within the diocese of Glasgow rather than of Galloway. Interpretations of this arrangement varied greatly, but two main schools dominated. One saw this ecclesiastical division as the residual trace of a once wider jurisdiction, with all of Galloway formerly falling beneath the bishops of Glasgow, but a partition had been effected on the revival of the Galwegian see in the 1120s.[27] The second viewed it as a forcible partition, probably dating from Malcolm IV's invasion of Galloway in 1160, intended to improve the royal supervision of the conquered lordship.[28] The value of such a division, however, is not obvious, as Desnes Ioan remained firmly within the sphere of the lords of Galloway. Of these two interpretations, the former carried more weight, as it seemed logical to propose that in the absence of a bishop at Whithorn the Galwegians would naturally have looked to the nearest convenient bishop for provision of certain services, such as consecration, reconciliation and provision of chrism. This argument, however, overlooked the traditional ties with the Northumbrian Church. Indeed, the weight of the evidence concerning the revival of the Galwegian see points towards York as the main source of initiative.[29] Whatever the scenario for the creation of this division, however, it was recognised that implicit within inclusion in the see of Glasgow was subjection to the overlordship of the ruler of Strathclyde. From 1107 that meant overlordship by Prince David.

Further evidence for the submission of Galloway to the rulers of Strathclyde appears to lie in David's exercise of rights to fiscal levies from south-western districts of his domain. The earliest references are to tithes of his cain of certain foodstuffs from four districts, Carrick, Kyle, Cunninghame and Strathclyde,[30] which correspond approximately with the later sheriffdoms of Ayr and Renfrew. Malcolm IV's great charter to Kelso Abbey appears to allude to these districts when it refers to 'that part of Galloway' held by King David.[31] This implies clearly that part of Galloway was *not* held by him. The automatic reaction would be to claim that the lordship was the portion which lay outwith his control, yet certain factors would seem to indicate otherwise. The principal objection from Fergus's lifetime is his apparent provision of forinsec service in the armies fighting in northern England down to 1138. This provision of military levies appears as early as the reign of Malcolm III, who used Galwegians in Northumberland in the 1080s and 1090s.[32] In no instance, however, is it made clear on what basis troops were provided, and that it was through forinsec service is simply an assumption based on the belief in Galwegian subjection to Scottish overlordship. It is generally overlooked that in the campaign of 1137-8 Fergus had a personal interest at stake, in that he was fighting at least nominally in support of Matilda, half-sister to his wife. Only in William the Lion's campaign of 1174, which followed the conquest of the lordship, can provision of military service be seen as a service obligation to the crown. On what basis, then, were troops provided in earlier periods?

Throughout the Middle Ages, Galloway was seen as a reservoir of military man-power, providing contingents to Scottish and English armies and establishing its rulers as power-brokers in the political manoeuverings of their day. This position is demonstrated most clearly in the lifetime of Alan of Galloway in the early thirteenth century. He provided major forces to the armies of both Alexander II of Scotland and John of England, as well as conducting his own military ventures in Ulster, Man and the southern Hebrides.[33] Service obligations appear to have been of little importance to Alan, and it is clear from his dealings with King John and Reginald of Man that his assistance did not come without a price.[34] With resources of good quality man-power and a fleet at his disposal, Alan commanded a valuable commodity much in demand by neighbouring rulers. It would not be stretching the evidence too thinly to suggest that Galloway was an early source of gallowglasses, major contingents of essentially mercenary troops fighting under foreign banners.[35] It could be argued, therefore, that the Galwegians serving in the eleventh- and twelfth-century Scottish armies were present on occasion as hired troops, not as the product of a military levy.

Counter to this proposal, some scholars would point to the direct evidence for payment of fiscal renders by the lords of Galloway to the Scots, referred to explicitly in two twelfth-century sources. The earlier of these is a charter of Uhtred, granting land in Desnes Ioan to Richard, son of Troite, datable to the late 1160s or early 1170s.[36] It states clearly that Uhtred was paying cain to the crown. The second source records a judgement made by Roland in the 1180s in a court at Lanark, which confirmed the royal right to cain from Galloway.[37] Both documents are of vital importance, but their significance has been consistently misinterpreted. In Uhtred's charter it is made clear that the cain was being levied only on Desnes Ioan and its subdivision of Cro, not Galloway in general. This, it should be remembered, was also the district which fell beneath the jurisdiction of the see of Glasgow. Here, then, would appear to be direct proof for the subjection of Galloway to spiritual and temporal dominance by the rulers of Strathclyde and their Scottish successors. There is, however, sufficient independent evidence to suggest that Desnes Ioan was something of an anomaly. In other sources it is treated as a distinct unit with clear boundaries, whilst the remainder of the lordship appears simply as an amorphous whole until the reorganisation of the administrative pattern after 1234. In addition to this, Uhtred seemed to indulge in an almost prodigal alienation of lands and privileges within Desnes Ioan,[38] making no such inroads on his inheritance elsewhere in the lordship. His grants were such that his successors possessed little demesne in this region. This attitude towards Desnes Ioan begs an explanation.

Analysis of the pattern of lordship estates shows an overwhelming concentration of lands in the Ken-Dee Valley and the Machars peninsula. Blanks in this distribution can be explained by the nature of the topography, with most such areas corresponding with expanses of upland or moor. Desnes Ioan, however, was a fertile and apparently populous district, but contained few manors held personally by the lords. The distribution of such estates suggests that the bulk of the lordship inheritance lay in Galloway west of the Urr, with particular foci at Kirkcudbright and Cruggleton. Whilst estates elsewhere in the lordship passed in and out of the direct possession of the lords and their successors, the grouping around these two foci remained in the hands of the senior line.[39] The clear implication is that these represented the heartland, the capiti of the two main portions of Galloway east and west of the Cree. The regular granting away of other estates, especially in Desnes Ioan, suggests that they were of secondary importance, perhaps reflecting a distinction between inherited and acquired land. That Desnes Ioan as a whole is treated in this manner suggests that it may have been a late acquisition, perhaps only added to the lordship in the time of Uhtred. The general lack of Galwegian charters from before 1160 makes this difficult to confirm, but certain features of the later documentation and some characteristics in the archaeological record indicate strongly that this must be the case.

In his paper, Derek Craig indicated the sharp dichotomy in sculptural remains within Galloway.[40] Various stylistic schools are known from the region west of the Urr, with major groupings corresponding approximately to the ecclesiastical divisions of the medieval diocese. Desnes Ioan, however, has produced no such monumental sculpture, which suggests a wholly different cultural tradition. It is probable, therefore, that the lands east of the Urr fell under an alternative spiritual and temporal influence in the period when the sculptures were being produced in the tenth and eleventh centuries. The most viable agency is Strathclyde, whose political power expanded southwards into Annandale, Nithsdale and the Carlisle region as Northumbria disintegrated. It was probably at the time of this expansion that Desnes Ioan was drawn into the sphere of the bishops of Glasgow. Scottish inheritance of the Strathclyde kingdom after 1018 is unlikely to have seen any diminution of its territories and, down to 1093, Malcolm III was to take an active interest in the south-western portion of his domain, attempting to consolidate his grip on Carlisle. It is unlikely that Malcolm would have jeopardised his position in this region by allowing Desnes Ioan to slip from his grasp, let alone permit it to fall under Galwegian rule. It is only after Malcolm IV's loss of Carlisle in 1157 that there is any suggestion that this region formed an integral part of the lordship.

Evidence for control of Desnes Ioan by the Galloway dynasty does not appear in concrete form until after *c*.1165. The earliest material lies in a group of Uhtred's charters, none of which predates the beginning of the reign of William the Lion. Significantly, Uhtred's possession of Desnes Ioan coincides with the disappearance of Radulf, son of Dunegal, lord of lower Nithsdale, and the apparent extinction of his line.[41] There is reason to believe that royal interest in Dumfries, Radulf's probable caput, dates from the 1160s,[42] over twenty years earlier than the foundation of the burgh, and it would appear that the stronghold there may have been viewed as a replacement for Carlisle. As Reid pointed out, Desnes Ioan goes naturally with Dumfries, forming both a buffer and a commercial hinterland.[43] It is reasonable to assume that Radulf had controlled that district, but that on his death a carve-up of his domain had occurred. The crown seized Dumfries and the lands east of the Nith, while the remainder west of the river was given to Uhtred. Coming probably little more than five years after Malcolm IV's conquest of Galloway, this major gift of territory might seem awkward to explain, but Scottish treatment of the lordship suggests that Fergus had been the principal target and that the king bore little grudge against his sons. Indeed, the evidence for family discord in the Galloway dynasty in the 1150s[44] could support the argument that Uhtred and Gilbert had either assisted in their father's downfall or had done little to prevent it. Desnes Ioan, then, may have formed a reward of sorts. A more likely explanation, however, is that William required assistance in the establishment of a military and administrative framework for his new acquisition in Nithsdale. Uhtred, as the nearest great lord, was clearly in a position to provide such assistance. His establishment of knights on land in Desnes Ioan can be linked to garrison service at Dumfries,[45] and there is some evidence to support the view that the region formed part of an administrative unit, perhaps a sheriffdom, based on the new royal castle. For this district, then, Uhtred and his successors would have been liable to cain and other dues.

The second reference to cain from Galloway, that made in Roland's judgement of 1187, has been taken as concrete proof of the rigorous application of this tribute in the years immediately after the death of Gilbert and the seizure of the lordship by the pro-Scottish son of Uhtred. The scale of the payments has been taken as indicative that it was the higher nobility, the supporters of Gilbert, who were being targeted for punishment rather than the body of the populace.[46] The application, moreover, has been seen as general, reaching all districts of the lordship. This, however, cannot be the case. Although it has been recognised for a number of years that Roland may have retained control of some of eastern Galloway following his father's murder in 1174,[47] and that he speedily gained control of his uncle's lands in 1185, it is clear from his submission to Henry II in 1186[48] that he was not the free agent which has normally been assumed. It can be shown that from c. 1176 until the Quitclaim of Canterbury in December 1189, the lordship lay under the direct and active overlordship of the king of England, vassal status having been accepted by Gilbert as the price for English assistance in escaping the wrath of William the Lion.[49] Roland had attempted to avoid such a submission in 1186, but the chronicles cannot disguise the fact that he submitted to superior military force and took oaths of fealty and homage as binding as those performed by his uncle. In 1187, therefore, Roland was in no position to acknowledge a general right to cain from Galloway as a right of the Scottish crown. Such a grant, however, is recorded and dated to c. May 1187.[50] What, then, were the circumstances of the grant? Two possibilities present themselves. Firstly, Roland was justiciar of 'Galloway'.[51] This is generally taken to mean all of southern Scotland south and west of Clydesdale and Annandale. The 'Galloway' of the 1187 judgement, therefore, could be this extended region, from which the crown had long drawn cain.[52] The second possibility is that the record gives only general details of an originally more specific judgement concerned with those regions which Roland had retained after his father's murder. The most obvious of these is Desnes Ioan. Only after 1189 could a more general grant be made.

Based on this later evidence, the lordship as ruled by Fergus appears as a compact territory, focussing upon two main centres at Kirkcudbright and Cruggleton. It was served by bishops whose see corresponded exactly with the secular unit, an arrangement which further illustrates its independent character. It appears, moreover, to have been free from obvious Scottish influences until the acquisition of a portion of the old lordship of lower Nithsdale, itself a subdivision of the kingdom of Strathclyde. This territorial expansion probably occurred no earlier than 1165. It did, however, bring tenurial complications, with the lords of Galloway recognising their status as vassals of the king of Scots for this district, whilst at the same time continuing to exclude them from Galloway proper.

In conclusion, therefore, it must be recognised that there are still major unanswered questions concerning the origins of the lordship and the ruling dynasty, but there are several factors which argue against significant Scottish interferences until after 1160. There are no recorded antecedents for Fergus, but his interests in the Irish Sea zone and association with those portions of Galloway colonised by Scandinavians indicate a possible descent from Norse-Celtic stock. No weight can be attached to claims for his advancement by David I, and their association in the 1130s appears to stem from coincidental political interests in the English succession dispute rather than from any personal bond. Fergus certainly did not introduce Scottish elements into Galloway, the influx of settlers commencing only with his son's acquisition of Desnes Ioan. Fergus's political activities show significant independence from superior control. His marriage to an illegitimate daughter of Henry I put him on a par with Alexander I of Scots, and gave him some social distinction over his supposed mentor, David I, whose wife, although of royal stock, was a widow with family already. Henry clearly regarded Fergus as a power worth wooing, presumably on account of his resources of man-power. Finally, the evidence of subjection to Scottish overlordship and the payment of tribute has been called into question, with no proof for such burdens being available for any periods other than the brief interludes when Galloway suffered military conquest. In contrast, the Galloway of Fergus appears as a potent force, ruled by an independent lord, wooed by foreign powers. As long as the dynasty remained strong, Galloway remained free from Scottish control, but every sign of weakness was exploited by the Canmore kings. It was the failure of the male line of the House of Fergus that sealed the fate of the lordship.

Appendix

Simplified family tree of the House of Fergus

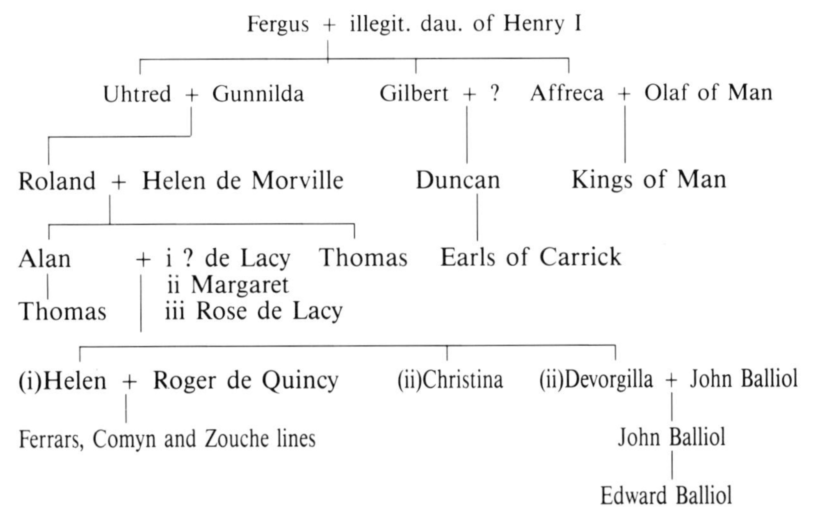

Notes

1. e.g. Reid, R. C., *Wigtownshire Charters,* xi.
2. Anderson, A. O., *Scottish Annals from English Chroniclers* (London, 1908), 100-101.
3. Mackenzie, W., *The History of Galloway from the Earliest Period to the Present Time* (Kirkcudbright, 1841), i, 167-8; Chalmers, G., *Caledonia* (new edition Paisley, 1887), i, 366; M'Kerlie, P. E., *The History of the Lands and Their Owners in Galloway* (2nd edition Paisley, 1906), i, 109-11; Huyshe, W., *Grey Galloway: Its Lords and Its Saints* (Edinburgh, 1914), 107-8; Robertson, J. F.,

The Story of Galloway (Castle Douglas, 1964), 41-3; Duncan, A. A. M., *Scotland, The Making of the Kingdom* (Edinburgh, 1975), 86.

4. M'Kerlie, *Lands and Their Owners,* i, 109-11.
5. Huyshe, *Grey Galloway,* 107.
6. *Chron. Holyrood,* 136-7.
7. Given-Wilson, C. and Curteis, A., *The Royal Bastards of Medieval England* (London, 1984), 71; see also Robert de Torigni, *Chronica,* in Chronicles of Stephen etc., ed. Howlett, R., iv (1889), 229.
8. See for example, *Glasgow Registrum,* i, Nos. 3, 9, 10.
9. e.g. *RRS,* vi, No. 235.
10. Guillaume le Clerc, *The Romance of Fergus,* ed. Frescolin, W. (Philadelphia, 1983.
11. Legge, M. D., 'Some notes on the Roman de Fergus', *TDGAS,* 27 (1948-9), 163-72; Legge, M. D., 'The Father of Fergus of Galloway', *SHR,* 43 (1964), 86-7.
12. e.g. Legge, 'Father of Fergus of Galloway', 87.
13. *The Romance of Fergus,* 13-15; Legge, 'Notes on the Roman de Fergus', 163-5; Greenber, J., 'Guillaume le Clerc and Alan of Galloway', *Proceedings of the Modern Language Association,* 66 (1951), 524-33; Webster, K., 'Galloway and the Romances', *Modern Language Notes,* 55 (1940), 363-6; Owen, D. D. R., 'The craft of Guillaume le Clerc's Fergus', in *The Craft of Fiction; Essays in Medieval Poetics,* ed. Arrathoon, L. (Rochester, Michigan, 1984), 47-81 at 48, 77.
14. Legge, 'Notes on the Roman de Fergus', 163, 166-7.
15. Schmolke-Hasselmann, B., 'Der arturische Versroman, et "Le Roman de Fergus": technique narrative et intention politique', in *An Arthurian Tapestry: Essays in Memory of Lewis Thorpe,* ed. Varty, K. (Glasgow, 1981), 342-53.
16. Owen, 'The craft of Guillaume le Clerc's Fergus'.
17. Greenberg, 'Guillaume le Clerc', 526-8, 532.
18. Legge, 'Notes on the Roman de Fergus', 163.
19. Agnew, A., *A History of the Hereditary Sheriffs of Galloway* (Edinburgh, 1864), 613; Kevan McDowall, J., *Carrick Gallovidian* (Ayr, 1947), 34; McGill, J. M., 'A Genealogical Survey of the Ancient Lords of Galloway', *Scottish Genealogist,* 2 (1955), 3-6.
20. *Chron. Man,* 61.
21. Hill, P. H., *Excavations at Bruce Street, Whithorn, 1984; Interim Report* (Edinburgh, 1985), 36-7; Hill, P. H., *Whithorn 1. Excavations 1984-1986. Interim Report* (Whithorn, 1987), 6-9.
22. Duncan, *Making of the Kingdom,* 163.
23. See my contribution to the forthcoming revised Scottish Historical Atlas, on the demesne estates of the lords of Galloway.
24. See e.g. *RRS,* i, Nos. 1, 3, 5, 6.
25. e.g. *Glasgow Registrum,* i, No. 1.
26. Shead, N. F., 'The Origins of the Medieval Diocese of Glasgow', *SHR,* 48 (1969), 220-5.
27. Skene, W. F., *Celtic Scotland* (Edinburgh, 1876), ii, 375-6.
28. Reid, R. C., 'The feudalisation of lower Nithsdale', *TDGAS,* 34 (1955-6), 102-110, at 105-6.
29. Restrictions on space do not permit reproduction of the full argument in support of this view. This is set out in full in my PhD thesis, *The Lordship of Galloway, c.1000-c.1250 (University of St Andrews, 1988).*

30. *Glasgow Registrum,* No. 9.
31. *RRS,* i, No. 131.
32. Anderson, *Annals,* 100-101.
33. e.g. *CDS,* i, Nos. 529, 533; *CDS,* v, No. 9; The Saga of Hacon, in *Icelandic Sagas,* trans Dasent, G. W., iv (Rolls Series, 1894), 150.
34. Greeves, R., 'The Galloway Lands in Ulster', *TDGAS,* 36 (1957-8), 115-21; MacNeill, T. E., *Anglo-Norman Ulster: The History and Archaeology of an Irish Barony, 1177-1400* (Edinburgh, 1980), 6, 14-15.
35. I am indebted to Professor A. A. M. Duncan for pointing out this possibility to me in the course of the ASHS conference in St Andrews in October 1987.
36. Cumbria Record Office, Lowther Archive, D/Lons/L5/1/S1.
37. *APS,* i, 378, xxiii.
38. e.g. *Holyrood Liber,* Nos. 23, 27, 49, 73; *Holm Cultram Register,* Nos. 120, 133, 140a; *CDS,* ii, No. 1606. These represented only a few of his grants to ecclesiastical institutions. No charters of Lincluden Nunnery survive, but it was founded by Uhtred and endowed with extensive lands in Desnes Ioan.
39. The inquest post-mortem into the lands of Elena la Zouche, grand-daughter of Alan, and youngest daughter of Helen de Quincy, the senior Galloway heiress (*CDS,* ii, No. 824), shows the concentration of her share of the Quincy third of Galloway. More significantly, the *Brevis Descriptio Regni Scotie* of *c*.1296 described Kirkcudbright, the chief lordship centre, as belonging to William de Ferrars, who was descended from Alan's eldest grand-daughter, Margaret, countess of Derby (*Miscellany of the Maitland Club,* iv (Glasgow, 1847), pt i, 34).
40. See Craig, 'Pre-Norman sculpture'.
41. For the disappearance of Radulf see: *Scots Peerage,* vi, 286-7; Reid, 'Feudalisation of Nithsdale', 103.
42. Scott, J. G., 'An early sheriff of Dumfries?', *TDGAS,* 57 (1982), 90-91.
43. Reid, 'Feudalisation of lower Nithsdale', 109.
44. Walter Daniel, *Life of Ailred of Rievaulx,* ed. Powicke, F. M. (Oxford, 1950), 45.
45. Scott, 'An early sheriff?'
46. Duncan, *Making of the Kingdom,* 185-6.
47. Ibid., 183-4.
48. *Benedict of Peterborough,* i, 348-9.
49. Ibid., i, 126.
50. *APS,* i, 378, xxiii.
51. *RRS,* i, Nos. 309, 400, 406.
52. Duncan, *Making of the Kingdom,* 203-4.

THE LAWS OF GALLOWAY
A PRELIMINARY SURVEY*

Hector L. MacQueen

In 1244 Alexander II and his council enacted an assize whereby the justiciar of Lothian was to hold inquests in each sheriffdom within his bailiary in order to find out those who had committed crimes. But it was provided that this should not apply in Galloway, 'which has its own special laws'.[1] Eighty years later Robert I granted to the captains and men of Galloway that in future when a Galwegian was accused of a crime he should have a good and faithful assize and should not need to purge or acquit himself 'in accordance with the old laws of Galloway'; but these laws were still to apply where the accusation was against one of the king's Galloway sergeants or officers, or concerned with one of the four pleas of the Crown, treason, or the killing of foreigners.[2] Despite this, the laws of Galloway were still in use as late as 1384 when parliament agreed that they should be preserved as against the provisions of a statute just enacted, which provided that if a person accused in one sheriffdom should flee into another then the first sheriff should write to the second who could then cite the fugitive to appear before a court.[3]

What were these laws of Galloway? So far as I know, this question had never been fully answered, although there have been valuable studies of what were undoubtedly vital elements of the laws — notably the articles by George Neilson and W. C. Dickinson on *surdit de sergaunt,* and a number of remarks on the same topic by Geoffrey Barrow in the course of more general works.[4] This essay is not an attempt at a definitive study but should be regarded as a report on work in progress on medieval Galwegian law and customs with reference also to the neighbouring province of Carrick, from where there is evidence for a virtually identical system and form of society in the same period. It focuses in particular on the subject of *kenkynnol* but also ventures a few remarks on other aspects of the law in Galloway, the study of which seems worth pursuing in more detail than has been done to date.

The word *kenkynnol* is found in a number of well known medieval documents relating to Carrick.[5] It is a form of the Gaelic phrase *ceann cineail* meaning 'head of the kindred',[6] but Professor Barrow has pointed out that it is also cognate with the Welsh *pencenedl,* which has precisely the same meaning.[7] It is also found in documents coming from Scotland north of the Forth, sometimes in the form 'kenkynie'.[8] The evidence that *kenkynnol* was also a feature of the laws of Galloway is a single entry in the *Formulary E* collection of royal writs printed by Professor Duncan, a style *ad constituendum capitaneos super leges Galwidie.*[9] In translation it reads:

> The king to all etc. Know that we have constituted X captain (*capitaneus*) of all his kin (*parentela*) or, of a certain kin, of which by right and according to the customs of Galloway used hitherto he ought to be captain. Wherefore we command all others who are of the said kin that they submit to X their captain in everything just as it was done according to the said laws and customs of all his kin.

The importance of the document is that it is a style used in the king's chapel; in other words, it was not unusual for clerks of the chapel to have to produce such a writ. In the reign of David II there are references which probably illustrate the *Formulary E* style in use: appointments of Donald Edgar as chief of the Clan MacGowin, of Gilbert Maclellan as chief of the Clan Connan, and of Michael MacGorth as chief of the Kenelmen.[10] And there were many other clans, or kin groups, with captains in Galloway and Carrick. For example, the 1282 inventory of the royal muniments referred to an undertaking made to the king by the captains and freeholders of Carrick.[11] The chief men of Clan Afren in Galloway submitted to Edward I at Wigtown in 1296,[12] while various clans within Carrick brought themselves under the captaincy of the Kennedies of Dunure at different times in the fourteenth and fifteenth centuries: the Muntercasduf, the Makmaykanis, the Werichsach and possibly the Kynchaldiis.[13] The treasurer's accounts of 1473 referred to a composition with 'MacDowele for the resignacioune for the . . . hed of kyne in the partis of Galwaye',[14] while in 1490 parliament considered certain customs 'usit be heedis of kin' in Galloway and Carrick.[15] It seems likely that when the mid-thirteenth-century English chronicler, Matthew Paris, wrote of the *duces ac magistrates* of Galloway, he was referring to men who were the chiefs of their clans.[16] Presumably all these captains, chief men and heads of kin exercised the rights of *kenkynnol,* whatever these may have been.

Our only direct clue, apart from the literal meaning of the word, as to what *kenkynnol* involved lies in the phraseology of some charters and confirmations giving it to the Kennedies of Dunure in Carrick. In 1372 Robert II issued three confirmations, all apparently in favour of John Kennedy of Dunure. Only two of these need concern us here. By the first he confirmed a confirmation of Alexander III, dated January 1275/6, of the gift by Neil, earl of Carrick, to Roland (Lachlan) of Carrick and his heirs, that he should be head of all his kindred both *in calumpniis* and the other matters pertaining to *kenkynnol,* together with the office of bailie of Carrick and the leadership (*duccione*) of the men of that district under whomsoever should be the earl of Carrick.[17] Secondly, King Robert confirmed the charter by which Earl Neil had made his grant to Roland, the terms of the grant being exactly as outlined in King Alexander's confirmation.[18] Earl Neil's charter must have been made before 1256, the year of his death; probably it was occasioned by the requirement that the head of a kin-group be male, while he himself had only female issue

(Marjorie, who succeeded him as countess of Carrick in accordance with the feudal rules of inheritance which had become the common law of Scotland by the mid-thirteenth century). The verbal formula first used in this document — to be the head of the kindred *in calumpniis* and all other matters pertaining to the office — remained virtually unchanged in subsequent grants of *kenkynnol* to the Kennedies up to 1455.[19] Additionally, the holding of weapon-showings is mentioned as a further duty in some of the fifteenth-century grants.

Thus the only specific item in the early charters is the right to *calumpniis.* What were they? Since Lord Hailes in the eighteenth century, historians seem to have thought that this meant the taking of *calps.*[20] *Calp* in Galloway was a form of the tribute-render which Sir John Skene described as follows at the end of the sixteenth century:[21]

> Calpes in Galloway and Carrick signifies ane gift, sik as horse or other thing, quhilk an man in his win lifetime and liege poustie gives to his Maister, or to onie uther man that is greatest in power and authoritie, and speciallie to the head and chiefe of the clann, for his maintenance and protection . . . (Skene then goes on to show his Edinburgh lawyer's disapproval of this) . . . like (he says) as for the samin effect and cause sinderie personnis payis Black maill to thieves, or mainteners of thieves, contrair the lawes of this realme.

Whatever one may think of *calps,* I am not convinced that this is what we should understand by *calumpniis* in the *kenkynnol* documents. The word *calumpnia* means 'charge', accusation' and its primary use in medieval Scotland was in a legal context to describe what was done by somebody commencing a litigation — the complaint against the defender, or, in a criminal context, the charge against the accused person.

Discussion of charges and accusations in the south-west of Scotland brings to mind another important feature of that area's legal history, the *surdit de sergaunt* or *superdictum servientium.* There is much thirteenth- and fourteenth-century evidence that in Galloway and Carrick there existed a class of functionaries called sergeants, whose role was basically policing the countryside. Their policing function consisted in the finding and accusing of criminals. The evidence of a royal charter of 1364 granting Terregles on the borders of the Stewartry and Dumfriesshire to John Herries suggests that they also had powers to carry out summary justice — that is, they could execute robbers taken red-handed. Otherwise, the accusation of the sergeant laid upon the accused the burden of proving his innocence of the crime. Hence the *surdit* (French) or *superdictum,* the 'saying upon' somebody, the accusation. They seem to have operated in small groups and to have travelled widely, perhaps on some kind of circuit, and not to have been confined in their operations by territorially-defined jurisdictions like baronies. They had a right to claim one night's hospitality wherever they happened to be, to sustain them in this role; this privilege was termed *sorryn et frithalos,* Gaelic words meaning 'quartering and attendance'.[22] In all this there is a clear parallel with the serjeants of the peace still to be found in Wales and northern England in the thirteenth century.[23] It is clear that when Archibald Douglas, lord of Galloway, obtained exemption of his lordship from the act of 1384 about the pursuit of fugitive criminals, parliament agreed to it because in Galloway there already existed a system which could ignore jurisdictional frontiers.

There is no doubt that these sergeants held office under the control of some lord. Thus, in 1225 the earl of Carrick agreed that the clergy in his earldom should not be liable to give hospitality to his sergeants (who, we are told, are also called *kethres*).[24] In 1285 Robert Bruce, as earl of Carrick by virtue of his marriage with Countess Marjorie, exempted the Carrick tenants of Melrose Abbey from the *superdictu* or accusation 'of our sergeants'.[25] In 1305 the community of Galloway explained to the conquering Edward I of England that the barons and great lords were using the strange and tortious custom called *surdit de sergaunt* to the grievance of the land.[26] We can see therefore that the lords had control of these sergeants; further, we can see that the earl of Carrick in particular had, in addition to *kenkynnol* prior to 1256, sergeants with accusatorial powers. It is the powers of these sergeants which I suggest are indicated by the *calumpniis* of the *kenkynnol* charters.

It is important to note that the sergeant's charge compelled the accused to clear himself by compurgation at the period with which we are principally concerned, perhaps by battle as an alternative earlier on. Compurgation meant getting a number of people to swear one's innocence. Probably this took place in the court of the lord; certainly the failure to clear oneself would mean at the very least some sort of fine to the lord, as the 1285 Bruce charter suggests.[27] Outwith Galloway from the mid-thirteenth century onwards, criminal actions were increasingly made only on private appeals or by presentment and indictment by a jury (it is this which is referred to in the assize of 1244 mentioned at the beginning of this paper). Elsewhere in Scotland, of course, a person indicted of a crime by the jury of presentment would then have his guilt or innocence determined by an assize or visnet, but a Galwegian had apparently to make a special request for this prior to 1324.[28] In that year, as we have seen, Robert I granted to the captains and men of Galloway that, subject to certain exceptions, anyone accused by a sergeant might have a good and faithful assize rather than being required to purge himself under the old laws of Galloway.[29] Neilson appears to misunderstand this grant as introducing the jury of presentment to Galloway,[30] but it seems clearly to preserve the accusatory role of the sergeant and to be only an attempt to offer the assize to the accused as an alternative to compurgation. Sergeants could therefore continue to be a significant source of income for the lords in the south-west after 1324, and there is no sign of their being formally abolished at any stage in the fourteenth or fifteenth centuries.

It is obvious that many south-western lords apart from the earls of Carrick had sergeants with the power to force people to clear themselves of criminal charges and the right to claim hospitality; and it is likely that many of these lords also claimed *kenkynnol* within their kindred groups. I would argue that sergeants were one of the means by which a *kenkynnol* fulfilled his obligation to protect the members of his kindred, assisting them in the righting of wrongs against them. It may be the fact that the sergeants exercised jurisdiction on a kin rather than on a territorial basis that explains the 'assize of Galloway' enacted by William I and referred to in his brieve in favour of Melrose Abbey; it provided that the lords of Galloway were to assist in the pursuit of thieves.[31] The Melrose brieve suggests that the aim of the assize was the integration of outside settlers like the monks and their men into the kin-based system in Galloway. This may also explain some of the later complaints against the sergeants; claiming criminals wherever they might be for the court of the *kenkynnol* might have trespassed on other jurisdictional claims based on territorial rather than kindred rights. This is surely what lies behind the Melrose exemption from the Carrick sergeants in 1265: the abbey wanted to justice it own tenants. [32] Similarly, the Terregles charter laid great stress on baronial freedom from outside interference.[33]

All this suggests that the *kenkynnol* and his sergeants played an important role in the blood-feud and the system of compositions between kin-groups for homicides and other injuries, which probably survived into the later medieval period in Galloway or elsewhere in Celtic Britain.[34] It has also been argued that the text known as the *Leg es inter Brettos et Scotos* is a written version of the composition tariffs used in Galloway because it employs a curiously mixed terminology to describe different types of compensation payment. The words used include *cro, galanas* and *gelchach or kelchin,* which are found variously in Irish and Welsh sources as terms for compensation payments; this combination of different linguistic traditions reflects, it is said, the racial mixture existing in medieval Galloway.[35] But other views are possible. Professor Jackson believes that the text was produced at the end of the eleventh century as part of the integration of Strathclyde within the kingdom of the Scots and that this explains its multi-lingual character;[36] this would also suggest that it formed part of the general law of Scotland. Further, the text found its way into the treatise *Regiam Majestatem.*[37] If we accept that it formed part of the original *Regiam Majestatem* and that the *Regiam* was an attempt to set out the general Scots law (and it must be admitted that these are both debateable points),[38] then it is difficult to see why the compiler chose to incorporate into such a work a text with a purely provincial application. Moreover, the words *cro* and *galanas* turn up in another chapter of

Regiam,[39] suggesting that these were terms known as part of the general law. On the other hand, the text is found on its own and in French in the thirteenth-century Berne MS, where it follows immediately after three chapters all relating to Galloway, possibly indicating a Galwegian connection.[40] On the whole question, therefore, the verdict must be one of Not Proven.

A few other points about the nature of the *kenkynnol*'s lordship may be made. The giving of *calps* was of course an important recognition of the lordship of the head of the kin which at the same time imposed on him the duty to provide protection to the giver; it survived in Galloway and Carrick until 1490 at least, when parliament sought its abolition.[41] Then it was described as a custom used by the heads of kin. *Calps* can be found elsewhere in the Celtic world, in Scotland north of the Forth and in Ireland.[42] But its character differed in Galloway from northern Scotland, where *calp* was paid on the death of the client and took the form of the best eighth of his goods and his gear or his best brindlebeast. In this respect it was like the feudal due of *herezeld* or heriot due from a deceased tenant's estate to his lord and found in use throughout Scotland. But the definition of Galwegian *calps* given by Skene is clear that the payment was made by the client 'in his awin lifetime'. This contrast may wholly explain why only in Galloway and Carrick was it abolished in 1490 (it was 1617 before it received its quietus north of the Forth).[43] Here, therefore, Galloway appears distinct from the rest of Scotland, and in particular from Gaelic Scotland.

The other matters mentioned in the *kenkynnol* charters, apart from the office itself (that is, the office of bailie of Carrick with the following of the men of Carrick and the holding of weapon-showings), seem to bring us back into line with the rest of Scotland. These tasks surely suggest the duty of common army service owed to the king by the men of Carrick, which is specifically mentioned in a charter of Robert Bruce as earl in 1302.[44] Such military service is found throughout Scotland and has pre-feudal origins; it was the *mormaer* or *toisech* of each province who was originally responsible for calling out his men, whose service was return for his protection.[45] But this duty was not, I think, related to being *kenkynnol*; it was a public task performed for the king involving all able-bodied men in the province, not merely the kin of the officer concerned. Presumably there were similar obligations on the Galwegians who in the twelfth century seem to have claimed the right to hold a special place in the Scottish army.[46]

Other officers who appear in Galloway and Carrick are apparently the counterparts of ones found elsewhere in Celtic Scotland. There are several references to *judices* in Galloway and Carrick, who no doubt functioned much like the *judices* of the other provinces of Scotland, that is, as the repositories of the traditional laws and customs of the region.[47] If so, some of their recorded judgements in the twelfth century (for example, on the burden of cain, a food render to the king found all over Scotland, and on trial by combat) raise interesting questions about the relationship between Galloway and the Scottish crown in the early medieval period and about whether judicial duels were really a Norman innovation in Scotland, as has usually been held.[48] In another case we find the *judices* of Galloway sitting with the *judices* of Scotia in Edinburgh finding one Gillespie Mahonegen liable to the king for failure to find hostages (possibly cautioners for good behaviour).[49]

The judgement about cain refers to 'mairs' as the executive officers responsible for its collection in Galloway. Again, officers with this title are found all over Scotland in fairly similar roles.[50] David Sellar in his 1985 O'Donnell lecture has drawn attention to the interesting note by Skene in his 1609 edition of *Regiam Majestatem,* referring to a grant of the *officium serjandie comitatus de Carrik, quod officium Toschadorech dicitur, vulgo ane mair of fee.*[51] Were the mairs collecting cain in the twelfth century simply the sergeants with the power to accuse of crime under another name? The grant noted by Skene appears to be the same as one entered in the indices to the Great Seal rolls of the fourteenth century;[52] there also survive in the Great Seal register two further grants of the office of sergeant of the earldom of Carrick, registered in 1440 and 1450 respectively.[53] The reference to the officer as a *toiseachdeor* is made only by Skene, who as Lord Clerk Register would have had access to the original roll and was presumably quoting from it.[54] The office of the *toiseachdeor* is one for which there is again evidence from many other parts of Scotland, including Nithsdale, as well as in the Isle of Man. Part of their function seems to have involved the pursuit of criminals.[55] No evidence for the word *toiseachdeor* in Galloway has been unearthed as yet, but on the information now available it seems that this is most likely accidental. We may also note in this context reference in the Terregles charter to the king's coroners and their sergeants, who had rights to 'ransel' and to arrest,[56] and another entry in the Great Seal indices recording a grant of the office of coroner west of the Cree in the reign of David II.[57] Whether or not any of these officers were known as *toiseachdeors,* it should not be forgotten that in Carrick some were called *kethres.*[58]

There is some evidence for the existence and late survival in Galloway of customs relating to marriage, status and the rearing of children, which were at variance with the norms of the Church as expressed in the canon law. Again in this the Galloway evidence is consistent with that for the rest of Celtic Scotland and also Ireland and Wales.[59] The disapproving comment in Walter Daniel's *Life of Ailred,* that in Galloway '. . . chastity founders as often as lust wills and the pure is only so far removed from a harlot that the more chaste will change their husbands every month and a man will sell his wife for a heifer',[60] suggests the ready dissolubility of marriage in Galloway. One or two other pieces of evidence allow further inferences about customs regarding status which were inconsistent with the canon law. When Alan of Galloway died in 1234, he left three daughters, who were legitimate under canon law rules, and a son, Thomas, who was not. Perhaps Thomas was the son of a concubine; Galwegian recognition of him as Alan's successor, which was still strong enough for Edward I to seek to use it at the end of the thirteenth century, surely implies a relaxed concept of legitimacy by comparison with that of canon law.[61] Another practice disapproved by the Church was fosterage,[62] but there can be no doubt that it occurred at the highest levels of society in both Galloway and Carrick; there is mention of Gillechatfar, the foster brother (*collactaneus*) of Uhtred, in the twelfth century, while Barbour's *Brus* refers to the foster brother of Robert I several times.[63] Both Uhtred and Robert must have spent much, if not all, of their childhood in foster homes. Finally, a late source refers twice to fosterage amongst the Kennedies in the fourteenth and early fifteenth centuries;[64] although the second story has been correctly characterised as 'a tissue of untruths' from the historical point of view,[65] the familiarity of the custom in the south west is evident.

This is also an appropriate point at which to quote in full A. O. Anderson's fine translation of Matthew Paris's colourful description of the entry into blood-brotherhood by the chiefs and men of Galloway in 1235 when they rose in support of Thomas, the bastard son of Alan:[66]

> And that in attempting this they might more surely attain to their desire they made an unheard-of covenant, inventing a kind of sorcery, in accord nevertheless with a certain abominable custom of their ancient forefathers. For all those barbarians, and their leaders and magistrates, shed blood from the precordial vein into a large vessel by blood-letting; and moreover stirred and mixed the blood after it was drawn; and afterwards they offered it, mixed, to one another in turn, and drank it as a sign that they were thenceforth bound in a hitherto indissoluble and as it were consanguineal covenant, and united in good fortune and ill even to the sacrifice of their lives.

While the tone of this passage reflects the biases of a self-perceived higher civilisation, it may contain the essence of events and perhaps another aspect of Galwegian custom.

The decline of the laws of Galloway is not a matter for which there is any direct evidence. It has been suggested that the well-known statute of 1426, which provided that the king's laws were to prevail over 'particulare lawis . . . speciale privilegis (and) the lawis of uther cuntries and realmis', was directed at the laws of Galloway but it seems more probable that if there was any immediate occasion for the act, it was either a preliminary to the attack on barratry which developed in the following years, or an attempt to nullify the law of the Clan Macduff which might otherwise have been used to benefit the adherents of the recently executed Murdoch

Stewart, duke of Albany and earl of Fife.[67] It also seems clear that another statute enacted in 1504 in terms like those of 1426 was aimed at Celtic laws and customs, not within Galloway, but in the Western Isles.[68] In any event, it is certain that elaborate structures of customs like those that we have been examining could not have been abolished at a stroke by mere acts of parliament; it is a striking testimony of the efficacy of such attempts that the law of Clan Macduff was still in operation in 1548.[69]

The disappearance of the laws of Galloway is much more likely to have been a long and slow process brought about by shifting concepts of law and morality, and by changes in the power structure within Galloway, in particular the gradual replacement of native lords working within the traditional system by those who recognised different rules and values. The two most important influences in this process were probably the monarchy and the Church. Galloway was first brought firmly under direct Scottish authority in the twelfth century, and from then on came into increasing contact with the institutions and rules of the developing common law of Scotland. The settlement of outsiders who employed norms of tenure and jurisdiction which cut across the kin-based system in Galloway, and who saw that system as 'strange and tortious' began to restrict its scope. *Kenkynnol* and *surdit de sergaunt* survived where there was continuity of native settlement and also, we may suspect, because of its value to the crown in maintaining elementary order in what was a difficult area. But by 1455 when the Douglas lordship of Galloway fell to the crown by virtue of forfeiture, its legal administration could be incorporated into the general system with barely a hiccup, while in 1490 the custom of *calps* as used by heads of kin in Galloway and Carrick could be abolished because it was inconsistent with the common law. The history of the laws of Galloway was at an end.

Acknowledgement

*A version of this paper was read to the British Legal History Conference at Cardiff in July 1987. I am grateful to a number of friends who have kindly read and discussed this paper with me. I hope that the extent of my indebtedness is adequately reflected in the footnotes.

Notes

1. *APS,* i, 403 c.14.
2. *RMS,* i, app. i, No.59.
3. *APS,* i, 550-1.
4. Neilson, G., 'Surdit de sergaunt: an old Galloway law', *The Scottish Antiquary,* 11 (1897), 155-7; Dickinson, W. C., 'Surdit de Sergaunt', *SHR,* 39 (1960), 170-5; Barrow, G. W. S., 'Northern English Society in the twelfth and thirteenth centuries', *Northern History,* 4 (1969), 1-28 at 22-3; Barrow, G. W. S., 'The pattern of lordship and feudal settlement in Cumbria', *JMH,* 1 (1975), 117-38

at 128-30; Barrow, G. W. S., *The Anglo-Norman Era in Scottish History* (Oxford, 1980), 159-61; G. W. S. Barrow, *Kingship and Unity* (London, 1981), 11-13.

5. See below, nn. 17-19.
6. This seems to have been first pointed out by J. Bartholomew in *SHR,* 2 (1905), 190-1; See also W. D. H. Sellar, 'Celtic law and Scots law; survival and integration', *Scottish Studies,* xxix (1988), 1-27 at 8.
7. Barrow, *Kingship and Unity,* 12.
8. E.g. *Cawdor Book,* 130; *Black Book of Taymouth,* 185. 'Kenkynie' represents Gaelic *ceann cinidh.* Kenneth Nicholls tells me that neither of the forms *ceann cineil* or *ceann cinidh* is found in later medieval Ireland.
9. *Formulary E: Scottish Letters and Brieves 1286-1424,* ed. A. A. M. Duncan (University of Glasgow, Scottish History Department Occasional Papers, 1976), No.82.
10. *RMS* i, app.ii, Nos. 912, 913 and 982. See also Kermack, W. R., 'Kindred of the Bear', *Scottish Genealogist,* 19 (1972), 14-15, I am indebted to David Sellar for this reference.
11. *APS,* i, 109.
12. *CDS,* ii, No. 990.
13. See *RMS,* i, app.ii, No. 914 and SRO, GD 25/1/63. These clan names present a number of problems which cannot be considered here through lack of space, but Geoffrey Barrow has suggested to me that 'Muntercasduf', conventionally interpreted as 'the household of the black feet', should be 'the household of the servants of Duff', citing a late twelfth-century charter of Duncan, earl of Carrick to Melrose which is witnessed by Gillebride Macmekin Acnostduf and his brother Ean (*Melrose Liber,* i, No. 32). The lineage name 'Achostduf' seems to embody *quas,* 'servant, devotee' and the name Duf. My father suggests that the preceding 'A' should also be seen as a lineage term in the usual south-western form (cp Ahannay, Adair, etc.) like the Irish O'Neil, O'Donnell, etc. An example of the interchangeability of 'A' and 'O' in Galloway in this context is provided by the Okenental/Acconeltan family mentioned in *Melrose Liber,* i, Nos. 31 and 192. Finally, what is the relation between the Gillebride-Macmekin Acnostduf in *Melrose Liber,* i, No. 32 and the Macmaykanis who come under the captaincy of the Kennedies in 1455?
14. *Treasurer Accounts,* i, 6.
15. *APS,* ii, 214, c.5 and 222, cc.19 and 20.
16. Matthew Paris, *Chronica Majora,* ed. Luard, H. R. (Rolls Series, 1872-83), iii, 365. I owe this reference to Professor Alan Harding. See further below, text accompanying n.66.
17. *RMS,* i, No. 508.
18. *RMS,* i, No. 5009.
19. See *RMS,* ii, Nos. 379 and 414; SRO, GD 25/1/40, 52, 58, 60 and 66.
20. For Hailes see *The Additonal Case for the Countess of Sutherland* (Edinburgh, 1770), 108; also Cowan, D., *Historical Account of the Noble Family of Kennedy* (Edinburgh, 1849), 7; Paterson, J., *History of the County of Ayr* (Ayr and Paisley, 2 vols., 1847-52), ii, 273, 276; *Scots Peerage,* ii, 424.
21. *De Verborum Significatione* (Edinburgh, 1597), s.v. 'calps'.

22. See generally Dickinson, 'Surdit de sergaunt', and sources given therein for this account. The Terregles charter is *RMS,* i, No. 192.
23. Stewart-Brown, R., *The Sergeants of the Peace in Medieval England and Wales* (Manchester, 1936), throws much light on the Scottish evidence.
24. *Glasgow Registrum,* i, No. 139. There is a virtually identical grant by the earl of Lennox two years later: *Glasgow Registrum,* i, No. 141.
25. *Melrose Liber,* i, No. 316. It is explained that the tenants received this privilege because they claimed *legem Anglicana.* Dr P. A. Brand has suggested to me that the *lex Anglicanum* (i.e. English *written* law) in question may have been clause 38 of Magna Carta, which provided that no bailiff should put someone to his law by a simple complaint but should lead faithful witnesses to it. See Holt, J. C., *Magna Carta* (Cambridge, 1965), 226, 326-7.
26. *Memorando de Parliamento,* ed. Maitland, F. W., Rolls Series (London, 1893), 171-2.
27. It talks about the goods and escheats and damages falling to the earl by the exercise of his jurisdiction.
28. See *APS,* i, 56, c.22: 'Nullus Galwidiensis debet habere visnetum nisi refutaverit leges Galwidie et visnetum postulaverit'. The provenance of this law is uncertain (see Duncan, A. A. M., *Scotland: The Making of the Kingdom* (Edinburgh, 1975), 185, note) but the term 'visnet' is early. *Pace* Dickinson, 'Surdit de serguant', 172, n.5, the law is not found in the Berne manuscript.
29. *RMS,* i, app.ii, No. 59.
30. Neilson, 'Surdit de serguant', 176.
31. *RMS,* ii. No. 406.
33. *Melrose Liber,* i, No. 316.
34. On the bloodfeud generally see Wormald, J., 'Bloodfeud, kindred and government in early modern Scotland', *Past and Present,* 87 (1980), 54-97; also Black, R., 'A historical survey of delictual liability in Scotland for personal injuries and death', *Comparative and International Law Journal of South Africa,* 8 (1975), 46-70; Davies, R. R., 'The survival of the bloodfeud in medieval Wales', *History,* 54 (1969), 338-57; Nicholls, K. *Gaelic and Gaelicised Ireland in the Middle Ages* (Dublin, 1972), 54-7.
35. The different versions of the text may be studied most conveniently in *APS,* i, 663-5. For the theory of a connection with Galloway see *APS,* i, 49 and Barrow, G. W. S., *Robert Bruce and the Community of the Realm of Scotland* (3rd ed., Edinburgh, 1988), 135-6. I am indebted to my friend William Windram who several years ago drew my attention to a number of problems concerning the *Leges* which make any conclusion about them somewhat hazardous. In particular we should not make too much of the title. Our only medieval evidence that there was a law so called in the 1305 ordinance of Edward I concerning the governance of Scotland which abolished 'l'usages de Sots et de Brets' (*APS,* i, 22). It was Sir John Skene who in 1609 identified certain chapters near the end of *Regiam Majestatem* as the *Leges inter Brettos et Scotos* (see p.103 of his Latin edition of the text). Skene probably knew nothing of the 1305 ordinance, which was not printed until 1661 (Ryley, W., *Placita Parliamentaria,* 503-8). He also noted that in certain MSS the chapters were grouped separately under this title and were written in French rather than in the Latin of the *Regiam.* This comment is borne out to the extent that there is an early text of these

laws separated from *Regiam Majestatem* and written in French, amongst the miscellaneous collection of *leges Scocie* in the thirteenth-century Berne MS. However, there the laws have no title at all. It is of course perfectly possible that Skene saw another MS like the one he describes but which is now lost; until it is recovered, we must accept that the identification of the usages of the Scots and the Bretts abolished by Edward I with the texts labelled by Skene rests on uncertain grounds.

36. Jackson, K. H., 'The Britons of Southern Scotland', *Antiquity,* 29 (1955), 77-88 at 88. See also Duncan, *Scotland: The Making of the Kingdom,* 107-8.
37. See the versions of *Regiam* in *APS,* i at 640-1, in *Stair Society,* 11 at 275-8.
38. See Duncan, A. A. M., '*Regiam Majestatem:* a reconsideration', *Juridical Review,* 6 (1961), 199-217 at 204; Harding, A., '*Regiam Majestatem* amongst medieval lawbooks', *Juridical Review,* 29 (1984), 97-111.
39. *APS,* i, 637, *Stair Society* 11, 269.
40. For discussion of the Berne MS see my article on Scots law under Alexander III.
41. Skene, W. F., *Celtic Scotland* (2nd ed., 3 vols., Edinburgh, 1886-90), iii, 319-21; Duncan, *Scotland: The Making of the Kingdom,* 108-9.
43. *APS,* iv, 548, c.21.
44. *Melrose Liber,* ii, No. 351.
45. Duncan, *Scotland: The Making of the Kingdom,* 110-11, 378-83.
46. Anderson, *Scottish Annals,* 193, 199-200, 202-3, 247. Note also the royal *citacio exercitus* addressed to *omnes capitaneos Gallowidiae (Formulary E,* No. 88).
47. *Fife Court Book,* introduction, lxvi-ix. For a discussion of the lists of *judices,* including those of Galloway and Carrick, see Barrow, G. W. S., *The Kingdom of the Scots* (London, 1973), 69-82. See also Nicholls, *Gaelic and Gaelicised Ireland,* 46-7; Davies, R. R., 'The administration of law in medieval Wales: the role of the *ynad cwmwd* (*judex patrie*), in *Lawyers and Laymen,* ed. Charles-Edwards, T. M., et al (Cardiff, 1986), 258-73.
48. *APS,* i, 378, cc.22 and d 23. See Duncan, *Scotland: The Making of the Kingdom,* 185-6, and Bartlett, R., *Trial by Fire and Water: The Medieval Judicial Ordeal* (Oxford, 1986), 49. The judicial duel was known in early Irish law (see Kelly, F., *A Guide to Early Irish Law* (Dublin, 1989), 211-3, a reference for which I am indebted to Kenneth Nicholls), although not in early Welsh law (Jenkins, D., *The Law of Hywel Dda* (Llandysul, 1986), xxxii).
49. *APS,* i, 398, c.3. See Duncan, *Scotland: The Making of the Kingdom,* 529.
50. See *Fife Court Book,* introduction, lxii-vi.
51. Skene, *Regiam Majestatem,* 13. I am grateful to David Sellar for allowing me to read a typescript of his lecture, 'Celtic law and Scots law: survival and integration', and to draw upon it here. It was delivered in Edinburgh on 9th May 1985 and is published in *Scottish Studies,* 29.
52. *RMS,* i, app. ii, No. 1032.
53. *RMS,* Nos. 231 and 413.
54. See also Murray, A. L., 'The lord clerk register', *SHR,* 53 (1974), 124-56, especially at 139; Murray, A. L., 'Sir John Skene and the Exchequer 1594-1612', *Miscellany I* (Stair Society, 1971), 125-55, especially at 135.
55. Dickinson, W. C., 'The toschederach', *Juridical Review,* 53 (1941), 85-109; see further Sellar, 'Celtic Law', 9-11.

56. *RMS,* i, No. 192. For ranselling see Dickinson, 'Surdit de sergaunt', 175 and *n.l.;* Anglo-Norman Era, 159, n.81.
57. *RMS,* i, app. ii, No. 1303. Note also the coroner between the rivers Ayr and Doon (ibid., No. 844) and the resignation of the 'crounareschipe . . . in the partis of Galwaye' by MacDowele in 1473 (*Treasurer's Accounts,* i, 6).
58. See above, text at n.24.
59. See Sellar, W. D. H., 'Marriage, divorce and concubinage in Gaelic Scotland', *Transactions of the Gaelic Society of Inverness,* 51 (1971-80), 463-93, for Scotland and Ireland, and Davies, R. R., 'The status of women and the practice of marriage in late medieval Wales', in *The Welsh Law of Women* ed. Jenkins, J. (Cardiff, 1980), 93-114, for Wales.
60. Ed. Powicke, F. M. (Nelson Medieval Classics, 1950), 47; MacQueen, J., 'The Picts in Galloway', *TDGAS,* 39 (1962), 127-43 at 131; Sellar, 'Marriage', at 475.
61. See Duncan, *Scotland: The Making of the Kingdom,* 530-1; Barrow, *Robert Bruce,* 112.
62. See Goody, J., *The Development of the Family and Marriage in Europe* (Cambridge, 1983), 68-9.
63. *Holyrood Liber,* No. 23; *Barbour's Bruce,* ed. MacDiarmid, M. P., and Stevenson, J. A. C., fostering as a Gaelic custom see Skene, *Celtic Scotland,* iii, 321-3; Cameron, J., *Celtic Law,* 66, 220-1; Nicholls, *Gaelic and Gaelicised Ireland,* 79; and Sellar, 'Celtic law', 12.
64. *Historical and Genealogical Account of the principal families of the name of Kennedy from an original manuscript,* ed. Pitcairn, R. (Edinburgh, 1830), 3 and 6.
65. See Agnew, A., *The Hereditary Sheriffs of Wigtownshire* (2 vols., Edinburgh, 1893) i, 238.
66. Anderson, *Scottish Annals,* 341-2, translating the *Chronica Majora,* iii, 365. See above n.17. For Matthew Paris see Vaughan, R., *Matthew Paris* (Cambridge, 1958, reissued 1979) especially at 143-5.
67. The Statute is *APS,* ii, 9, c.3. For discussion see Nicholson, R., *Scotland: The Later Middle Ages* (Edinburgh, 1974), 309, and (on barratry) 293-5; also Balfour-Melville, E. W. M., *James I King of Scots 1406-1437* (London, 1936), 130-36; Duncan, A. A. M., *James I 1424-1437* (2nd ed., University of Glasgow, Scottish History Department Occasional Papers, 1984).
68. *APS,* ii, 252, c.24. See Nicholson, *Scotland: The Later Middle Ages,* 546; Murray, A. L., 'Sinclair's practicks', in *Lawmaking and Lawmakers in British History,* ed. Harding, A. (Royal Historical Society, 1980), 90-104 at 102 n.49; Donaldson, G., 'Problems of sovereignty and law in Orkney and Shetland', in *Miscellany II,* ed. Sellar, W. D. H. (Stair Society, 1984), 13-40 at 26.
69. See *The Practicks of Sir James Balfour of Pittendreich,* ed. NcNeill, P. G. B. (Stair Society, 2 vols., 1962-3) ii, 511-12.

Devorgilla's Bridge, Dumfries: view from south.

MEDIEVAL BUILDINGS AND SECULAR LORDSHIP

Geoffrey Stell

PATRONAGE, CONTINUITY AND CHANGE

In Galloway, as elsewhere, the nature and chronology of lay patronage can be measured directly by secular structures, and indirectly by churches and Christian monuments. Here also a number of these buildings and monuments can be seen to represent different facets of the power and wealth of a single family, kindred or corporation. But in Galloway, the indirect evidence provided by church archaeology and architecture is especially vital because of the comparative lack of documentary records relating to the Galloway monasteries.

Another special characteristic of Galloway is that old habits evidently died hard. The long survival or adaptation of sites, building traditions,

Fig.9.1 Motte of Urr; aerial view. (Crown Copyright, RCAHMS)

and styles among it medieval monuments show that a strong degree of continuity has underlain even the most dramatic upheavals in Galwegian society. When, and in what form, new beginnings manifested themselves within this society is thus a matter of special interest.[1]

SECULAR STRUCTURES

The beginnings of feudalism in Dumfries and Galloway in the twelfth century appear to mark a new departure in the outward physical form of lordship, the motte and bailey castle. At the latest count almost one quarter of known mottes in Scotland, seventy-four out of three hundred and seventeen, are to be found in the south- west. Many of those in Galloway probably originated in the military campaigns of Malcolm IV, only to be 'destroyed' in the rebellion of 1174. A second phase of motte-building was promoted after 1185 by Roland, lord of Galloway, who ruthlessly reunified the divided lordship. Following earlier royal example, 'he built castles and very many fortresses'.[2]

Distinguishing native imitations from genuine Anglo-Norman products is not easy.[3] Indeed, the mottes of Galloway continue to pose far more questions than answers to problems of feudal geography, largely because only part of one of them, the Motte of Urr, has been the subject of modern archaeological investigation.[4] It still remains to be tested how far this, the most extensive motte and bailey castle in Scotland, may retain physical characteristics from earlier, pre-feudal times, particularly in the nature of its bailey ditch and rampart which enclose an area of about five acres and embrace the motte with its own surrounding ditch. Although it does not occupy a particularly commanding site on the valley floor of the Urr Water, perhaps originally an island, the earthwork itself is most impressive, its deep ditches being reminiscent of an Iron Age hillfort.

Continuity in the principles and techniques of fortifications is deducible here as elsewhere, for there does not seem to have been much that Anglo-Norman sappers could have taught their predecessors about the construction of ramparts and ditches, including rock-cut ditches, and the employment of different combinations of earth, timber and stone for their superstructures. The fact that early fortifications are now seen in much reduced condition, either as low earthen mounds or heaps of stony debris, sometimes heat-fused or vitrified, should not make us underestimate the organisation, skill and tools which went into their construction. Locally, excavations at sites such as Mote of Mark, Trusty's Hill, and much further east at Burnswark, testify to the relative sophistication of earthwork defences before the Anglo-Norman era.[5]

Some of the earliest castles of stone and lime in the region also appear to have been shaped out of older fortifications in traditional centres of Galloway lordship. Buittle and much of eastern Galloway came into the possession of the Balliol family through marriage to Devorgilla, third

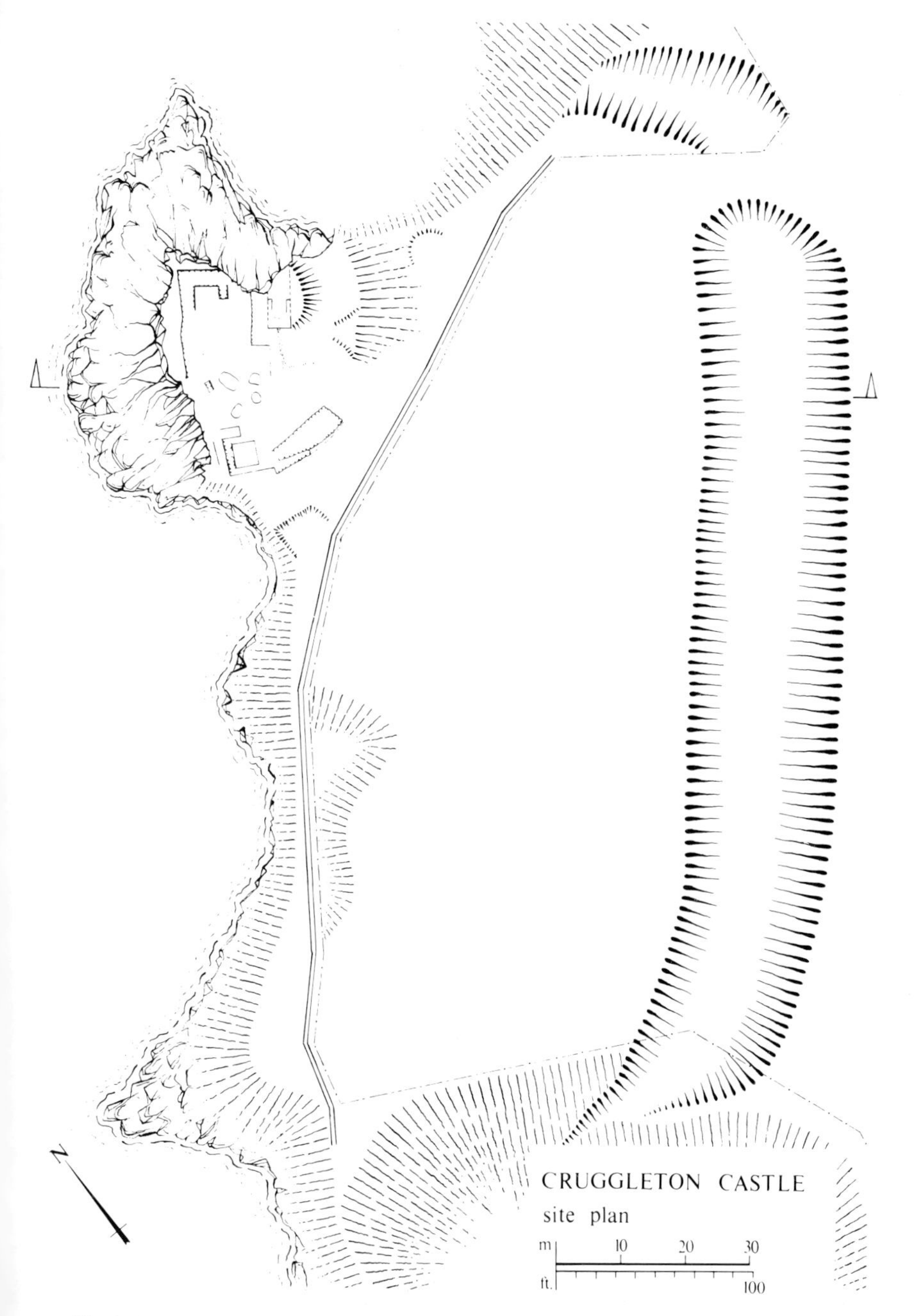

Fig.9.2a Cruggleton Castle; plan. (Crown Copyright, RCAHMS)

daughter of Alan, last native lord of Galloway (d.1234)[6] The castle occupies an extensive, low-lying site close to a later bridge across the navigable Urr Water, about two miles downstream from the Motte of Urr. The most conspicuous remains are the ditches and stone defences (including a substantial gatehouse) around the main castle mound, recently cleared of vegetation, but there are less obvious outer enclosures which may perpetuate the form of an earlier earthwork fortification.[7] Excavations at the ditched promontory fortification of Cruggleton have shown that it too entered a stone-built phase in the later thirteenth century, probably at the hands of John Comyn, earl of Buchan, descendant of one of the other Galloway co-heiresses; the occupation of the site, though, goes back to the late Iron Age.[8]

It is also worth mentioning in parenthesis that Morton Castle in Nithsdale, like Buittle, betrays an ancient ancestry by reason of its name, and the surviving hall-gatehouse block which is probably of mid- to late fourteenth-century date, appears to overlie the remains of an earlier promontory fortification.[9] These remains go back to the 1170s when the lordship of Morton first came on record; it was then in the possession of Hugh Sansmanche ('Sleeveless'), possibly acquired through the marriage to a daughter of Radulf, son of Dunegal, native lord of Nithsdale.[10] They may be even earlier; without systematic excavation it is impossible to tell.

A significant proportion of prehistoric and post-Roman sites in this region show signs of later reoccupation, and the habit of living or taking refuge on commanding hilltops, promontories or islands obviously commended itself in medieval and later times.[11] South-west Scotland is well known for its crannogs, and has produced rich evidence of structures and relics dated to the Roman Iron Age. But the most conspicuous surviving remains are those of medieval towers and rectangular buildings on natural

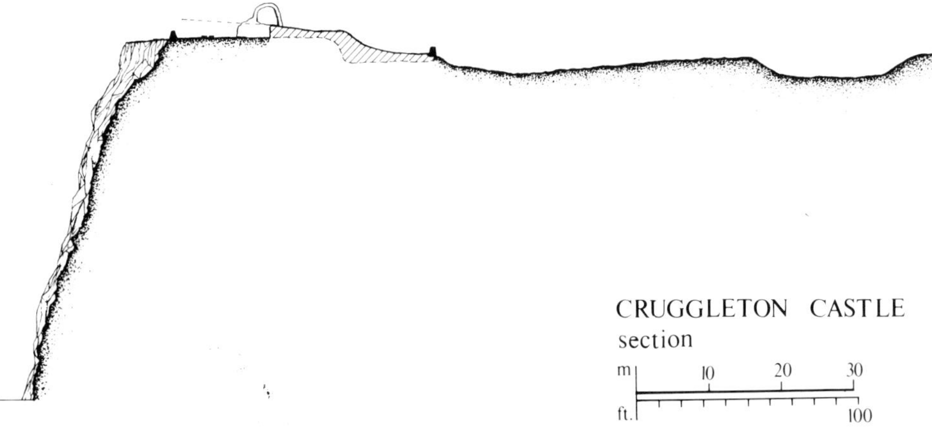

Fig.9.2b Cruggleton Castle; section (Crown Copyright, RCAHMS)

or man-made islands.[12] Visitors to the mighty Threave Castle cannot fail to observe that it is heir to this long insular tradition. Occupying an island site that may have been an early centre of Galloway lordship, the tower was built after the acquisition of that lordship in 1369 by Archibald Douglas.[13]

The massive 26m-high tower on Threave Island represents another important departure in building practice for the region. Compared to later Scottish towers, there are some peculiarities in its design, but the entry/stair and kitchen/service relationship suggests that the Douglases and their masons may have derived their ideas from Norman or Angevin models. Like some of its first generation counterparts elsewhere in Scotland, Threave was upas-like in its domination and isolation, for with the possible exception of Corsewall Castle and a tower on an island at Lochnaw, both in the far west of the Rhinns, there are scarcely any surviving Galloway towers that can be securely dated to the period of Douglas dominance.

Upon the collapse of the Douglas empire after 1455, however, tower-building practices became more widespread socially and geographically. This second generation of Galloway towers is roughly ascribable to the later fifteenth and earlier sixteenth centuries, some such as Cardoness Castle being impressive in quality and size, as well as in the density of their distribution. This local group includes the unique and diminutive Orchardton which, probably on account of an Irish connection that has not yet been clarified, is the only known cylindrical tower house in Scotland.[14] The group also includes the early sixteenth-century nucleus of Dunskey Castle which occupies the site of an earlier coastal promontory fortification invested and burnt as a result of a feud with the fearsome McCullochs of Myrton. In general, however, the relationship of these towers to earlier structures are rarely as clear, for example, as those at Torthorwald and Lochwood in neighbouring Nithsdale and Annandale.[15]

Later alterations and additions in a number of these towers illustrate significant points of change in, for example, late sixteenth- or seventeenth-century stair design.[16] More unusually, at Old Place of Mochrum an independent and self-contained T-plan tower was built by the Dunbar family in the later sixteenth century, a short distance away from their oblong tower of *c.*1500.[17] The linking section is modern, so this double-towered establishment may well be a local manifestation of the unit system, that is, the provision of independent residences for different branches of one family, a not unexpected product of a kin-based society. Likewise, outside Galloway in Annandale, the late medieval tower at Amisfield, whose upperworks were altered in *c.*1600, received the addition of a separate three-storeyed range in 1631.

The 1631 block at Amisfield represents one of the first dated stages in the emergence of houses of regular and formal design in the south-west, but it was not until the eighteenth century that the majority of Galloway lairds began to provide for themselves houses which seem to us to be wholly domestic in appearance and arrangement.[18] Even then there remained a lingering respect for the stout qualities of the older buildings and a conservative adherence to their settings. Many of the extant towers, which number over eighty in the whole of Dumfriesshire and Galloway,[19] are encapsulated within later buildings, the proportion being greater than in many other parts of Scotland.

A good example in western Galloway is Lochnaw Castle, ancestral home of the Agnews, one-time hereditary sheriffs of Galloway. It was massively enlarged in two stages in the early nineteenth century, but now stands reduced to its nucleus, an early sixteenth-century oblong tower with adjacent dwelling ranges of 1663. A fragment of its predecessor, possibly dating back to the early fifteenth century, occupies an island site in the nearby loch.

Indeed, the policies of few great houses are without the remnants or known sites of their predecessors, and detailed investigation of many a modern-looking house or farmstead often brings traces of older buildings to light. The farmsteads of Wigtownshire, and the Machars in particular, are rich in this kind of evidence.

CHURCHES AND CHRISTIAN MONUMENTS

Of the forty-five parishes of the Galloway diocese at the time of the Reformation, only a small proportion has bequeathed the remains of parish churches or chapels. An even smaller number, reduced mainly to foundations or fragmentary ruins, can be ascribed to the main period of parish formation in the twelfth and thirteenth centuries. The most complete are the restored Romanesque church at Cruggleton and the Early Gothic structure at Buittle. Given the proprietorial nature of early church buildings, it is no coincidence that these two bicameral structures correspond with principal centres of Galloway lordship, and would have been relatively well-endowed at an early date.

Which of the twelfth-century lords of Galloway, owners of the nearby castle, was responsible for the work at Cruggleton Church is not known, although Fergus (d.1161) seems the most likely. In 1427 its modest revenues were appropriated by the bishop of Whithorn, and in the seventeenth century the small parish was united with that of Sorbie.[20] The apparent physical isolation of the church may be deceptive, although no traces of a village settlement have been found in the vicinity.

There is a tradition that the church of Buittle parish was originally at Kirkennan where remains of burials, but not buildings, have been found.[21] Buittle Old Church itself consists of a plain, unaisled thirteenth-century nave, to which a wider and more elaborate chancel has been added in the late thirteenth or early fourteenth century, the belfry and other minor alterations being of the post-Reformation period.[22] It may date substantially from the era of Balliol lordship of Buittle between 1234 and 1296, although it is possible that the chancel belongs to the period of Douglas possession after 1325. In 1347 the parish and its church were appropriated by the abbot and convent of Sweetheart Abbey.

The principal church of the medieval diocese of Galloway is itself a somewhat disjointed and enigmatic ruin compared to other Scottish cathedrals of less wealthy sees. What would have been a large and elaborate aisled choir was in keeping with the status of the church, and would have provided an appropriate setting for the shrine of St Ninian, object of a lucrative pilgrimage traffic in the later Middle Ages. In other respects, however, Whithorn was of modest scale and was almost alone among major Scottish cathedrals in possessing a narrow unaisled nave.

Small though it may have been, the nave does provide independent witness to a significant phase of building activity in the middle of the twelfth century. The most obvious result of this activity is the ornamented doorway set within four orders at the west end of the south wall where it was repositioned, possibly in late medieval times. Excavations have shown that this Romanesque church was cruciform plan with a short aisleless nave and an eastern arm of unknown extent.[23] Unfortunately, the historical evidence does not provide a firm context for this work. The bishopric was revived in 1128, possibly at the instance of Fergus, lord of Galloway, but the status of the church and the community which served the restored see for the first fifty years of its existence is not clearly defined. Whether the body of regular canons converted into Premonstratensians in about 1175-77 had been inherited from an old minster-style organisation or from a short-lived Augustinian establishment founded between 1154 and 1161 is a matter of informed speculation.[24]

Although amongst the least wealthy of the twelve Scottish houses of their order and lacking most of their historical records, the three Cistercian monasteries in Galloway present a marked contrast in size and sophistication with the poverty of architecture associated with the secular clergy, a contrast that reflects an imbalance in patronage and a financial system based on appropriated parish revenues.

The ruins of Dundrennan Abbey constitute the most accomplished piece of medieval architecture in the province. It is perhaps a little surprising that work of this quality was organised and funded in the heart of semi-independent Galloway in the middle or later decades of the twelfth century, although its foundation in about 1142 as a daughter-house of Rievaulx Abbey in Yorkshire must have been to the mutual political advantage of King David I, Fergus of Galloway and the Cistercians themselves. A letter of 1165 refers to Dundrennan as 'the abbey which the brethren of Rievaulx built', no doubt using the skills developed in the completion of the church at Rievaulx itself.[25] The later twelfth-century work, however, shows closer stylistic affinities with other Yorkshire Cistercian monasteries, most notably Roche and Byland. [26]

These later operations were presumably funded by the wealth of its own estate, particularly from the profits of sheep-farming and the production of wool.[27] The abbey probably enjoyed a generous landed endowment from the native lords of Galloway, the last of whom, Alan (d.1234), was buried there. A tomb recess at the north end of the north transept contains a mutilated effigy of a knight, possibly of thirteenth-century date and said to represent Alan of Galloway himself.

Fig.9.3 Threave Castle; aerial view. (Crown Copyright, Historic Buildings and Monuments (SDD))

The creation of two further major dependencies seems to show that Galloway was to the Cistercians' liking. Glenluce Abbey was founded as a daughter-house of Dundrennan in 1191/2 by Roland, lord of Galloway, but little is known of its endowments. In the sixteenth century its buildings and possessions were prey to the conflicting ambitions of local landed families, most notably the Gordons of Lochinvar and the earls of Cassillis, through their protégés, the Hays of Park.[28] In the partly-tiled floor of the church there are monuments to the Gordons and the Hays, rivals even in the commemoration of death, and the surviving piers and bases are reminiscent of the original link, through Dundrennan, with the building styles of Byland and Roche Abbeys in Yorkshire.[29]

The romantic circumstances surrounding the foundation of New Abbey ('new' in relation to the mother-house of Dundrennan) are reflected in its alternative name of 'Dulce Cor' (Sweetheart), the rich and pious Devorgilla de Balliol having founded this Cistercian monastery in 1273 in fond memory of her husband, John (d.1268).[30] His embalmed heart in a casket was buried with her on her death in 1290, and the effigy of the foundress bearing a representation of the heart casket surmount the reassembled fragments of a copy of her tomb in the south transept chapel. The foundation charter, which survives in an inspection by David II dated 1360,[31] endowed the monastery with the lands of Loch Kindar and part of Kirkpatrick Durham, but there is no record of other endowments from Balliol possessions outwith the province.

A change in the expression of lay patronage is marked by Archibald Douglas's establishment of Lincluden Collegiate Church in 1389.[32] This was a college of secular priests (in this case, a provost and eight prebendaries, later increased to twelve) endowed to celebrate masses for the souls of the founder and his family, thus fulfilling spiritual needs on a more personal and intimate basis than the increasingly sclerotic monasteries. In an age of conspicuous consumption, churches of this kind also provided an opportunity for a show of wealth and status.

The architecture and sculpture in the choir is accordingly of a considerable richness and quality, giving some measure of the patronage of the powerful Douglas family. Authorship may be attributed to John Morow, a Parisian-born master-mason whose early fifteenth-century work at Melrose Abbey was accompanied by an inscribed panel listing other Scottish commissions, including work in 'Nyddysdayl' (Nithsdale).[33] Some details show close affinities with Melrose, and would have coincided with the acquisition of French interests and tastes by the founder's son, Archibald, fourth earl of Douglas and duke Touraine, who was killed at Verneuil in 1424. It is the effigy and tomb of his widow, Princess Margaret, eldest daughter of King Robert III, which takes pride of place on the north side of the choir, and her status is denoted by the magnificence of the tomb-surround.

Outside Lincluden and Dundrennan, however, Galloway cannot claim a particularly strong tradition in late medieval sculpture of tombs, effigies and grave-slabs. The cult continued, though, and is well displayed in post-Reformation funerary monuments such as that which commemorates Sir Thomas MacLellan of Bombie and his wife (1597) in the former church of the Greyfriars in Kirkcudbright, or the enormous early seventeenth-century stone sarcophagus of the Gordon family which dominates the interior of Anwoth Old Church, or even the large slab effigial monument of 1568 inside Terregles 'Queir'.

This 'queir' (choir) itself was built as a mortuary chapel by the fourth lord Herries in 1583, and with its mixture of pointed and round-headed openings and three-sided apse, it perpetuates some of the traditional Gothic forms of the later Middle Ages. Much restored in 1875, it stands at the eastern end of the parish church which was built in 1799 on the site of an earlier nave. Its special significance lies in the fact it was erected in the immediate post-Reformation era by a Roman Catholic family, and is a tangible reminder of the persistence of the old faith among leading Catholic families and their followers as the Protestant Reformation ran its rough and often bitter course.[34]

Lay patronage and the protection it gave to Christian rites must have mattered equally in earlier centuries, but the social context of the early crosses of the region is difficult to establish. Of the distinctive Whithorn school of monuments, for example, which probably belong to a period of settlement in the Machars from the early tenth century onwards, about twenty crosses would have served as headstones for individual graves, the majority having come from Whithorn. Only one survives complete, and only one bears a decipherable inscription (in runes): 'The monument (or cross) of Donfert'. The taller crosses are mainly from the surrounding district, and probably marked religious centres, the most complete of these cemetery crosses being the tenth-century Monreith Cross which stands 2.3m high.[35]

In 1973 the cross was transferred to Whithorn Museum from the grounds of Monreith House, home of the Maxwells of Monreith since its completion in 1791. The Maxwells had lived in this vicinity from at least the later fifteenth century, first at 'Dowies' (also known as Ballingrene or Old Place of Monreith,[36] then after 1684 at Myrton Castle. Sir Herbert Maxwell, who succeeded to Monreith in 1877, related how, when Sir William Maxwell, purchaser of the lands of Myrton-MacCulloch in 1684, moved from Ballingrene:

> he designed to bring thither the Celtic cross which stood beside the old House of Ballingrene on an elevation known as the Mower. In transporting it the cart capsized in crossing the burn between the baronies of Monreith and Myrtoun, the shaft of the cross broke in two, and the story goes that flames burst forth from the fracture, and

an aged woman who witnessed the incident cried out, warning the laird that ill-fortune would befall him and his family if that cross were taken away from the old house. Sir William took the warning in earnest, and caused the cross to be replaced on the Mower. There or thereabouts it remained until my father, finding that it had been set up over the burial place of a favourite horse, thought he would treat it more honourably and had it erected where it now stands in front of Monreith House. Some persons may discern the fulfilment of the wise woman's warnings in the break-up of the estate of Monreith following upon the cross being removed from the old house.[37]

It is difficult to believe that an undistinguished site near Dowies, a house dating from about 1600, was the original setting for the cross. But since the later Middle Ages proprietorial links had joined the possessors of Monreith to what Sir Herbert picturesquely called 'the ancient God's acre

Fig.9.4 Dundrennan Abbey; lithograph by W. Spreat from a drawing by Reverend A. B. Hutchison, c.1857.

beside the sea at Kirkmaiden'[38] where his ancestors were buried, and where he himself had the chancel of the medieval church rebuilt. A centre of its own parish in medieval times, now part of Glasserton parish, Kirkmaiden is the certain source of other sculptured crosses of the Whithorn school, and Collingwood considered that it was next in importance to Whithorn and St Ninian's Cave among sacred sites in tenth-century Galloway.[39] It is thus reasonable to believe that this sea-shore burial-ground was also the first site of the Monreith Cross, even though the identities and habitations of the Maxwell's tenth-century predecessors remain as yet unknown.

Notes

1. The references cited here are supplementary to the standard detailed descriptions of buildings and monuments contained in MacGibbon, D. and Ross, T., *The Castellated and Domestic Architecture of Scotland* (5 vols, Edinburgh, 1887-92), also their *Ecclesiastical Architecture of Scotland* (3 vols, Edinburgh, 1896-7), and in the Royal Commission on the Ancient and Historical Monuments of Scotland (RCAHMS) *Inventories* of the counties of Wigtownshire (1912) and the Stewartry of Kirkcudbright (1914), supplemented by RCAHMS *Archaeological Sites and Monuments Series* 24-5, West and East Rhins, Wigtown District (1985). Popularised accounts are provided by Geoffrey Stell, *Dumfries and Galloway* (Edinburgh, 1986), and the guide books and leaflets to monuments in the care of Historic Buildings and Monuments (Scottish Development Department).
2. Simpson, G. G. and Webster, B., 'Charter evidence and the distribution of mottes in Scotland' in Stringer, K. J. (ed.), *Essays on the Nobility of Medieval Scotland* (Edinburgh, 1985), 1-24 at 9-10, 18-19 and 21; for the translation of the chronicle account (*Gesta Regis Henrici Secundi*) see Anderson, *Scottish Annals,* 256, 288.
3. Examples in Tabraham, C. J., 'Norman settlement in Galloway: recent fieldwork in the Stewartry' in Breeze, D. J. (ed.), *Studies in Scottish Antiquity* (Edinburgh, 1984), 87-124.
4. Hope-Taylor, B., 'Excavation at Mote of Urr, Interim Report: 1951 Season', *TDGAS,* 29 (1950-51), 167-72; see also Reid, R. C., 'The Mote of Urr', *TDGAS,* 21 (1936-38), 14-17.
5. Thomas, C., 'Excavations at Trusty's Hill, Anwoth, 1960', *TDGAS,* 38 (1959-60), 58-70; Curle, A. O., 'Report on the excavations at the vitrified fort . . . at Mote of Mark', *PSAS,* 48 (1913-14), 125-68; Laing, L. R., 'The Angles in Scotland and the Mote of Mark', *TDGAS,* 50 (1973), 37-52; Laing, L. R., 'Mote of Mark', *Current Archaeology,* 4 (4) (1973), 121-5; Laing, L. R., 'The Mote of Mark and the Origins of Anglian Interlace', *Antiquity,* 49 (no. 194), June 1975, 98-108; Christison, D., Barbour, J., and Anderson, J., 'Account of the excavations of the camps and earthworks at Birrenswark Hill', *PSAS,* 9 (1898), 195-249; Jobey, G., 'Burnswark Hill', *TDGAS,* 53 (1977-78), 57-104.
6. Stell, G. P., 'The Balliol family and the Great Cause of Scotland 1291-2' In Stringer (ed.), *Essays,* 150-65; Nicolaisen, W. F. H., *Scottish Place-Names: their study and significance* (London, 1976), 77.

7. See also Coles, F. R., 'The Motes, Forts and Doons of the Stewartry of Kirkcudbright', *PSAS,* 26 (1891-2), 117-70 at 132-5; Reid, R. C., 'Buittle Castle', *TDGAS,* 11 (1923-4), 197-204.
8. Ewart, G. J., *Cruggleton Castle, Report of Excavations 1978-1981* (Dumfries, 1985), especially 12-14, 22-36; see also Reid, R. C., 'Cruggleton Castle', *TDGAS,* 16 (1929-30), 152-60.
9. Stell, G. P., 'Castles and Towers in South-Western Scotland, some recent surveys', *TDGAS,* 57 (1982), 65-77 at 73; see also Reid, R. C., 'Morton Castle', *TDGAS,* 12 (1924-5), 255-61; Simpson, W. D., 'Morton Castle, Dumfriesshire', *TDGAS,* 22 (1943), 26-35.
10. *RRS,* ii, 241, no. 183.
11. e.g. Williams, J., 'Tynron Doon, Dumfriesshire . . .', *TDGAS,* 48 (1971), 106-20; Barbour, J., 'Notice of a stone fort, near Kirkandrews . . . recently excavated by James Brown, Esq., of Knockbrex', *PSAS,* 41 (1906-7), 68-80.
12. e.g. Loch Maberry (NX 285751), Castle Loch, Mochrum (NX 293541), Loch Ochiltree (NX 3174), Loch Urr (NX 762845), Lochrutton (NX 898730) and Loch Arthur (NX 903690). Note also Castle (site) and Stable Isle, Loch Fergus (NX 698507), early castles on islands at Lochnaw, Inch (Castle Kennedy), and the numerous later towers such as Craigcaffie and Ravenstone built in marshy surroundings.
13. Good, G. L., and Tabraham, C. J., 'Excavations at Threave Castle, Galloway, 1974-78', *Medieval Archaeology,* 25 (1981), 90-140.
14. Gourlay, W. R., 'Orchardton Tower . . .', *TDGAS,* 15 (1928-9), 149-57. The cylindrical tower was evidently designed to serve as a solar block to an adjacent hall range; it was not intended to stand alone.
15. RCAHMS, *Dumfries* (1920), nos. 315, 316, 590; Maxwell-Irving, A. M. T., 'Lochwood Castle — a preliminary site survey', *TDGAS,* 45 (1968), 184-99. See also the erstwhile tower and motte at Castlemilk illustrated in the 'platte' of 1547 (Merriman, M., 'The Platte of Castlemilk', *TDGAS,* 44 (1967), 175-81.
16. e.g. Carsluith and Drumcoltran Castles.
17. Reid, R. C., 'Old Place of Mochrum', *TDGAS,* 19 (1933-5), 144-52; Cormack, W. F., and Truckell, A. E., 'Inventory of the estate of the late Sir John Dunbar of Mochrum', *TDGAS,* 60 (1985), 62-72.
18. Lochryan House (NX 065688), built for Colonel Agnew of Croach (Lochryan) after 1701, was probably the first of the symmetrically-planned lairds' houses of western Galloway, although its present castellated roof-line is unlikely to be genuine. In 1792 it was noted that 'for the last forty years, it has been uninhabited . . . Several fine paintings have been left to fade and moulder away, on the staircase . . . The partitions still remain; and the roof, although ruinous, is not yet entirely destroyed; but, the lapse of a few years will leave nothing but the bare walls' (Robert Heron, *Observations made in a Journey through the Western Counties of Scotland in the autumn of 1792* (Perth and Edinburgh, 1793), ii, 297).
19. The number of surviving towers probably represents only a very small proportion of the whole, for, to take the example of Eskdale and Ewesdale, out of a possible forty-one tower sites in existence in the late sixteenth century only one, Gilnockie or Hollows Tower, probably a former Armstrong residence, survives intact. Intense cattle- and sheep-rustling activities made this area a special case, but

the general pattern may equally apply to the minor lairds of Galloway. RCAHMS, *Archaeological Sites and Monuments Series,* 12, Upper Eskdale (1980), 13, Ewesdale and Lower Eskdale (1981), Annandale and Eskdale District.

20. Radford, C. A. R., 'Cruggleton Church', *TDGAS,* 28 (1949-50), 9-25; Cowan, I. B., *The Parishes of Medieval Scotland* (1967), 40.
21. Macfarlane, *Geographical Coll.,* ii, 58.
22. Reid, R. C., 'Buittle Church', *TDGAS,* 11 (1923-4); Cowan, *Parishes,* 23.
23. Radford, C. A. R., 'Excavations at Whithorn, First Season, 1949', *TDGAS,* 27 (1948-9), 85-126 at 123-6; Radford, C. A. R., 'Excavations at Whithorn (Final Report)', *TDGAS,* 24 (1955-6), 131-94 at 183-5.
24. Watt, D. E. R., *Fasti Ecclesiae Scoticanae Medii Aevi* (1969), 133-4. See also Radford, 'Excavations at Whithorn, First Season', 183-5.
25. Stringer, K. J., 'Galloway and the Abbeys of Rievaulx and Dundrennan', *TDGAS,* 55 (1980), 174-7.
26. Fergusson, P., 'The Late Twelfth Century Rebuilding at Dundrennan Abbey', *The Antiquaries Journal,* 53 (1973), 232-43.
27. Dundrennan may have had interests in Balmaclellan in the Glenkens, Galloway's major sheep-run, *CPL,* 10 (1447-1455), 156, but cf. Cowan, *Parishes,* 13. Its endowments also included land in Ireland, *CDS,* ii, nos. 967, 969, 1157.
28. Henry, D., 'Glenluce Abbey', *Ayr-Galloway Coll.,* 5 (1885), 125-88; Reid, R. C. (ed.), *Wigtownshire Charters* (SHS 3rd series, 51, 1960), 37-84; Cowan, I. B., and Easson, D. E., *Medieval Religious Houses of Scotland,* 75 and refs. cited. See also Morton, A. S., 'Glenluce Abbey', *TDGAS,* 21 (1936-8), 228-36; Reid, R. C., 'Some processes relating to Glenluce Abbey', *TDGAS,* 21 (1936-8), 290-309.
29. For further accounts of the archaeology and architecture of Glenluce see *Ayr-Galloway Coll.,* 10 (1899), 199-208; *TDGAS,* 19 (1933-5), 141-3 *TDGAS,* 21 (1936-8), 310-11; *TDGAS,* 25 (1946-7), 176-81; *TDGAS,* 29 (1950-1), 177-94; *TDGAS,* 30 (1951-2), 179-90.
30. Stell, 'Balliol Family', 157; Cowan and Easson, *Religious Houses,* 78; Huyshe, W., *Devorgilla, Lady of Galloway and her Abbey of the Sweet Heart* (Edinburgh, 1913); Bradford, C. A., *Heart Burial* (London, 1933), 14.
31. Cowan and Easson, *Religious Houses,* 223; and for the suppression of the Benedictine nunnery on the site, Easson, D. E., 'The Nunneries of Galloway', *TDGAS,* 23 (1940-5), 190-9 at 190-5.
33. Richardson, J. S., *The Medieval Stone Carver in Scotland* (Edinburgh, 1964), 57-8, pl. 109; Fawcett, R., *Scottish Medieval Churches,* (1985), 52.
34. The date is usually and incorrectly given as 1585; Hay, G., *The Architecture of Scottish Pre-Reformation Churches 1560-1843* (Oxford, 1957), 31, 151-2. Cf. Anson, P. F., 'Catholic Church Building in Scotland from the Reformation to the Outbreak of the First World War, 1560-1914', *Innes Review,* 5 (1954), 125-40 at 125, 'It is probable that the chapel at Stobhall near Perth, erected in about 1578, was the last place of Catholic worship built in Scotland until the chapel at Preshome, Banffshire, arose in 1788'.
35. Stuart, J., *Sculptured Stones of Scotland,* ii (Aberdeen, 1867), 50-51, pls. 96-7; Allen, J. R., and Anderson, J., *The Early Christian Monuments of Scotland* (Edinburgh, 1903), pt. iii, 485-6 (fig. 517); Collingwood, W. G., 'The early crosses of Galloway', *TDGAS,* 10 (1922-3), 205-31 at 222.

36. *RMS,* ii, no. 1499; Reid, R. C., 'Dowies', *TDGAS,* 25 (1946-7), 36-43; Stell, 'Castles and Towers', 73-4.
37. Maxwell, H. E., *Evening Memories* (London, 1932), 355.
38. Ibid., 145.
39. Stuart, *Sculptured Stones,* ii, 51-67, pl. 120; Allen and Anderson, *Early Christian Monuments,* 484-5; Collingwood, 'Early Crosses', 226.

Dundrennan Abbey: the north transept.

BURNS, BANNOCKBURN AND THE ARCHAEOLOGY OF THE EVANESCENT

Ian A. Morrison

It is said that Robert Burns wrote 'Scots wha hae . . .' while staying in the Murray Arms, the very inn at Gatehouse-of-Fleet which was the base for the conference from which the present book arises. There are many who would favour that song as a national anthem for Scotland. Of its more obvious rivals, 'Scotland the Brave', though a fine brash march, lacks the ultimate panache of the Marseillaise and is all too easily reduced to a squeeze-box parody of itself. The droplets of saccharine in 'Flower of Scotland' can turn bitter on the tongue. Like many of the best of Scottish traditional tunes, the air Burns ensured would live into our century as 'Scots wha hae . . .' sounds well whether played fast or slow. Played contemplatively, it has the necessary gravitas to dignify solemn occasions; played briskly and with a Scots snap, it can have the spunk and swagger to celebrate victory at Cardiff Arms Park.

As the words make clear, Burns' aim in writing the lyric was political. Though published under such titles as 'Bruce's address to his Army' or 'Bruce to his men at Bannockburn' the motivation and style had as much to do with 1789 as 1314, that is, with the French Revolution as much as the Scottish War of Independence. When Burns moved to Dumfries in 1791 he made new friends who included a Dr William Maxwell. The doctor had been in France during the revolution and had come back full of enthusiasm for common folk asserting their independence. Burns joined him in this, like many another Scottish and English liberal at that time. What Burns wrote in 'Bruce's address' was not so much a work in the Scottish folk tradition as a rhetorical poem of slogans and exhortations. It is typical of its period rather than its place. As David Daiches has pointed out,[1] 'The Scots (language) in the poem is not integral . . . and by the last two stanzas it has been given up and the poem is revealed as an English sentimental poem on liberty in the eighteenth century sense'.

> By oppression's woes and pains!
> By your sons in servile chains!
> We will drain our dearest veins,
> But they shall be free!
>
> Lay the proud usurpers low!
> Tyrant fall in every foe;
> Liberty's in every blow!
> Let us do, or die!

Soon the guillotining of the French royals and then the outbreak of war between France and Britain in 1793 made such sentiments seem subversive rather than liberal. Burns had been outspoken, and had put more of what he felt down on paper than a judicious civil servant should. He lost some of his more genteel friends, but contrived to keep his job when called to book by the Excise service.

To a cynical twentieth-century eye, these Anglified verses are pompous rather than persuasively incendiary. Though the preceding Scots-flavoured stanzas have more of a swing to them, they are hardly Rabbie at his best:

Scots wha hae wi' Wallace bled,
Scots wham Bruce has aften led,
Welcome to your gory bed,
Or to victory.

Now's the day, and now's the hour;
See the front of battle lour;
See approach proud Edward's pow'r
Chains and slavery.

Wha will be a traitor knave?
Wha can fill a coward's grave?
Wha sae base as be a slave?
Let him turn and flee!

Wha for Scotland's king and law
Freedom's sword will strongly draw,
Free-man stand, or free-man fa'
Let them follow me!

Even that so-familiar opening line is not immune to criticism. Sir James Murray has pointed out that if the aim was indeed to put the words into Bruce's mouth, the correct Middle Scots idiom would not be 'Scots wha hae . . .' but 'Scots that has wi' Wallace bled . . .'

The merit of the case for regarding this as a potential anthem for Scotland, therefore, rests with the tune rather than the words. And the case is given historical depth by the fact that this tune is not merely an eighteenth-century confection, but seemingly one of the older elements in Scotland's musical heritage. Robert Burns suspected that this was so, and though as Murray indicated, the poet was not our best guide through the thickets of early verbiage, we owe him more than is generally realised for his sustained activity in seeking out and preserving our folk music. It was not just his expertise in using old tunes as vehicles for his poetry. From 1787 until his death in 1796, he collaborated with James Johnson in producing the six-volume *Scots Musical Museum.* As Johnson proved increasingly dilatory (it took him over six years to produce the final volume after Burns died), the poet assumed ever increasing responsibility for keeping the project moving, both in the collection and in the editing of material.

Among the tunes which he encountered was one known as 'Hey, tuttie taitie . . .' (in some sources '. . . taittie'). Of this he wrote 'I have met the tradition universally over Scotland, and particularly about Stirling . . . that this air was Robert the Bruce's March at the Battle of Bannockburn, which was fought in 1314'. He therefore adopted the tune, and wrote the 'Bruce's address' words to it. In practice, this association with Scotland's most popular poet has guaranteed the survival of this tune into our electronic age. It was, however, a near run thing. The high-handedness of publishers in printing his poems in conjunction with melodies of their own choice, and not those for which he actually conceived the verses, is notorious. In some cases, sound recordings of performances reconstructing the settings which he intended are only now becoming available. Sometimes the last lines of verses of this song were padded out:

> . . . Wha sae base as be a slave?
> Traitor! Coward! turn and flee.
> (instead of: Let him turn and flee!)
>
> . . . Free-man stand, or free-man fa'
> Caledonian! on wi' me!
> (Let him follow me!)
>
> . . . We will drain our dearest veins,
> But they shall be — shall be free!
> (But they shall be free!)
>
> . . . Liberty's in every blow!
> Forward! Let us do, or die!
> (Let us do or die!)

Though the publisher persuaded Burns to rewrite so that the lyric could be fitted to an alternative tune, happily for the survival of 'Hey, tuttie, taitie . . .' as part of our musical heritage, when the original pairing came to light, public opinion forced George Thomson to print it. Burns' intended version soon became sufficiently well-known outside the salons to be sung by Scots soldiers during the battle of Waterloo.[2]

It is one thing for the tune to have survived the two centuries which lie between Burns and ourselves, once it had got into print. But what of the prospects for the air actually having previously come down through a period twice that length, as Burns and many eighteenth-century Scots would have liked to have believed, that is, from Bannockburn until his lifetime? One twentieth-century reaction might perhaps be to utterly dismiss this, without serious consideration. We are dealing with a class of popular music which was literally unrecorded in those pre-electronic centuries. As a creation of the musically illiterate, it is true that it would not have had the chance of being circulated and carried between generations in manuscript staff notation or tablature, as first some religious, then latterly art music was. But such a blanket rejection of the feasibility of long-term oral/aural transmission of a folk-music theme would in fact be injudicious.

Occasionally, evidence crops up which gives us some indication of what is possible. For example, we should not disregard the unwritten survival of Elizabethan ballads still being sung in twentieth-century Appallachian rural communities, in versions which show remarkable fidelity to the stylistic traits of four hundred years earlier. Sometimes, as there, words and music have transcended centuries as an integral whole. Often, however, the verbal content has lost its relevance or become unfashionable, and it is the tune which has persisted. Burns was by no means the only one to go in for re-cycling. Contemporary Orangemen who still raise the banner of 1690 and march off to 'Now we shall sing of Billy the King . . .' are perhaps unaware that during the lifetime of their hero their anthem had rather different words, which made it sufficiently popular to merit (or de-merit?) a place in Thomas D'Urfey's 'Pills to Purge Melancholy'; try singing these stanzas to 'Lilliburllero':

I, a young maid, have been courted by many
Of all sorts and trades, as ever was any.
A spruce haberdasher first spoke me fair,
But I would have nothing to do with small ware . . .
My thing is my own, and I'll keep it so still,
Yet other young lasses may do what they will.
(Refrain twice)

A fine dapper tailor, with a yard in his hand,
Did proffer his service to be at command.
He talked of a slit I had above knee:
But I'll have no tailors to stitch it for me . . .
(Refrain twice)

One suspects that Rabbie, himself the author of such songs of transparent double-entendre as 'The Rantin' Dog the Daddie o't . . .', would have enjoyed this. As Daiches notes,[3] 'Burns was a master of bawdry and produced for the private edification of his friends some of the finest examples of underground art ever to have reached the expert in what is politely classified as curiosa'.

Francis Collinson in his survey of *The Traditional and National Music of Scotland*, gives attention to the deep roots of the many folk melodies which Burns borrowed, reinforcing the point that we do not have to go furth of Scotland for instances of good tunes being passed from generation to generation by ear. The sound archives of the School of Scottish Studies are indeed replete with examples, and those who explore the musical manuscripts in the National Library of Scotland or Edinburgh University Library can also make tuneful discoveries, as the writer has found on more than one occasion. For example, his grand-uncle knew an Edwardian music-hall song, 'Oh! Where's me fourpence, Charlie?'. This was clearly a parody of of an over-sentimental Jacobite song by William Glen (d.1824), which had the refrain, 'Oh! Wae's me for Prince Charlie . . .'. The tune was, however, not Glen's, but was known to Burns as that of the tale of Johnnie Faa, or the Gypsie Laddie (after one who caused consternation in the

Cassillis family). This ballad figures in the Skene manuscript of about 1615-30 ('Lady Cassilles Lilt').

It is seldom clear how old such tunes may already have been by the time their music first happened to be jotted down in anthologies such as that of Skene, or of Sir William Mure of Rowallan (who filled his notebook with lute tablature sometime between 1612 and 1628). These were personal scores for people to play from, not academic works; tunes, as Sir William put it, 'for kissing, for clapping, for loving, for proving'. Such domestic compilers were not concerned to note the date and provenance of their favourite songs and airs for the convenience of posterity. Although some formally-composed Scottish music has come down to us in notation in earlier sources, the Rowallan lute book takes us towards the limits for written-down tunes of our traditional popular music.

Sometimes, however, titles or fragments of lyrics are quoted in texts which are not themselves primarily musical. These allow us to trace material farther back, though not giving us the burden of the tune directly. It is remarkable where musical references do crop up: though those who believe that the Deil has a' the best tunes may not be surprised to find that the official report on the meeting of witches at North Berwick in 1591 cites the tunes 'Cummer goe ye on before' and 'The Silly Bit Chicken'. The writer of that glorious girn, the *Complaynt of Scotland*, enjoyed making lists, and he gives a useful indication of what songs and ballads were current in the 1540s. He merely names them, however, whereas George Bannatyne in his 1568 manuscript anthology of Scots poems gives us the complete words of songs, and in some cases (such as 'The wowing of Jock and Jenny') these can be matched to the traditionally associated tune, which is known from later sources.

Happily, a similar matching operation seems possible for the air to which Burns set 'Scots wha hae . . .'. Through the sixteenth-century court poet Alexander Montgomerie it appears possible to identify pre-Burns words previously set to 'Hey tuttie taitie'. These then give us a verbal hook with which to fish in literary sources for yet earlier mentions. Montgomerie was born around 1550, an impecunious cadet of Eglinton. He lived until *c.*1602, and was almost the last of the courtly poets to use Scots. He is best remembered for 'The Cherry and the Slae', but as Jack has pointed out,[4] he also reworked the words of a folksong sung to our tune 'Hey tuttie taitie', and these have been preserved in the Drummond MS. His stanzas have been published in various versions; the aim here is not to provide a definitive edition, but rather to ease the way of the reader who may wish to try singing these rather attractive lyrics to our familiar melody. Thus, while a substantial amount of sixteenth-century spelling has been retained to give an impression of the texture of the original, modifications have been made to this and to punctuation. (Similar liberties have been taken with the other extracts, in the interests of clarity for the casual reader).

Hey, now the day dawis,	
The jolie Cok crawis,	
Now schroudis the schawis[5]	5. (mist) shrouds the woods
Throu Nature anon.	
The thissell-cok[6] cryis	6. thistle-cock = thrush
On lovers wha lyis;	
Now skaillis[7] the skyis,	7. clears
The nicht is neir gone.	
The feilds owerflowis	
With gowans that growis	
Whair lilies lyk lowe[8] is	8. like flame
Als red as the rone.[9]	9. rowan
The turtill[10] that trew is	10. turtle-dove
With notes that renewis	
Hir pairtie[11] persewis;	11. mate
The nicht is neir gone.	
Now hartis with hindis	
Conforme to thair kyndis,	
Hie tursis their tyndis[12]	12. toss their antler tines
On grund whair they grone.	
Now hurcheonis with hairis[13]	13. hedgehogs, hares
Aye passis in pairis,	
Whilk duly declairis	
The nicht is neir gone.	
The sesoun excellis	
Thru sweetnes that smellis;	
Now Cupid compellis	
Our hairts each one	
On Venus wha waikis,	
To muse on our maikis[14]	14. mates
Syne sing for thair saikis,	
The nicht is neir gone.	
All courageous knichtis	
Aganis the day dichtis[15]	15. rub-up
The breist-plate that bright is	
To fecht with thair fone.	
The stonit steed[16] stampis	16. stallions
Throu courage and crampis[17]	17. and curvettes
Syne on the land lampis;[18]	18. leaps
The nicht neir is gone.	
The freikis on feildis[19]	19. fighting-men
That wicht wapins[20] weildis,	20. weapons
With schyning bright shieldis	
At Titan in trone,[21]	21. throne
Stiff speiris in restis[22]	22. in shield-notches
Ower coursaris crestis[23]	23. coursers =
Are brok on thair brestis;	warhorses, plumes

The nicht neir is gone.

So hard ar their hittis,
Some swayis, some sittis,
And some perforce flittis[24]
On grund whair they grone.
Syne groomis that gay[25] is
On blonkis that brayis[26]
With swordis assayis:
The night neir is gone.

24. departs

25. cheery

26. white steeds that neigh

Helena Mennie Shire[27] has discussed the nature of the occasions for which such court poets produced different categories of material. She cites evidence assembled by Stevens[28] that it was sixteenth-century practice to mark the dawning of a day of tournament with a song of joyous entry, summoning the protagonists to the play of arms and the running at the ring. She classified this as just such a martial aubade, and it would clearly have been very appropriate for Montgomerie to have adopted a traditional song beginning 'Hey, now the day daws . . .' for his courtly reworking as the dawn introit commissioned from him.

She concludes[29] that 'probably the tune was a popular tune with this opening line known as far back as The Gude and Godlie Ballatis'. As its title page puts it, this was 'ane compendius buik of godly and spiritual sangis, collectit out of sundrye partes of the Scripture, with sundrye uther Ballatis changeit out of prophaine sangis in(to) godly sangis, for auoyding of sin and harlatry . . .' . Emerging from the fervour for Reformation in the 1560s, it ran through various editions. Although only words and not musical notation are given, many folk songs and love songs may be identified among the 'changeit' songs, despite the way these secular works have been bowdlerised and parodied in the interests of religious propaganda.[30] 'Hay now the day dallis' is indeed there with its refrain of 'The nicht is neir gone'. Most of the stanzas are clearly the creation of those concerned with ending what they conceived of as the night of popery: 'Wo be to yow, Paip and Cardinall . . .' . The first verse, however, has the same content as Montgomerie's, and Helena Shire suggests that the Gude and Godlie compilers had adopted 'a spring aubade that was probably an old song'.[31] She points out that while the later propaganda verses do not match well, the initial stanza does match Montgomerie in metre and would indeed sing to the same music as his piece. The suggestion is that both versions had as their common starting point a song that was already established by the 1560s.

We can indeed trace it back further than that. Gavin Douglas died in 1522, around thirty years before Montgomerie was conceived, and he himself had been born in the fifteenth century, in 1474. Yet we find that he not only knew 'The Day Daws', but expected his readers to be so familiar with it that he could allude to the song without explanation. He did so in the course of his *Eneados*, which he eventually completed in 1513. This massive work was his Scots version of Virgil's *Aeneid*, and it is still considered to be one of the greatest Renaissance works of translation of a Latin classic into any vernacular. He added his own vivid prologues, and the part of The Proloug of the Threttene Buke which mentions the song runs thus:[32]

> Soon over the feildis schynys the lycht cleir,
> Welcum to pilgrim baith, and laborer;
> Tyte on hys hyndys gaif the greive a cry,
> 'Awaik, on foot, go till our husbandry';
> And the hyrd callis furth apon hys page,
> 'Do drive the cattal to thair pasturage'.
> The hynd's wife clepes up Katheryn and Gill,
> 'Yea, dame', said thai, 'God wot, with a gude will'.
> The dewy grain, powderit with daiseys gay,
> Schew on the sward a colour dapill gray;
> The mysty vaporis spryngand up full sweet,
> Maist confortabil to glad all man's spreit,
> Tharto, thir byrdis syngys in the schawys,
> As menstralis playng The Joly Day Now Dawys.

William Dunbar also uses the song title, and in a way which offers an even clearer indication of the extent to which we must regard this as a very well known air indeed, more than three-and-a-half centuries before Robert Burns. Dunbar, like Douglas, was involved with the court life of James VI. Some of his works were celebrations, such as 'The Thrissil and the Rose' marking his sovereign's wedding. But some of his most memorable songs are his flytings: essays in that particularly Scottish art form, vituperation. Here are just three from the many verses with which he singes the lugs o' the Merchants of Edinburgh:

> Quhy will ye, merchantis of renoun,
> Lat Edinburgh, your nobill toun,
> For lak of reformatioun
> The commene proffeitt tyine[33] and fame?
> Think ye not schame,
> That onie uther regioun
> Sall with dishonour hurt your name!
>
> May nane pass throw your principall gaitis[34]
> For stink of haddockis and of skaittis,
> For cryis of carlingis and debaittis,
> For fensum[35] flyttingis of defame:
> Think ye not schame,

33. tyine = lose

34. gaitis = ways

35. fensum = offensive

Before strangeris of all estaittis
That sic dishonour hurt your name!

Your commone menstrallis hes no tone[36]
But 'Now the Day Dawis' and 'Into Joun';[37]
Cunningar men man serve Sanct Cloun,[38]
And nevir to uther craftis clame:
Think ye not schame,
To hald sic mowaris[39] on the moyne,[40]
In hurt and sclander of your name!

36. tone = tune
37. Joun = June
38. Cloun = Clown
39. mowaris = jesters
40. on the moyne = moon = lunatics

It is evident that for the purposes of this verbal assault he is citing 'The day dawis' as one of the most hackneyed airs that the denizens of the despised capital of Scotland are likely to be able to conceive of. These would seem persuasive grounds for believing that to those of his generation, ours was a kenspeckle tune indeed.

It is generally reckoned that Dunbar was born around 1460. His rival, Kennedy, asserts specifically 'Thou was consavit in the grete eclips', and there was such an event on 18th July 1460. But Kennedy was flyting with him in making this statement and may merely have been linking Dunbar's origin abusively with an eldritch event. Be that as it may, like Gavin Douglas, Dunbar (who died in 1514) certainly lived out the greater part of his life in the fifteenth rather than sixteenth century. From the fifteenth back to the fourteenth, when the battle of Bannockburn took place, is hardly an inconceivable leap in terms of the kind of track record Scottish traditional airs have established for surviving the centuries.

It would appear that most of our seemingly more substantial artefacts or possessions prove less durable than our best tunes; tower houses may crumble (and tower blocks, too), but the seemingly evanescent lilt which blows down the wind can show extraordinary stamina, catching the ear and the imagination generation after generation.

It is in the nature of things impossible to prove that the tradition encountered by Burns regarding the use of this particular tune at Bannockburn is true. Sir Herman Bondi once remarked that the notion of 'Truth' is an emotional concept, with no place in science. In music, however, we are in a realm which combines emotion with intellect, not least when elements of national sentiment are involved. We can surely allow ourselves to feel it agreeable that what has come to light since Rabbie's day at least does not eliminate the possibility that the old tradition is right, and that this fine air may indeed be deeply rooted in the genesis of the Scottish nation.

BIBLIOGRAPHY

Collinson, F., *The Traditional and National Music of Scotland* (London, 1966).
Daiches, D., *Robert Burns* (Edinburgh, 1981).
Elliot, K., and Rimmer, F., *A History of Scottish Music* (BBC Publications, 1973).
Jack, R., *A Choice of Scottish Verse 1560-1660* (London, 1978).
Shire, H. M., *Song, Dance and Poetry of the Court of Scotland under James IV* (Cambridge, 1969).
Stevens, J., *Music and Poetry in the Early Tudor Court* (London, 1971).
Winstock, L., *Songs and Marches of the Roundheads and Cavaliers* (London, 1971).

Notes

1. Daiches, *Robert Burns,* 30.
2. Winstock, *Songs and Marches.*
3. Daiches, *Robert Burns,* 274.
4. Jack, *Scottish Verse.*

5-26. See above.

27. Shire, *Song, Dance and Poetry.*
28. Stevens, *Music and Poetry.*
29. Shire, *Song, Dance and Poetry,* 149.
30. Ibid.; and Elliott and Rimmer, *Scottish Music.*
31. Shire, *Song, Dance and Poetry,* 19.
32. 13th Book, Bannatyne Club edition, 1xiv, pt.ii, 851.

List of Abbreviations

Abbreviations used follow mainly the conventions adopted by the *Scottish Historical Review.*

Primary Sources

Annals of Ulster	*Annals of Ulster,* ed. and trans. W. Hennessy and B. McCarthy (London, 1887-93).
APS	*The Acts of the Parliaments of Scotland,* ed. T. Thompson and C. Innes (London, 1814-75).
Benedict of Peterborough	*Benedict of Peterborough,* ed. W. Stubbs (London, 1867).
CDS	*Calendar of Documents Relating to Scotland,* ed. J. Bain, i-iv (Edinburgh, 1881-8).
Chron. Holyrood	*A Scottish Chronicle Known as the Chronicle of Holyrood,* ed. M. O. Anderson (Scottish History Society, 1938).
Chron. Man	*The Chronicle of Man and the Sudreys,* ed. P. A. Munch and Rev. Dr. Goss (Douglas, 1874); *Cronica Regum Mannie et Insularum,* trans. G. Broderick (Belfast, 1979).
Dryburgh Liber	*Liber S Marie de Dryburgh* (Bannatyne Club, 1847).
Glasgow Registrum	*Registrum Episcopatus Glasguensis* (Bannatyne and Maitland Clubs, 1843).
Holm Cultram Register	*Register and Records of Holm Cultram,* ed. F. Grainger and W. G. Collingwood (Cumberland and Westmorland Antiquarian and Archaeological Society, 1929).
Holyrood Liber	*Liber Cartarum Sancte Crucis* (Bannatyne Club, 1837).
Jocelin of Furness	*The Life of S Kentigern, by Jocelinus, a Monk of Furness,* ed. and trans. A. P. Forbes (Edinburgh, 1874).
John of Hexham	John of Hexham, Continuation of Symeon of Durham's Historia Regum in *Symeonis Monachi Opera Omnia,* ed. T. Arnold (Rolls Series, No. 75).
Lebar Brecc	*Lebar Brecc,* ed. W. Stokes (Royal Irish Academy, 1876).
Martyrology of Oengus	*Martyrology of Oengus,* ed. W. Stokes (1905).
Martyrology of Tallacht	*Martyrology of Tallacht,* ed. Best and Lawless (1931).

Melrose Liber	*Liber S Marie de Melros* (Bannatyne Club, 1837).
RMS	*Registrum Magni Sigilli Regum Scotorum,* ed. J. M. Thomson and Others (Edinburgh, 1882-1914).
RRS	*Regesta Regum Scottorum,* ed. G. W. S. Barrow and Others (Edinburgh, 1960-).
Reginald of Durham	*Reginald Monachi Dunelmensis Libellus de Admirandis Beati Cuthberti Virtutibus* (Surtees Society, 1835).
St Bees Register	*The Register of the Priory of St Bees,* ed. J. Wilson (Surtees Society, 1915).
William of Malmesbury	William of Malmesbury, Historia Novella in *Gesta Regum Anglorum,* ed. W. Stubbs, ii (Rolls Series No. 90).

Journals and Institutions

ASHS	*Association for Scottish Historical Studies.*
BJRL	*Bulletin of the John Rylands Library.*
EHR	*English Historical Review.*
JCHAS	*Journal of the Cork Historical and Archaeological Society.*
JMH	*Journal of Medieval History.*
MGH	*Monumenta Germaniae Historica.*
PSAS	*Proceedings of the Society of Antiquaries of Scotland.*
RCAHMS	*Royal Commission for the Ancient and Historical Monuments of Scotland.*
SDD	*Scottish Development Department.*
SHR	*Scottish Historical Review.*
SHS	*Scottish History Society.*
SRO	*Scottish Record Office.*
TDGAS	*Transactions of the Dumfriesshire and Galloway Natural History and Antiquarian Society.*